POST-TRUTH

HOW BULLSHIT CONQUERED THE WORLD

JAMES
BALL

POST-
TRUTH

HOW BULLSHIT
CONQUERED
THE WORLD

Biteback Publishing

First published in Great Britain in 2017 by
Biteback Publishing Ltd
Westminster Tower
3 Albert Embankment
London SE1 7SP
Copyright © James Ball 2017

ISBN 978-1-78590-214-7

10 9 8 7 6 5 4 3 2

A CIP catalogue record for this book is available from the British Library.

Set in Minion Pro

Printed and bound in Great Britain by
CPI Group (UK) Ltd, Croydon CR0 4YY

'To those who can hear me, I say…'

CONTENTS

INTRODUCTION

The US government stockpiled 30,000 guillotines, stored in internment camps – including one in Alaska large enough for two million people – ready to wipe out Second Amendment supporters at a rate of three million an hour.[1] Trump supporters at a New York victory rally chanted, 'We hate Muslims, we hate blacks, we want our great country back'.[2] Denzel Washington endorsed Donald Trump[3] – and Trump actually won the popular vote in the US election, despite the mainstream media telling you otherwise.[4]

Everything above is grabby, easy to understand, easy to share – and false. All serve as examples of the long-existing but newly discussed phenomenon of outright fake news: easily shareable and discussable stories, posted to social media for jokes, for ideology, for political reasons by groups connected to foreign nations, such as Russia, or – most commonly – to make a bit of money.

These examples are classics of the genre: possible to invent in minutes, but taking hours to debunk. Even the most obvious nonsense claim takes time and effort to prove false. Take the internment camp supposedly prepared to jail two million opponents of Hillary Clinton. If the world's largest manufacturing building – a Boeing aircraft factory in Washington[5] – had the entirety of its internal space converted to confinement cells, it could only house one million people, and that's without any corridor space, kitchens, room for security or anything else. An actual site for two million would need to be three or four times larger, constructed entirely in secret, and somehow hidden from any kind of passer-by, whether by land or air. But none of this matters to someone already convinced. What actual proof do I have the site doesn't exist? Of course the answer is none.

For the determined debunker, just battling outright and obvious falsehoods, from anonymous blogs and hoax sites, would be a losing battle. But there's a far wider problem than these actual hoaxes – the whole range of stories that are essentially untrue, but arguable to people who believe them or can convincingly pretend to.

The UK's debate over whether to leave the European Union – the Brexit debate – was littered with such claims. The UK pays £350 million a week to the EU, and voting to leave would mean this money could be given to the NHS. The then Chancellor, George Osborne, would raise income taxes by 2p should the UK vote to leave. Voting to stay in the EU would open the UK to uncontrolled immigration from Turkey, from where twelve million people plan to migrate.[6]

These claims are, to most who dig into them, just as false as the first group, but with two main differences. The first is that there's enough core of truth to each to make them essentially arguable: the short version of the claim put on a leaflet may be an outright lie, but once they drilled down into the detail, two politicians arguing in the media could run the argument to a draw. The second is that these claims aren't made by anonymous figures – they're made by the politicians and the staffers at the centre of the rival campaigns.

Needless to say, this is a problem the US has had plenty of time to grow familiar with: Donald Trump can generate more political nonsense in an hour than most of his rivals can produce in a year. Trump's versatility in generating half-truth, untruth and outright spectacular mendacity borders on genius.

The subjects range from the trivial to matters of major national policy, and no statement is bound by anything that came before it. Take Trump's evolution on his flagship policy of building a border wall, which Mexico would pay for – the country's statement that it would do nothing of the sort was easily ignored. After his election, Trump acknowledged he'd be going to Congress for money for his wall – yet still insisted Mexico would pay for it.

Trump has accused the media of lying about the crowd size for his inauguration by quoting it at 250,000 rather than the 1,000,000+ he claims; pollsters of fabricating his low approval numbers; the CIA of fabricating evidence that Russia intervened in the election in his favour; and unknown authorities of allowing millions of fraudulent votes to be cast in an election he nonetheless won. Trump can even comfortably and casually lie about incidents captured on video: when caught during the campaign imitating the disability of *New York Times* reporter Serge Kovaleski,[7] Trump routinely states the incident – which happened at the front of a televised rally – didn't happen, or that he'd never met the reporter concerned (he had, repeatedly).

In markedly different ways, the world was reshaped in 2016 by two contests typified by anger against elites, a breakdown in trust in the media, widespread (and wrong) belief among pundits that the contests were foregone conclusions – and the routine use of what for the rest of this book we're going to call bullshit.

Britain's vote to leave the EU ends a relationship of more than forty years between the UK and the world's largest trading bloc. It will involve reforging the country's security partnerships and trading relationships with new and existing partners, and will leave the EU reassessing its own future.

The US election outcome is, if anything, even more significant for the world. At the start of his term, Donald Trump said that he'll try to reshape the country's healthcare system, redefine its relationship with Russia and with NATO, consider ripping up its trade deals, change the USA's long-standing China policy, end Obama's climate change measures and deport far more 'illegal immigrants' than his predecessor.

The consequences of each vote could hardly be more serious, and yet the campaigns that decided them – and masses of the media coverage – were based on trivia, half-truths and lies. It would be a gross oversimplification to claim that either electorate was tricked into their vote, but nor can we rule out that bullshit swung votes, especially as both were relatively close: had just 55,000 voters (out of more than 130 million nationwide) in three states voted differently, Hillary Clinton would be President.[8] Fake news stories alone – leaving out poor-quality information, biased coverage or mainstream media repeating dubious Trump claims – reached orders of magnitude more people than that.

The Brexit vote is less clear-cut, as it was less close: Leave won by a margin of 52 per cent to 48 per cent, or about 1.3 million votes. But analysis of who actually voted shows that the crucial margin of victory came from left-behind, low-income people who don't usually turn up to vote.[9] The question of what urged this group to vote in the referendum when they stayed at home in the previous year's general election remains an open one, but in a contest where one side offered complex economic forecasts for 2030 and the other gave clear-cut messages on handing money to EU bureaucrats versus the NHS, messaging is an obvious possibility.

Had bullshit been confined to the fringes, to fake news sites which didn't reach significant audiences, such questions could be ignored – but what happened in reality was that mainstream coverage became dominated by repeating and regurgitating claims which were often entirely untrue. The long-standing media habit of leaving campaigns to duke it out over who was telling the truth worked in favour of the liar: make a claim, have it echoed in print, on TV and online, and then get further coverage as the rival campaign challenges its truth.

What effort the major outlets make towards challenging the truth of political claims tends to be confined to specialist fact-check columns, or dedicated political shows – rather than leading the main news broadcasts, or shorter mainstream radio bulletins. The result is – superficially at least – bullshit works: if challenged, it provokes a story about the row that repeats the claim for days at a time; if unchallenged, the claim seems unanswerable.

Before we go further, it's worth explaining why this book talks about 'bullshit' rather than lies or untruth or some other term. One reason is simply that we need a catch-all word to cover misrepresentation, half-truths and outrageous lies alike. The other stems from the Princeton University philosopher Harry Frankfurt, who wrote a full book defining the term in 2005: *On Bullshit*.

Frankfurt's argument, roughly speaking, runs as such: to tell a lie, you need to care about some form of absolute truth or falsehood, and increasingly public life is run by people who don't care much either way – they care about their narrative.

'One who is concerned to report or conceal the facts assumes that there are indeed facts that are in some way both determinate and knowable,' he argues. 'His interest in telling the truth or in lying presupposes that there is a difference between getting things wrong and getting things right, and that it is at least occasionally possible to tell the difference.'

If someone rejects that idea then there are two options: to never again claim anything as fact, or to bullshit – say things are so, but with no recourse to reality.

Frankfurt concludes:

Someone who lies and someone who tells the truth are playing on opposite sides, so to speak, in the same game. Each responds to the facts as he understands them, although the response of the one is guided by the authority of the truth, while the response of the other defies that authority, and refuses to meet its demands.

The bullshitter ignores these demands altogether. He does not reject the authority of the truth, as the liar does, and oppose himself to it. He pays no attention to it at all. By virtue of this, bullshit is a greater enemy of the truth than lies are.

In other words, a bullshitter will say what works to get the outcome they want, and care little whether it's true or not. To many (this author included), this serves as a relatively fair description of many modern political campaigns, and its effect seems to be as damaging as Frankfurt's philosophical text would surmise.

The resultant mass-produced bullshit is too much even for the earnest media outlets who try to report fairly and accurately to attempt to deal with: their culture and norms simply cannot keep up with the onslaught, especially given their bone-deep habit of trying to give a hearing to both sides of a political argument. When it comes to dealing with bullshitters, the mainstream media may be bringing a knife to a gun fight.

But there are plenty of large outlets making no such effort. Many could easily be accused of being part of the bullshit machine themselves, some clearly intentionally. Just as outlets rage at fake news, stories on a wide range of issues are routinely angled to suit the prejudices of the audience – in the UK, right-wing tabloids have been made by regulators to apologise time and again for distorted reporting about Muslims,[10] refugees and immigrants.

Some outlets run front pages which it's almost impossible to believe they could ever think were true. In the run-up to the EU referendum, the *Daily Mail* ran a front page showing a lorry full of people smuggling themselves into the UK. 'WE'RE FROM EUROPE – LET US IN', the headline said. As the *Daily Mail* would surely be aware, EU citizens have a right to live and work in the UK and would have no need to travel illicitly into the country – the person quoted had in fact said 'We're from Iraq'.[11]

Some newspapers will go still further on their websites, to pick up any kind of traffic. The *Daily Express* – which sells 400,000 copies and has 1.5 million unique browsers a day – routinely runs online headlines like 'Chemtrails "will wipe out humans" causing biblical-style floods, says expert',[12] referring to a widely discredited conspiracy theory that planes leave behind chemicals designed to keep populations docile.

Such a culture is hardly confined to the UK. US supermarket tabloids have run front pages including 'HILLARY: 6 MONTHS TO LIVE!', 'HILLARY FAILED SECRET FBI LIE DETECTOR!' and 'HILLARY HITMAN TELLS ALL!'[13]

Concerns about media accuracy are hardly new: relatives of the ninety-six football fans killed in the crush at Hillsborough stadium in 1989 were faced in the immediate aftermath by a front page in *The Sun* falsely stating – based on untrue accounts from police – that fans had attacked police, robbed the wounded and dying, and had urinated on police officers.

So it goes too with fake news online – a phenomenon the journalist John Diamond had spotted twenty-one years before it hit the mainstream. 'The real problem with the internet is that everything written on it is true,' he wrote in 1995.[14] 'Or rather, there is no real way of discerning truth from lies. The net is a repository of facts, statistics, data: unless anything is palpably wrong, we tend to give all facts on our computer screens equal weight.'

What broke in 1995 has not been fixed in 2017. If a site has a plausible name and a design which looks roughly like a mainstream news site, we tend to believe it – one now-defunct site called the Boston Tribune, a plausible newspaper name for a non-existent paper, ran articles claiming Obama had bought a retirement home in the Middle East, had given his mother-in-law a lifetime pension for babysitting, and that an elderly man had been arrested for shooting a man who was attempting to abduct a seven-year-old child.

What Diamond, who died in 2001, could not have predicted was how the effect he already saw (that everything looks equally credible online) would be compounded by what's routinely called the 'filter bubble'. In short, we tend to click on things that suit what we already think, and we'll rarely try to fact-check a story that suits our preconceptions. In other words, a liberal will likely Google for a fact-check of a claim that Obama was born in Kenya (he wasn't), but is much less likely to do the same for a claim that Trump once called Republicans 'the dumbest group of voters in the country' (he didn't).[15]

Given that most of us are friends with people with a broadly similar worldview to ours, we see more and more unchecked news we're predisposed to agree with. The result? Where once right- and left-wing partisans disagreed over their interpretations of a roughly shared narrative, now a portion of each side see different, polarised and largely untrue narratives about the other – and each thinks the other is uniquely afflicted by 'fake news': those on the left point to Breitbart or pro-Trump hoax sites, while those on the right flag The Canary or the hoax sites designed to catch anti-Trumpers.

Politicians – in general – have not suddenly become more mendacious. The media have not suddenly become more inclined to lie. And despite suggestions otherwise, the public have not become more stupid or distracted (on the contrary, on average, we're more educated than we've ever been). So why is bullshit now in the ascendency?

In the US, Trump is exceptional in his repeated and tenacious disconnection from reality – but he hardly acts against a political trend on both sides of the Atlantic for focusing on messages that cut through, rather than getting too bogged down in boring-but-important details.

The big and systematic reasons for bullshit's triumph lie in large part on the media side of things, both with traditional outlets and with the new economics of the internet. Most of the time we discuss such things, we focus on the new technologies and platforms and their effect on us. That misses another seismic shift: the economics.

The business model of 'serious' outlets is under sustained pressure, especially so in the case of print media. Circulation numbers are falling, which simultaneously starves outlets of both circulation revenue (cash from the cover price) and advertising revenue, as people pay less as they reach an ever-smaller audience. This advertising drop is compounded by companies switching their ad spend to digital outlets – meaning numerous papers are seeing print revenue fall by 15 per cent or more each year. Less money means fewer reporters, each doing more work than ever with lower budgets, making regurgitating what politicians say a much more cost-effective proposition than digging into what they're saying.

There are knock-on effects too. Some outlets shift their coverage to suit their dwindling and ageing reader base, giving up entirely on ever reaching a younger audience in print.

Most have turned to their online coverage to compensate for their revenue, often compounding the bullshit problem. The biggest and most specialised outlets – places like the *New York Times* or *Financial Times* – have the prospect of getting enough people to pay online subscriptions for their news, allowing something akin to their traditional business model to continue.

Many others are instead in the game of reach: each visit to a news story generates fractions of a penny through display advertising, not nearly enough on its own to fund a news story. The way to make such small amounts pay is to generate huge audiences – millions a day – and to try to make each story as low-cost as possible.

This is not a business model designed to combat bullshit, but rather to propel it as far as possible across the world. Assigning a reporter to spend hours looking into a claim, then writing a cautiously worded article on its truth leads to more cost for fewer clicks. The easier and more lucrative alternative is to write up the original claim, unchecked, within minutes, followed by any angry reaction to it, alongside rebuttals. Any debunk can simply be cribbed from another outlet. The result can be six or more stories – some of them directly contradictory – with zero original reporting.

This model lends itself too to new media and fake news. If the goal is to maximise an audience (and therefore ad revenue) already facing a glut of down-the-middle serious news, then the trick is to hype and promote any kind of row to get a huge influx of partisan readers. While the hyper-partisan right-wing site Breitbart may be the poster child of this movement, the left-wing UK blog The Canary works on just the same model – which also benefits from sowing doubt as to the veracity of the mainstream media, thus promoting sharing and future clicks: 'Here's what you won't read' is a strong sell.

Fake news sites are the logical conclusion of this particular business model: if a story is going to be unchecked, or exaggerated, why not make it up entirely and reduce the costs even further? One ultra-successful fake story may generate money through advertising revenue, but may also be used to promote affiliate schemes such as casino sign-ups, get-rich-quick schemes, dubious health products or similar programmes. These generate a much more generous income than ad views to fake sites for each new person who signs up to the product or service, providing another lucrative revenue stream to hoaxers.

There's a twist to this: almost every major news site profits from these fake sites, too, even while wondering how to tackle them and warning of the risk they present. The 'sponsored links' present at the foot or side of posts on almost every major site give the outlet a small amount of revenue for each click, but almost universally link to fake or hyped news. Traditional media boosts and profits from fake news, even as it tries to fight it.

The above is the short version of the mess this book is trying to untangle. Part I will set out how bullshit – in different forms – shaped two of 2016's central political campaigns, tracking down the detail of how the Brexit battle was fought and how Trump rose to take the White House. These accounts will dissect the outright falsehoods, but also show how just the right dose of bullshit – coupled with a credulous media response – helped some narratives run for weeks, while others withered on the vine.

Part II then looks in turn at each of the key players involved in the process: politicians, old media, new media, fake media – and us, the consumers of news. What contribution has each made to what's happening? What are the limits of what each group will do? And, crucially, what reasons does each group have for acting as they do?

Then in Part III, we turn to looking at why bullshit works as a tactic – the toxic mixture of bullshit often playing well into the psychology of the audience, feeding our existing beliefs and reinforcing our social groups, furthering the goals of political actors, and serving the business models and long-standing culture of the media groups standing between the two.

Finally, we look at what's already being done to challenge fake news – if not bullshit – and why it's not working, and what else we might do to tackle the underlying issues that can perhaps turn back the tide.

Fact-checking won't be nearly enough. The media theorist Clay Shirky said in July 2016 that 'we've brought fact-checkers to a culture war'. This isn't to doubt the good that fact-checking can do, but all too often the people reading the debunks are not only far fewer in number, but also nothing like the same people who read the initial false claim. Not only do debunks of this sort do little to heal divides, they can inadvertently enhance them. We will need to go outside of our comfort zone to tackle bullshit.

Is bullshit an issue we even need to tackle, though? 'Fake news' is nothing new, and while 'post-truth' may have been the word of the year in 2016, there's plenty of seemingly bigger things going on: fears about the rise of populism, nationalism, a growing partisan gulf and accompanying erosion of the political centre.

I don't think the rise of bullshit coming at the same time as a rise in populist sentiment is a coincidence – each feeds the other. A corrosive effect of our casual attitude to truth is that there's no agreed way to test our conflicting narratives against one another: all we can say is that those who disagree with us are malicious, corrupt or liars. Donald Trump slams the media; left- and right-wing outlets call rival politicians (and each other) liars or 'fake news'; and supporters of each group turn on one another as dupes or traitors.

Fake news is more a symptom of this vacuum of trust than a cause: bullshit is indeed the enemy of the truth, and without a sense of truth we have no way to debate across the political fence – we can only shout our conflicting narratives. The end result of such an environment gives no more weight to the BBC or the *New York Times* than to a Facebook status or AmericanPatriotDaily.

com. Such an environment cannot help but be corrosive to the long-term health and stability of a democracy.

One theme of this book is that we all have our biases and we read, share and respond to news in accordance with them – whether we acknowledge them or not – which means it's only reasonable to share my own, especially as I've worked across a range of outlets which are mentioned throughout.

While writing this book, I'm employed as a special correspondent by BuzzFeed News. Prior to that, I've worked at *The Guardian* in the US and the UK, at the *Washington Post*, at the Bureau of Investigative Journalism, and for a time, during the 2010 Chelsea Manning leaks, at WikiLeaks. Additionally, I've freelanced for a range of UK newspapers and collaborated on projects with the *New York Times*, International Consortium of Investigative Journalists and ProPublica. If you're looking to call me an MSM shill, the evidence is all there. Beyond that, I've tried to source and evidence all claims in this book – if there's anything you'd like to pick up on from it, do get in touch via Twitter: I'm @jamesrbuk.

This book can't make any claim to have all the answers to tackling the rise of bullshit. What it hopefully does do is set out the scale of the problem, why it's happening, what motivates those engaged in it and why what's being done so far is inadequate, and to suggest some first steps in tackling the problem.

PART I

THE POWER OF BULLSHIT

CHAPTER ONE

TRUMPED: HOW THE DONALD WON AMERICA

US presidential campaigns have never been a bastion of honesty, highbrow political debate and detailed exchange of ideas. The 1800 presidential election saw supporters of John Adams say a Jefferson presidency would mean 'murder, robbery, rape, adultery and incest will openly be taught and practiced', while Jefferson's supporters slurred Adams as a 'gross hypocrite' and even a hermaphrodite.[1]

The modern presidential campaign is characterised by relentlessly targeted expensive attack ads, PACs (Political Action Committees), and surrogates on the offensive. In recent years, Senator John Kerry saw his military record attacked, while President Obama received sustained attack – albeit much of it from Donald Trump – over whether or not he had been born in the US. Anyone looking to imagine a golden era of wonderful presidential contests in the time span in between has to contend with Watergate, racist allegations in contests in the run-up to the civil war, and much more besides.[2]

So, of course, it's nothing new that a presidential contest is nasty or dishonest. But even against the low bar of recent contests,

2016's feels like something new: Donald Trump's rhetorical clusterbombs of nonsense 'facts', unprovable allegations, his rotating cast of enemies, and his ability to provoke divisions even among his ardent rivals – which of Trump's speeches should be taken seriously? Which ignored? – has left the US not just culturally divided or in disagreement on issues, but disagreeing about the fundamentals of its election.

Should the US public trust its President or its intelligence agencies over Russian hacking? How do parties contend elections when one party says the other benefited from millions of fake votes (despite losing anyway)? The result isn't simply a set of credulous Trump supporters who believe fake news on the one hand and a group of informed liberals who oppose him on the other. The bizarro world fuelled by Trump leaves both sides unable to separate truth from fiction, and sees conspiracy theories and fakery abound on social media, in crowds and elsewhere on all sides – with much of the media stuck in the middle, with little idea how to respond.

Donald Trump's arrival on the political scene did not herald an immediate change from a long era of honesty in presidential primaries: in a crowded field of colourful characters, Trump's sometimes outlandish claims weren't all outside of the norms. Trump's primary rival – and eventual Cabinet nominee – Ben Carson variously claimed the Holocaust would have been less successful if Jews had had access to guns; that there should be a religious test for the Presidency to exclude Muslims; and that Obamacare was the worst thing to happen to America 'since slavery'.[3]

Rival candidate Mike Huckabee spoke in terms as evocative and overwrought, claiming Obama's Iran deal would 'take the

Israelis and march them to the door of the oven', a Holocaust comparison immediately condemned as offensive by Democrats and Jewish groups.[4] Huckabee was also accused of exaggerating his accomplishments as governor, wildly exaggerating unemployment figures and wrongly claiming Obamacare would gut Medicare.[5]

In the context of this kind of hyperbole, many of Donald Trump's claims, especially during primary season as he contended as a rank outsider for the Republican nomination, are quite close to business as usual. When Donald Trump claimed the US had an unemployment rate of 42 per cent, this might seem ridiculous (the actual rate is around 5 per cent). But this number has at least some basis in reality – it's just not a helpful way to count unemployment. Trump's figure includes retirees, stay-at-home parents, long-term sick and disabled people and others not looking for work, as well as those actually wanting a job and unable to find one. This isn't to say this number isn't misleading – very few voters would want to force retirees or parents into work, and the headline unemployment rate fell dramatically under Obama – but the figure has a basis in reality.[6]

Other Trump claims fall in this questionable-but-not-invented category, close to but not quite within the remit of politics-as-usual. When campaigning, Trump pushed a policy of better drug price negotiation for Medicare – a proposal also advocated by Democrat contenders Hillary Clinton and Bernie Sanders. Unlike his rivals, though, Trump claimed he could save around $300 billion a year on drugs this way – despite Medicare spending just $78 billion a year on drugs, a proposal likened by the *Washington Post*'s fact-checking blog as 'truly absurd' and 'like turning water into wine.'[7]

In other instances, Trump – alongside other candidates – appeared to simply invent figures out of whole cloth. Having made building a wall along the Mexico border and instituting a 'Muslim ban' as planks of his candidacy, Trump repeatedly stated that Obama had agreed to take in 200,000 Syrian refugees. In the wake of such remarks followed multiple (largely ignored) excoriations from commentators and fact-check blogs. Their only noticeable effect was to encourage Trump to up his invented figure to 250,000. The real figure is more than an order of magnitude lower, at less than 10,000.[8]

A final example in this category of policy-based untruths can be found in Trump's tax plan, a huge series of cuts in rates and increases of standard deductions for earners at all income levels, as well as eliminating the estate (or 'death') tax. The independent Tax Policy Center found the plan will come at a huge cost to public finances, costing more than $9,500 billion in lost revenue over its first decade and eventually expanding the US government's budget deficit by 80 per cent of GDP – well beyond levels seen as sustainable. Without enormous, unprecedented spending cuts, such tax cuts would be unsustainable.

But Trump's rhetoric on his cuts went much further. On a national level, he claimed the tax cuts could help boost US growth to something as high as 5 per cent or 6 per cent a year – levels dramatically above the average economic growth of the country over the past thirty years. Moreover, Trump claimed on multiple occasions that his plan would cost him personally 'a fortune', as it would reduce tax rates for the ultra-rich. Independent analysts found nothing to back up such claims, saying instead that 'the largest benefits, in dollar and percentage terms, would go to the highest-income households',[9] with considerable benefits likely to accrue to ultra-high net worth individuals such as Trump himself. In other words, contrary to his claims, Trump's tax break would require major cuts, benefit richer families more than poorer ones, and benefit Trump himself significantly.

The defining policy from Trump, which garnered perhaps more chaos and confusion than any other, was his plan to build a wall along the USA's 2,000-mile-long land border with Mexico, to tackle illegal immigration, despite the fact that more Mexicans are leaving the US than are heading in the opposite direction.[10] Trump claimed the wall would cost just $8 billion, which would be paid 'by Mexico'. When eventually the Department for Homeland Security revealed – after Trump became President – that the wall would more likely cost around $21 billion, Trump simply dismissed press reports of the study (which had not yet been presented to him) on Twitter, pledging: 'I have not gotten involved in the design or negotiations yet. When I do … price will come WAY DOWN!'[11]

As political pledges make promises about the future, it's fairly standard for rival candidates to be able to claim they're uncosted or unworkable, and fairly standard for campaigns to dismiss such criticism. While in some instances Trump's plans seem to go well outside the norms of what will be deliverable, they represent at most an exaggeration of an ongoing political trend. Some of Trump's other campaign claims, though, represent a stranger shift: clearly untrue (and sometime damaging) ideas which are easily falsifiable.

Some of these claims lead to chains of divisive arguments as Trump and his supporters double-down on blatantly untrue claims. One of the most prominent through the campaign began with Donald Trump's claim that 'thousands' of Muslims stood on rooftops and cheered as the Twin Towers fell after the terror attacks on 11 September 2001 – something Trump said he saw first-hand. The claim, coming in an environment of hostility to Muslims, concern over terror, and anti-immigration settlement, risked fuelling racial and religious tensions and had no basis in truth.

'I watched in Jersey City, NJ, where thousands and thousands of people were cheering as that building was coming down,' he told a rally.[12] 'Thousands of people were cheering.'

Offered the opportunity to walk the comment back the next day following police denials such cheering ever happened, as Politifact sets out, Trump insisted he saw the Jersey City celebrations 'on television' and that the celebrations were 'well covered at the time'. The fact-checking site's search for evidence found a report alleging such celebrations had happened, dated six days after the attack, despite the report stating the allegations were 'unfounded', and a *Washington Post* story referring to police questioning a number of people over 'alleged' celebrations.

It was this second story which led to Trump's next escalation. Despite having claimed to have seen the celebrations of 'thousands' of people on television, rather than having read about them, Trump seized on the *Post* story as proof of the veracity of his claim. This led one of the authors of the article, Serge Kovaleski, to tell factcheck.org his story did not prove the claim.[13] 'I certainly do not remember anyone saying that thousands or even hundreds of people were celebrating,' he said.

The report's other author told the site: 'I specifically visited the Jersey City building and neighborhood where the celebrations were purported to have happened. But I could never verify that report.'

Trump, characteristically, chose to attack the reporter rather than accept his contradictory position. This reached its height at a November 2015 rally in South Carolina, where, from the podium, in front of thousands of supporters – not to mention TV cameras – Trump chose to mock Kovaleski by imitating a condition the *New York Times* reporter has which limits the movement in his arms.

'Now the poor guy, now you got to see this, "Uhhh, I don't know what I said. Uhhh, I don't remember,"' Trump says, wildly jerking his arms and pulling comedy-grotesque facial expressions as he misquotes Kovaleski. 'He's going like "Uhhh, I don't remember, oh, maybe that's what I said."'[14]

Kovaleski, of course, had not claimed not to remember writing the piece: he had clearly said he tried to corroborate the claims that *any* Muslims were found in New Jersey celebrating the attacks and failed, and accurately stated that nowhere had he claimed 'thousands' had celebrated such an attack.

But the nature of Trump's attack quickly overtook the row that provoked it, as the *New York Times* and other organisations branded Trump's derisory attack on its reporter as 'outrageous'. Inevitably, Trump's next response was to claim he hadn't, in fact, mocked the reporter's disability. Trump first claimed never to have met Kovaleski, instead claiming he was instead making a 'general' imitation of a person grovelling. Trump and Kovaleski had met around a dozen times, including for an interview in Trump's office and a full-day interview at a product launch.[15] Even in January 2017, more than a year after the incident, Trump was provoked by Meryl Streep's condemnation of his mockery to deny it yet again.

'For the 100th time, I never "mocked" a disabled reporter

(would never do that) but simply showed him … "groveling" when he totally changed a 16 year old story that he had written in order to make me look bad. Just more very dishonest media!' the then President-elect tweeted.[16]

Again: Kovaleski did not change his original story, which had not even been the original evidence Trump cited. He had never grovelled. And the footage of Trump's mockery has been broadcast on multiple TV networks and sites across the internet. But this case forms a pattern for the new President which we'll see again: an aggressive but unevidenced claim is followed by a search for anything which seems to corroborate Trump's speech – then, once something's been seized on as the 'proof' of the claim, anyone attacking that claim faces a series of *ad hominem* assaults. The final position becomes a matter of faith: to support Trump, one generally has to believe the full stack – initial claim, its proof, and that Trump didn't attack the reporter. The items come as a package, facts and nuance be damned.

Trump has a playbook which helps him escape having to know any of the details or nuances on policy – a political gift for escalating any question of fact into an argument. This playbook served Trump faithfully as he claimed to have predicted 9/11 and to have consistently opposed the invasion of Iraq in 2003, and on defensive issues like his repeated failure to disclose his tax returns – claiming during the race they couldn't be released due to an audit (audits do not prevent the voluntary release of returns). Then, after his victory, Trump's team merely stated the public 'didn't care'[17] anyway when they simply dropped their long-standing promise to eventually release the documents.

But where Trump's gift really comes to the fore is in the case of two long and complex sagas involving email accounts of

Hillary Clinton, the Democratic nominee for President in his 2016 race.

Clinton ended up facing two largely separate controversies involving email. The first centred on her use of a private email server during her time as Secretary of State, a move introduced largely to allow the largely computer-illiterate Clinton to use her BlackBerry for emails, according to transcripts from an eventual FBI investigation.[18] Other Secretaries of State – notably Colin Powell – had held private email accounts while in office, but Clinton's server use became a particular scandal when it emerged that material which should have been classified had been discussed on the unofficial email channel, though without evidence of deliberate malfeasance.

Trump seized upon the row, and the FBI investigation, as part of his 'crooked Hillary' narrative of regularly painting his opponent as a corrupt candidate who should be locked up. During the second presidential debate, he referred to the decision of Clinton's team to securely delete – using free software – 33,000 personal emails from her private server before threatening to appoint a special prosecutor to investigate the matter.

'If I win, I am going to instruct my Attorney General to get a special prosecutor to look into your situation. Because there has never been so many lies, so much deception. There has never been anything like it. And we're gonna have a special prosecutor,' he said.[19]

When I speak, I go out and speak, the people of this country are furious. In my opinion, the people that have been long-time workers at the FBI are furious. There has never been anything like this where emails, and you get a subpoena. You get a subpoena

> … and after getting the subpoena you delete 33,000 e-mails and then you acid wash them or bleach them, as you would say. Very expensive process. So we're gonna get a special prosecutor and we're gonna look into it.

Note, in the above remarks, Trump never particularly sets out exactly what his opponent had done which would merit a special prosecutor, other than the apparently unprecedented deletion of some emails. But several months earlier, after a lengthy investigation, FBI director James Comey had publicly said that no legal action would be taken against Clinton, and specifically noted: 'We found no evidence that any of the additional work-related e-mails were intentionally deleted in an effort to conceal them' and 'We did not find clear evidence that Secretary Clinton or her colleagues intended to violate laws governing the handling of classified information,'[20] nor did he find direct evidence that the server had been hacked, though he did repeatedly criticise officials for 'careless' handling of information and leaving information at risk.

That Clinton herself had made a series of errors of judgement fed into a second email-related scandal: the hacking of email accounts belonging to her close aide John Podesta and other staff at the Democratic National Committee, which were then published over a series of weeks by WikiLeaks.

The whistle-blowing site had already published the emails from Clinton's servers which had been examined and then officially released, leaving a confusing amalgamation of multiple caches of Clinton-related email on the site – and consequently a high risk that anyone not following a months-long story extremely closely could easily believe the hacks and leaks were in some ways related to Clinton's own security failings.

In reality, the incidents were not linked. Emails from Clinton's private server were reviewed by officials and voluntarily published as part of a PR drive following the revelation of its existence. The publication of Podesta's emails came from a highly sophisticated and targeted phishing attack, in which Podesta received an email apparently from Google warning he was facing hacking attacks from Eastern Europe, and must change his password – which led to him disclosing his password to the attacker.[21] Despite claims to the contrary from Trump and his boosters, there is public domain evidence suggesting the attack was sophisticated and linked to Russian state actors.

Despite public evidence and statements from intelligence agencies that Russia was connected to the email hacking attacks, Trump was dismissive – saying it was 'probably China, or somebody sitting in his bed'[22] – though did appear to invite the Russians to hand over any Clinton emails they did have to US authorities, apparently inviting a foreign power to help influence a US election in which he was a candidate.

Trump and his campaign successfully kept emails and Clinton's 'corruption' routinely in the headlines in a series of campaign attacks heavy on invective if light on details. The campaign regularly used the emails, or facts contained therein, as part of a 'CROOKED HILLARY QUESTION OF THE DAY'[23] series of attack lines. Trump's approach not only ensured his opponent would be seen as corrupt and illegitimate by his own supporters, but – intentionally or otherwise – bundled in much of the rest of the establishment, making it appear as if intelligence agencies, the White House and others were gathering together to defend a corrupt politician, delegitimising institutions usually seen as untouchable in regular presidential races.

These efforts paid off when the FBI announced at the end of October in a letter to Congress that it was reopening part of its investigation into Clinton's email servers. The initial letter, which was shy on details, said emails had surfaced in an investigation 'unrelated to the [closed] investigation' on Clinton's email server,[24] sparking headlines everywhere on a story which had never really gone away. In the event, the emails had been found on computers belonging to the former congressman Anthony Weiner, who has been married to one of Clinton's closest aides and was facing investigation on sex charges. The FBI reported that investigators had found emails from Clinton's private server, but it had not at the time of notifying Congress – just days before the election – disclosed whether or not any of them were new or significant.

The new batch of emails were investigated and a few days later found to contain no significant new information, but had all the same served to bring the row back to the fore at a crucial phase of the late election. Trump's team also quickly refused to accept that the review had been fair: General Mike Flynn – a campaign advisor to Trump and his appointee as National Security Advisor – tweeted that it would be 'impossible' to scan hundreds of thousands of emails in a few days, a claim ridiculed by intelligence experts including NSA whistle-blower Edward Snowden.[25] It's difficult if not impossible to know whether the row significantly affected voters, but an ABC/Washington Post poll[26] taken in the days after Comey's announcement showed 34 per cent of voters stating the email scandal would make them less likely to vote Clinton – though headline voting intention moved only a fraction, if at all.

Trump's approach, with hindsight, appears to have been

effective in cutting through and keeping his two-word mantra – 'Crooked Hillary' – in circulation. Meanwhile, attempts to spark similar scandals against Donald Trump struggled to cut through beyond those already hostile to the candidate. On 1 October 2016, the *New York Times* published a one-page summary of Trump's 1995 tax return, which it had received in a reporter's mailbox. The 21-year-old document showed a $916 million loss for the year, potentially allowing Trump to use the losses to offset tax for a period of up to eighteen years.[27]

Inevitably, the Clinton campaign moved to capitalise on the leak, which could be used in a variety of ways: attacking Trump for not voluntarily publishing his own returns, for avoiding tax, or even for being an unsuccessful businessman whose failed casino ventures – which had racked up huge losses he could then offset against future taxes – had led to numerous job losses and unpaid contractors. But Clinton's campaign did not have the long and sustained history on any of those attack lines on Trump, harming the chances of the issue landing.

Similarly, months of forensic reporting by David Fahrenthold at the *Washington Post* showed a series of concerns around Donald Trump's charitable contributions and his foundation. Fahrenthold found – in contradiction to repeated claims by Trump that he gives millions of his own money to charity – no evidence of major charitable contributions from Trump's own pocket. The reporting also found a series of conflict of interest and ethics questions around Trump's foundation.

Despite, or perhaps because of, receiving years of scrutiny and questions about the Clinton Foundation, Clinton's campaign did little to capitalise on Trump's foundation as an attack line.

In the months following the election, much of the commentary on how to write about Trump has focused on the need to build up reporting and investigative capabilities, and use it to dig into America's unconventional President. This may well be a good thing, but it's important to remember that the election campaign contained plenty of original investigative reporting into Trump's taxes, business affairs and court allegations, and his lurid and offensive comments about women.[28] And then he won the election all the same.

Part of the answer may lie in the almost universally held view that Hillary Clinton was winning the election. Despite Trump's wall-to-wall free media and constant controversies, he consistently trailed his rival in the polls, leading several leading Republicans to feel able to publicly break from their presidential candidate, either condemning him or saying they would not vote for him.[29]

Clinton's team, like most pundits, were convinced their approach was working and she was winning the election. This view, coupled with fears that some Obama voters may not turn out for Clinton if she didn't run a positive campaign, may have prevented the campaign from trying negative campaigning or attack ads which could have changed the outcome. National polls showed a lead of between one and seven points for Clinton in the days before the election,[30] and the campaign appeared to be looking for a blowout win to fend off any challenges that her victory could be illegitimate. Just days before the election, Clinton was campaigning in Arizona, which has only voted Democrat in a presidential contest once since 1952, rather than the conventional battleground states which eventually decided the contest against her.

Concerns that Trump wouldn't necessarily accept an election

result were not baseless, despite being virtually unheard of in modern US politics – even in the extraordinarily close and acrimonious 2000 Bush *v.* Gore contest, Gore eventually conceded the election after a Florida court called a halt to his bid to have votes recounted. But in the days before the election, with little or no evidence to cite, Trump openly suggested the contest may be fixed against him.

Asked by the moderator of the third presidential debate whether he'd accept the result, Trump claimed Clinton 'should never have been allowed to run for the presidency' and listed reasons he felt he was facing a rigged field.

'I will look at it at the time. I'm not looking at anything now, I'll look at it at the time. What I've seen, what I've seen, is so bad,' Trump said in response to the question.[31]

First of all, the media is so dishonest and so corrupt and the pile-on is so amazing. The *New York Times* actually wrote an article about it, but they don't even care. It is so dishonest, and they have poisoned the minds of the voters…

If you look at your voter rolls, you will see millions of people that are registered to vote. Millions. This isn't coming from me. This is coming from Pew report and other places. Millions of people that are registered to vote that shouldn't be registered to vote. So let me just give you one other thing. I talk about the corrupt media. I talk about the millions of people.

Faced with a plea from moderator Chris Wallace, of Fox News, that the US had a long tradition of candidates accepting defeat even after bitter contests, Trump merely promised he'd 'keep you in suspense'. At a rally the day after the debate, and the subsequent furore, Trump declined to walk the comments back, telling his supporters: 'I will totally accept the results of this great and historic presidential election … if I win.'[32]

And win he did. Donald Trump obtained 304 of the USA's 538 electoral college votes, a close but relatively decisive victory – Hillary Clinton delivered her concession speech early on the morning after election day. Trump's attacking of the electoral system he was contending in before the election may have been morally questionable, but had some strategic merit: it could fuel indignant supporters to vote, or give a surge of popular support to any legal challenges against the result. There is no reasonable or rational reason – other than ego – to challenge the result of an election you have won. And yet that's exactly what Donald Trump went on to do, becoming possibly the first winner of an election to claim the contest was rigged.

The issue was Hillary Clinton's victory in the popular vote: in some of the states Clinton won, she won big, amassing just under 3 million votes more than Donald Trump. This was not what Donald Trump or his supporters wanted to hear. In the hours following the election, a website showing faked voter totals, declaring Trump the winner of the popular vote, topped Google results and was widely shared on social media as evidence of mainstream media fakery.[33]

Trump himself claimed he had won a 'massive landslide victory' at the electoral college[34] – an untrue claim – before making a more astounding claim: there had been 3 million false votes in the election he'd just won, conveniently around the margin of Clinton's popular vote victory.

The apparent source of Trump's claim seems extraordinary. In a tweet, he credits 'Gregg Phillips and his crew', who 'say at least 3,000,000 votes were illegal'. Phillips, a long-time Conservative and Tea Party activist, has frequently alleged voter fraud which other studies were unable to find.[35] Phillips's claim to have confirmed 3 million votes was picked up by the right-wing conspiracy site InfoWars, whose founder Alex Jones has, among other things, claimed that 9/11 was an inside job and that the shooting of twenty schoolchildren at Sandy Hook was faked.[36] Trump granted Jones one of the first interviews following his election victory.[37]

Phillips has refused to share his methodology or publish data supporting his claim, while numerous mainstream election experts have offered extensive evidence showing that the election was not faked. Trump has, nonetheless, while offering no other evidence to support his claim, ordered an official investigation into voter fraud and promised to crack down on people wrongly registering to vote in multiple states. Trump's cited expert – Phillips – is allegedly registered in three states,[38] as are several of Trump's inner circle and family.[39] Being registered to vote in several states is not uncommon, as those moving from one state to another often forget to specifically de-register as they move.

Donald Trump is not the only person attacking the legitimacy of the election he won, however. In the weeks following the election victory, the row over the hacking of emails of officials connected to Hillary Clinton came to the fore once again – but this time in a way problematic for Donald Trump.

Before the election, the Department for Homeland Security and Office of the Director of National Intelligence issued a statement on behalf of the USA's intelligence community that Russia had been behind hacking attacks designed to influence the US election.[40] After the election, leaked accounts detailed how the

CIA had come to a similar conclusion in a secret report, stating with 'high confidence' that Russia had influenced the election to boost Trump.[41]

In another move unprecedented in modern times, President-elect Trump opted to directly contradict the statements of the intelligence agencies he was about to take command of. 'These are the same people that said Saddam Hussein had weapons of mass destruction,' Trump said in one post-election statement. In another tweet, Trump appeared to prioritise WikiLeaks founder Julian Assange's denials over the CIA's statement: 'Julian Assange said "a 14 year old could have hacked Podesta" – why was DNC so careless? Also said Russians did not give him the info!'[42]

The effect of this row was not just to strike a divide between Trump's supporters and intelligence agencies, but rather to strike doubt and confusion across the US electorate. Blanket coverage of the row over Russia's involvement in influencing the US election was coupled with a huge crowdfunding effort by the Green Party's presidential candidate Jill Stein to secure recounts in three pivotal states narrowly won by Donald Trump.

In the weeks around those headlines, polls showed a nation completely divided on Russian hacking and electoral fraud. On fraud, according to a YouGov poll, 62 per cent of Trump voters said they believed millions of illegal votes had been cast in the election – while 25 per cent of Clinton voters said the same. On hacking, the results were starker still: 87 per cent of Clinton voters said it was true Russia had hacked emails to help Trump, while only 20 per cent of Trump voters said the same. But many went further: 50 per cent of Clinton voters said it was true that Russia had tampered with election counting machines to help Trump (*v.* 9 per cent of Trump voters).[43]

Here's the significant thing about the second claim – not only is there no evidence of any tampering with voting machines, almost no one has even been making that claim. Neither the Clinton campaign nor the Democratic National Committee alleged the actual vote counts were altered, while Obama specifically said it didn't happen:

'We were frankly more concerned in the run-up to the election to the possibilities of vote tampering, which we did not see evidence of and we're confident we can guard against,' he told the *Daily Show*.[44] If the polls are even remotely near correct, conspiratorial thinking is now part of mainstream political thought in America among both those who lean to the left and those to the right: millions of voters on every side believe their rivals would act illegally to win. Such a situation cannot be good for America's political institutions.

The rise of conspiratorial thinking and fake or polarised news is (arguably) easier to track on the right than on the left. Eight years of a President seen as illegitimate by many right-wing Americans fuelled the movement of hyper-aggressive online shows, fake news and conspiratorial sites, and the rise of the alt-right – of whom more later – a combination of racist and far-right groups. Such groups, often feeling poorly served by mainstream outlets, have long been happy to share alternative media – and people are happy to serve it up, whether for quick profit from ads or affiliate schemes, from a desire to prank, or to serve an ideological cause. Stories claiming that Pope Francis endorsed Trump, that Clinton sold weapons to ISIS, and that those investigating her had been found dead all found large and eager audiences.[45]

Though left-wing conspiracy sites have been around for a

long while, there was less of an obvious demand for such content while a relatively liberal Democrat occupied the White House – meaning 'fake news' is often discussed as a right-wing phenomenon. But left-wing conspiracies and fakes circulate all the same, even if they are called out less often. Fake stories circulating the political left are often just as aggressive as those on the right, including articles falsely alleging that Vice-President Mike Pence had said women would 'try to get raped' if abortion bans had a rape exception,[46] that Trump once said he'd run as a Republican because they have 'the dumbest' voters,[47] or – as discussed in the introduction to this book – that Trump's victory rallies featured a chant of 'we hate Muslims, we hate blacks'.[48]

These straightforwardly untrue stories – and how they get shared – have dominated much of the media debate on how to tackle the issues of polarisation or falling trust in the political process and media, and are one of the issues on the table. However, expectations that Trump as President-elect or President would be different from the Trump the nation discovered through the election campaign have proven unfounded – and the occupant of the Oval Office will inevitably have far more influence on the nature of public discourse than any fake news purveyor.

Trump's transition was characterised by arguments over vote fraud and by a public spat between Trump and his intelligence agencies. Hopes his administration would mark a change of tone had been fading – Trump hired Steve Bannon, the former editor of Breitbart.com and a man who once said he wanted to 'destroy the state' in a senior role, setting up his administration's staffing to be a struggle between establishment and insurgent factions.

Inauguration gave America the chance to see what type of

President Trump planned to be – and the early impression was one still given to easily discovered and unnecessary bullshit. Speaking to a crowd of around 10,000 at a concert at the Lincoln Memorial the evening before inauguration day, Trump said, 'I don't know if it's ever been done before. But if it has very seldom.' In reality, Obama held a concert in exactly the same venue in 2009, to a crowd estimated at anything up to forty times larger.[49]

Trump's staff briefed that he would write his own inauguration address – only for it to be briefed shortly afterwards that it had been written by Bannon and Stephen Miller, another hire from Breitbart.[50] This was followed by claims from Donald Trump that rain on the day only started after he finished his address, despite clear TV evidence to the contrary.[51] But the biggest and strangest row emerged over crowd size – Trump and his team decided to go against photographic and video evidence to claim his crowd had been the largest ever.

Let's be clear: there was little if any reason for Trump to do this. Washington DC is one of the most liberal cities in America, and the city is a long way from many of his heartlands. Given Trump's predecessor's election was such a historic occasion, it would be no surprise or issue for Trump to secure a smaller crowd than Barack Obama. Photographs clearly showed this was the case: areas which had been covered with crowds for Obama's first inaugural address were clearly lightly filled,[52] TV footage showed row after row of unoccupied roadside bleachers, and people on social media made much of the comparison – and Donald Trump seemed to notice.

The result was an extraordinary first press conference from newly installed press secretary Sean Spicer on his first day. Giving a statement and taking no questions, Spicer accused the media of 'deliberately false reporting' and 'intentionally fram[ing]' photos to 'minimise the enormous support' gathered on the mall – falsely claiming Trump's was the first inauguration to use grass coverings and saying this made the areas look emptier. Spicer concluded these efforts were 'shameful and wrong' and said the Trump administration would 'hold the press accountable'.[53]

The divide saw liberals and conservatives rowing over which photos showed larger crowd sizes, over whether or not a limo had been set on fire (despite footage showing that one had) – with a short-lived false claim that its real owner had been the Rev. Jesse Jackson[54] – and even over whether or not the National Park Service was improperly biased having tweeted a picture of crowd sizes.[55] A poll taken just after the weekend showed respondents two photographs side-by-side, showing crowds of different sizes on the national mall. The photos were unlabelled, but taken from Obama and Trump's inaugurations – and yet, when asked which was bigger, 15 per cent of Trump voters said the obviously smaller crowd was the larger of the two.[56] The researchers told the *Washington Post*: 'Some Trump supporters in our sample decided to use this question to express their support for Trump rather than to answer the survey question factually.'

When challenged about the various untruths Spicer had voiced during his first press statement, Trump advisor Kellyanne Conway archly said he'd merely used 'alternative facts'. These examples seem trivial, and they are – but they highlight the state of affairs that's been reached. The US government and media can't agree on crowd sizes, or events captured on television.

There's no agreement on whether or not Trump and his family

are breaching ethics rules covering benefiting from public office. There has been a temptation among those on the left to paint these as part of a genius master strategy by Trump and his team to 'distract' from issues of greater interest – though little agreement on which issues are the distractions and which merit attention. Such claims, without evidence, are counter-productive: Trump's tweets often follow cable news broadcasts on the issue he responds to. Imagining without any evidence that there's a masterful and malevolent master strategy behind any story is itself disempowering for reader and media alike – suggesting the media are always covering the wrong issues, and that everyone is constantly being outsmarted.

It may be the trivial issues that best highlight the challenges facing the media, but the early signs suggest the Trump administration will be pushing the boundaries where it matters, too. In its first weeks in office, the administration suggested taking Iraq's oil – a major breach of international law – would have been a good idea. The composition of the National Security Committee was changed to give political advisors permanent spots and sideline some career intelligence officers.

When the Trump administration issued an executive order preventing entry to the US for people from seven majority Muslim countries, even if they possessed valid visas or green-cards, it was blocked by judges. Trump and his officials were then quick to suggest those judges were acting illegitimately in those decisions, on multiple occasions. Even here, the trivial won out again: despite Trump repeatedly and publicly calling the measure a 'ban', Spicer insisted it had never been referred to as such, sparking further coverage of the discrepancy. Trump's early moves as President suggest he will test the limits of the powers of the presidency. It's far from clear how effectively the media or the political system will be able to challenge him.

Much of what has happened in the early days of Trump's presidency has set out the challenges which will face those who would try to hold him to account. But of all the incidents in the first weeks of Trump's presidency, it's his address to several hundred CIA staff on the first full day of his term which is perhaps the most revealing. Speaking to an audience of professionals whose career depends on closely tracking what people say and do – and separating the truth from lies – Trump said things which were not only untrue but also clearly and demonstrably false to anyone with access to Google. By denying ever having had any kind of rift with the intelligence agencies, Trump said what he imagined the audience in front of him wanted to hear, and perhaps in that moment what he wanted to be true, and – another running theme – to set out an alternative villain.

'I have a running war with the media. They are among the most dishonest human beings on Earth,' he said. 'And they sort of made it sound like I had a feud with the intelligence community. And I just want to let you know, the reason you're the number-one stop is exactly the opposite – exactly. And they understand that, too.'[57]

Trump's comments criticising the intelligence agency in terms unprecedented for any President-elect were, even as Trump was speaking, openly available to anyone on Twitter, including accusations of deliberate leaks and even likening their activities to those of Nazi Germany.[58] What he said wasn't true. What was also apparent was that he didn't care.

The cumulative effect of Trump's wall of lies, distortions,

bullshit and incomprehensibility has sent the media – and much of the public – into a tailspin. Responses included trying to ignore him until he went away, which is not a viable option for a President. For a time, the sage advice was to take Trump 'seriously, but not literally', but this once again started to fall apart as he reached the Oval Office: despite Trump's flamboyancy and his bullshit, his first few weeks as President saw Trump delivering many of the policies the supporters at his rallies were waiting for – the very policies that 'informed' commentators had spent months explaining he either couldn't or wouldn't attempt to deliver.

The result is a mess. The man behind the *Resolute* desk has been in the public eye for more than thirty years, and yet in many respects we know almost nothing about him. We don't know the full extent of his wealth. We don't know how much tax he's paid. We don't know how much business he's done in Russia. We don't – thanks to the strangeness of his initial doctor's report, which referred to his health as 'astonishingly excellent' – have a good picture of his health. And thanks to the nature of the campaign he's run, we don't agree on the basics of a country's health: whether crime is rising or not, whether the election Trump won was rigged with millions of fake votes. We don't even agree whether one crowd is bigger than another.

Trump has called the media 'enemies of the people'.[59] This is central to Trump's approach to politics: whether a deliberate strategy or the result of lifelong habit, Trump has no respect for the idea of the fourth estate, a media holding power to account. Everything must be a row, not a debate – the media aren't checking his claims, or his details; they're standing against him and his supporters. Trump's style of politics needs an enemy, and with

Clinton dispatched in the presidential election, the media are the perfect choice for the role.

This is America's version of the post-truth world. Britain's version of it, conducted through the Brexit campaign, is characteristically less dramatic – but its effects, as we're about to see, are just as real.

CHAPTER TWO

BREXIT: TAKING BACK CONTROL

Shortly after 10 p.m. on 23 June 2016, and much of the British establishment was breathing a gentle sigh of relief. After months of campaigning for a referendum which polls were indicating would be much closer than they'd initially expected, it looked like the UK had voted to remain a member of the European Union. An on-the-day poll from YouGov showed a close but comfortable 52/48 Remain victory,[1] while Nigel Farage – one of the leaders of the 'unofficial' Leave campaign Leave.EU – appeared to concede the race. 'Looks like Remain will edge it,' he said, citing 'friends in the financial markets who have done some big polling'.[2]

Ninety minutes later, as the first set of real results came, things looked very different. Sunderland, an area expected to be roughly 50/50 between Leave and Remain voted decisively to leave. In area after area across the country, Leave, it turned out, performed slightly stronger than expected. By 4 a.m., it was obvious the UK would leave the EU. A few hours later, the pound had fallen 10 per cent against the dollar, hitting a 31-year low. By 8 a.m., the nation's breakfast programming was interrupted with David Cameron's resignation as Prime Minister outside 10 Downing Street. And, most significantly of all, the UK would need to begin preparations to extricate itself from its 43-year bond with the European Union.

This wasn't what was supposed to happen. David Cameron made the EU referendum a manifesto commitment in 2015, in large part as a response to decades-long divisions among his backbenchers on EU membership. Some had questioned whether Cameron ever expected the referendum to happen – few had predicted the Conservatives securing a majority government in the 2015 general election. Once pledged, though, a referendum was likely unavoidable: the Liberal Democrats, seen as the Conservatives' most likely coalition partner if one was needed, had pledged support for an in/out referendum in their manifesto.

Despite his claims to be keeping an open mind on the question, almost no one expected David Cameron to do anything except support continued membership of the EU, and in the months running up to the referendum this seemed the overwhelmingly likely outcome. At the start of 2016, Remain had a comfortable polling lead of eight to ten points over Leave[3] – and every political mantra suggested their support would grow: people don't vote against their economic interests; people lean towards the status quo in referenda; and experts would line up on the side of Remain.

There were plenty of reasons to back either side of the referendum debate, and it would be a nonsense to claim voters on either side were tricked or fooled into their vote. But that should not be a reason to ignore how the two campaigns worked, and how one – perhaps inevitably – got bogged down in practicalities, details and defensiveness, while the other managed a slick campaign based on pledges few informed people ever believed could or should be delivered: something very close to our definition of bullshit.

The decision to vote in favour of Brexit broke every law of British political gravity – and grew out of a campaign unlike any other, one created on the basis of promises which those making them had no power to deliver – or indeed any intention of delivering.

Polling evidence has long suggested that the UK public hasn't cared a great deal either way about the European Union per se. Despite EU bureaucrats and regulations serving as a regular punching bag for UK media outlets and politicians, fewer than one in ten UK voters listed the EU among the top three issues facing the country in the run-up to the 2015 election.[4] However, as both campaigns did their early research, it became clear each had their own trump card on issues closely connected to EU membership that ranked highly for UK voters.

For Remain, the issue was economic stability. If the camp could convince voters that leaving would damage their finances, or present a major risk to them, they could win people over. For Leave, immigration was the strongest card in hand: the British public overwhelmingly believed immigration was too high and should be reduced – something that would be largely impossible while the EU dictated freedom of movement for EU workers to be a non-negotiable part of membership.

This shaped the early strategic decisions of both campaigns. At the core of Remain – officially named Britain Stronger in Europe, with its politically unfortunate acronym of BSE – was an awareness that few people in the UK would be receptive to an enthusiastic and passionate championing of the EU and its values. Instead, the campaign would rely on the assumption – for decades a very sound one in UK politics – that voters would not support anything that would hit their own family finances.[5] The Remain campaign had a number of advantages: expert and international support, access to civil service research until the purdah period began, and a reasonable poll lead coming into the campaign proper. It had a number of challenges too, though: the Conservative Party was anything but united, leaving the risk of civil war among the party – and the party's voters were generally Eurosceptic. To win, Remain would need to attract millions of voters who had opted for Labour, the Liberal Democrats or SNP rather than Conservatives – despite Labour having an unpopular leader who seemed ambivalent on the Remain cause.

The Leave camp faced its own divisions: its senior Conservative figures feared UKIP and its leader Nigel Farage, who had stood for Parliament on seven occasions and won on none, would alienate millions of voters who could potentially back Brexit. Then there was the question of how to play the immigration issue: should it be saved up for the final days of the campaign, as Dominic Cummings – the campaign director of the official Vote Leave campaign – wanted, or played from the outset, as Farage and his main donor Arron Banks preferred? The two groups went separate ways into separate campaigns, allowing Vote Leave to run with a message hinting at the immigration issue but making it much broader: 'Take Back Control', or 'Vote Leave, Take Control'.[6] The official Leave campaign was left not just fighting the Remain arguments but also shaking off their association with an outrider group which was happy to campaign on issues too rich for a mainstream campaign's taste. This may have eventually worked in their favour: given the obvious acrimony between the two Leave camps, few people could suggest under-the-table coordination between the two, but nevertheless Leave had the distinct advantage of having an outrider which could say things the mainstream campaign couldn't, allowing the two groups to target different audiences.

Both campaigns faced much that was novel. Both campaigns had a degree of support from MPs of various political parties, and from voters across the political spectrum. While support for Leave may have been concentrated on the right, a small but substantive portion of left-leaning voters supported Leave over concerns around globalisation and similar issues. However, holding together a tenuous coalition was likely a bigger issue for Remain – who had substantial numbers of MPs from four major parties onside – than Leave, whose support was largely concentrated among Conservatives, with just a smattering of Labour MPs onside. Another issue was dealing with an unusual media landscape: David Cameron could not count on the right-wing tabloids who would usually back a Conservative PM, while Leave contended with broadsheets' unclear affiliations through the campaign. Trying to run the EU referendum like a general election would simply be a non-starter for either side.

There was one extra obstacle for the Remain side which could only serve to help Leave: decades of accumulated bullshit about and scapegoating of the EU, dripped out through Eurosceptic papers and by politicians looking for an out year after year. Every politician has to pass an unpopular policy from time to time, and the EU made an ideal punching bag for many, or for policies which the UK could have stopped during EU treaty negotiations but chose not to. Rather than risk a political hit for explaining the UK had accepted a trade-off, it was expedient to instead blame inflexible EU bureaucrats, and EU institutions and officials, often tone-deaf to the UK's political climate, routinely made this all too easy.

Cameron and the Stronger In campaign were the ones left with the consequences of these decisions: a British public who had been told over the years (in some cases rightly, in some wrongly) that the EU had forced them to ditch their imperial units for metric, would ban acres, weaken vacuum cleaners and hairdryers, close off-licenses, forbid bendy bananas,[7] and far more – and that the EU was responsible for more serious and open questions of benefit and health tourism and the pressure of EU immigration on public services, as well as the question of whether immigration was keeping British people out of work.

This would not be a business-as-usual election: fittingly enough for a contest which would decide a four-decades-old issue, it would raise questions that crossed party lines, and settle scores which had run for far longer than just one four- or five-year parliamentary term.

The claim that came to define the Brexit campaign was not one that looked backwards: it was a simple and clear sentence which combined its campaign's main attack line with its main promise, and it was for week after week painted onto the side of a bus: 'We send the EU £350 million a week – let's fund our NHS instead'.

Without that slogan, Leave and Remain each had one of the UK electorate's top three issues on their side: Leave had immigration, Remain the economy. Vote Leave's bus slogan immediately attached their cause to the NHS, the third remaining 'top three' issue, and one of the country's most beloved institutions.

Leave's central pledge was one visibly adopted by its most prominent faces. During the campaign, Boris Johnson, then a Cabinet minister and now the Foreign Secretary, posed in a high-vis jacket with a giant £350 million cheque at a blast furnace in Staffordshire, before symbolically burning the cheque.[8] Michael Gove, once a close ally of Cameron's and then still a Cabinet minister, told ITV News: 'If that money is taken back, then that £50 million a day will be spent on British people's priorities and the NHS of course is top of people's list.'[9] A third Cabinet minister, Priti Patel, tied together the £350 million figure and immigration in remarks to the *Sunday Telegraph*.[10]

'It is becoming clear that our membership of the EU is putting the NHS under threat,' she said. 'Every week we send £350 million to Brussels – that's money that could be better invested in helping patients who rely on our NHS … Current levels of migration are causing unsustainable pressures on our public services and we can see that the NHS is creaking under the strain.'

The £350 million claim was cited daily in the media, was raised regularly by serving Cabinet ministers, and appeared in the visuals of almost every piece of Brexit coverage thanks to being printed on the side of a bus. And yet almost no one who said it could possibly have believed it to be true: as the months after the vote made clear, virtually no one at the core of the Vote Leave campaign believed in the literal truth of the campaign's central slogan. There would not be £350 million a week for the NHS.

And yet it was this that in many ways proved the claim's strength: it was irresistible bait for Remain campaigners and for media fact-checkers alike. Vote Leave had used the largest possible figure for the cost of EU membership it could defensibly choose. This led virtually every media outlet to run extensive pieces questioning the correct figure, and prompted multiple Remain-supporting politicians to try to explain the exaggerated figure.

One version of the explanation works as such: in raw terms, the UK sends the EU just over £18 billion a year, or £350 million a week. However, Margaret Thatcher secured a rebate from this amount which the UK has held ever since 1985, meaning the UK gets around £100 million reduced off this total – in practice, this is reduced before the UK ever sends the money. For various reasons, these amounts alter a little each year, so it's not clear exactly what they will be each year, but this £250 million is the highest that could be fairly said to be sent to the EU. Even then, though, that figure is arguably too high: the UK receives some direct benefits from the EU, such as spending for infrastructure or regional development projects and subsidies for farmers, totalling around £75 million a week – meaning the net amount the UK sends to the EU is around £175 million a week.[11]

This is a terrible argument to be trying to advance in a political debate: it's difficult to follow, relies on a knowledge of how EU spending works and what a rebate is, and, even if it's followed through completely, leaves you with the impression that even after everything it receives from the EU, the UK is still sending £175 million a week to the EU – confirming the Leave campaign's broader point that the UK would have more money for domestic priorities after leaving.

It hardly mattered that the UK's statistical authority asked the campaign not to use the £350 million figure – a rare intervention during election periods – warning the figures were 'potentially misleading'.[12] The simple truth is that to most of us, both £350 million and £175 million are simply incomprehensibly big numbers: whichever it is, it's a lot, and we're sending it somewhere.

Penny Mordaunt, then a defence minister, set out this line of reasoning masterfully at a pre-referendum BuzzFeed News event addressing an audience of young voters:[13] 'To put it in non-monetary terms, if I use the gross figure that's the sort of monetary equivalent of sending a warship a week to the EU,' she explained. 'That's the monetary equivalent of the gross figure. The net figure is a warship a fortnight to the EU. So the point I'd make upfront is it's still a lot of money.'

A warship a week or a warship a fortnight – either way, it sounds pretty damn expensive. Using the largest figure available had almost no downside risk – advertising regulators are unable to involve themselves in election advertising – and the claim served as bait for Remain supporters and neutral fact-checkers alike.

This was no accident: Vote Leave's campaign director Dominic Cummings knew exactly what he was doing, as he set out in a lengthy blog post months after the campaign was over.[14]

Stating that the £350 million NHS claim had been 'necessary to win', Cummings explained:

Sometimes we said 'we send the EU £350 million' to provoke people into argument. This worked much better than I thought it would. There is no single definitive figure because there are different sets of official figures but the Treasury gross figure is slightly more than £350m of which we get back roughly half …

Would we have won without immigration? No. Would we have won without £350m/NHS? All our research and the close result strongly suggests No.

The impression you may be left with after the above is that the debate was about whether Brexit would leave £175 million a week or £350 million a week for the NHS – a simple question of how much extra money would be available. In reality, it is highly unlikely there will be any extra money for the NHS, and it may even face further funding pressures due to Brexit – but it's not an argument Remain could have set out in a simple sound bite.

In essence, the amount of money the government has to spend is reliant on the size of the economy: by taking some tax on the amount of income we all earn, on the profits that companies make, and (through measures like VAT and fuel tax) on what we buy, the government raises its money. If the economy will grow more slowly, that means there will be less money to spend – and this is a much bigger effect than the direct cash transfers the UK makes to the EU. So even if Brexit causes no recession, and has low one-off costs, if it slows UK growth even slightly over the short- and medium-term, it will leave less money for the government to spend – including on the NHS. Unsurprisingly, this wonkish and forward-looking argument is not one that Remain and its spokespeople found easy to make.

£350 million a week for the NHS was the ultimate bullshit political claim: with no politician or party strictly accountable for it, punishment at the ballot box is tough. There was no official regulator or arbitrator to censure the campaign for using the figure, and any time people tried to tackle the details, they were forced to repeat the campaign's talking point. This system of laying bait with claims just too provocative to resist proved to be a persistent tactic throughout the campaign.

As we saw above, Vote Leave campaign director Dominic Cummings stated that both the NHS claim and immigration had been essential to Leave's victory. The campaign's central claim on the immigration issue centred on the alleged likelihood of Turkey – a country often in the news for political unrest, having a strongman leader (rapidly on his way to becoming an autocrat), and as a frontline in the conflicts with Syria and ISIS – becoming an EU member. Turkey, more than any other issue, showed how Leave's loose media and campaign ecosystem could take a claim and inflate it to reach different groups of voters.

The Vote Leave campaign on Turkey used a simple online poster which made only the subtlest of allusions to an influx of new immigrants – nothing that could be attacked as politically incorrect or aggressive. 'TURKEY (population 76 million) IS JOINING THE EU', it said. Strictly speaking, the poster could be described as true: Turkey is one of a group of nations being considered for EU membership. But it is nowhere near becoming a member at any point in the next decade or so. The process for joining the EU requires that prerequisites in thirty-five different areas be met. Turkey, at the time of the referendum, had met just one, and was not remotely close on many of the others. Even if all thirty-five criteria were met, Turkey's membership would be far from a given, as every EU member would have to agree to allow it to join.[15]

Vote Leave's misleading poster opened the way for claims which were still more audacious, though. Defence minister Penny Mordaunt repeatedly stated that no UK Prime Minister could veto Turkey's membership of the EU, implying to voters that the referendum would pose a final chance to prevent Turkish citizens gaining the unimpeded right to live and work in the UK. Mordaunt, though, was referring to her own political assessment that the UK – which has defence cooperation deals with Turkey – would never choose to veto membership. The UK as an EU member would retain full power to veto any new member, if it so chose.

The Eurosceptic media then served to amplify the effect of these political claims in ways the campaigns would have been unlikely to wish to be directly associated with. The most misleading (but stark) such claim was a banner headline in the *Daily Express*, perhaps the most ardent of the pro-Leave papers.

'12M TURKS SAY THEY'LL COME TO UK', said its banner headline, followed by a caption stating: 'Those planning to move are either unemployed or students according to shock new poll'. This poll made explicit what Vote Leave's poster stating Turkey's population left ambiguous: an influx of 12 million immigrants would be vast for the UK, which has net migration of around 300,000 a year.[16]

By flagging the unemployment of many of those allegedly planning to come to the UK, the *Express* article also implied a threat to jobs, or a need to pay benefits to the newcomers, stoking anti-immigration sentiment. The poll, though, was wildly misleading, asking respondents if they or *anyone they knew* would 'consider' a move. This is like asking a roomful of people if anyone they know would consider becoming a nurse, then saying anyone with a raised hand is a nurse. The story was 'clarified' on page two. Other papers ran stories on visa-free travel for Turks to the UK – on tourist visas – giving the impression, amid the broader atmosphere, that such deals were to allow long-term migration. The collective effect of these stories and attack lines was to plant the idea of Turkish immigration as an issue, inflate its scale out of all proportion, make it sound an inevitable effect of EU migration, and then to pose the referendum as the last chance to stop the threat – which in the short- or medium-term was simply non-existent.

This series of baffling and barely true or simply untrue claims continued to come from pro-Leave campaigns or newspapers. One line of attack centred on proposals to create an EU army, with the implication that this would lead to the end of the UK's military independence (despite the UK already being part of multiple international alliances). The army was indeed a real proposal, but one that has circulated and gone nowhere for more than a decade, and one the UK could easily have blocked – and had said it would likely do so.

A particularly baffling example came in a *Daily Mail* front-page splash, timed as Theresa May – then a Remain supporter – and George Osborne squabbled over whether the UK needed better border controls even if it stayed in the UK. Alongside a photo of a lorry full of people attempting to smuggle themselves into the country, the paper splashed the quote 'WE'RE FROM EUROPE – LET US IN!'. No one from an EU nation would ever need to enter the UK in this way, given their right to live and work here, so it's difficult to see why the *Mail* believed this to be what the people on the van said, or why the story was tied to the EU membership row. It quickly emerged, via a BBC reporter who had seen the footage in question, that the man quoted had in reality said, 'We're from Iraq.'[17]

Perhaps the most chilling of the misleading attack lines on immigration came from Nigel Farage and the unofficial Leave.EU campaign: a picture of a huge queue of people – coincidentally or otherwise, mostly made up of non-white people – headlined 'BREAKING POINT – the EU has failed us all', with the strapline 'We must break free of the EU and take back control'. The poster was widely condemned as offensive and even compared to some used in Nazi propaganda, which had similarly pictured large flows of refugees against an almost identical background.

The image was given no context in the Leave.EU poster, but was in reality a picture of refugees on the Croatia/Slovenia border. The UK's obligations on refugees are unrelated to its EU membership, and the UK had already opted out of EU refugee quota schemes. At the fringes of the campaign – largely spread through Twitter and Facebook – came the sorts of conspiratorial thinking now familiar from the Trump contest. Claims included the false assertions that various celebrities had endorsed Leave – including Victoria Beckham, based on a twenty-year-old out-of-context quote; that EU membership would mean the end of the monarchy; and even that people should take pens to polling stations in case authorities rubbed out and replaced votes for Leave made in pencil.

The Leave campaign worked very effectively as a sales pitch: no one tried to set out a detailed scheme of action for how the exit process would work, or what exact form Brexit would take – instead referring to those choices being up to the government of the time – but promising a bright, global trading future. On the present-day issues the official campaign and its rivals and outriders chose to highlight, a collection of exaggerated claims – some deliberate, some accidental – served to fuel rows which in turn sold their core message. Leave had few specific promises of its own that could be attacked, and had made sure attacks on the few specifics it did cite would serve its interests.

This should not have come as a surprise to anyone: it was exactly the tactic used in the only other UK-wide referendum in recent memory: the 2011 vote on whether to reform the UK's electoral system by introducing the Alternative Vote (AV) system. Matthew Elliott, the chief executive of Vote Leave, had also been the architect of the No to AV campaign – and some of his tactics should have been very familiar to his opponents.

Elliott's No2AV campaign used a series of emotive and hard-hitting posters to claim the UK couldn't afford to change its voting system. One showed a crying baby alongside the caption 'She needs a maternity unit NOT an alternative voting system'. Another showed a soldier's face with the words 'He needs bulletproof vests'. Their shared strapline: 'Our country can't afford it'.

For its main line of attack, No2AV avoided complex and detailed arguments about the rights and wrongs of different voting systems – the actual question under debate – and instead claimed the new system would cost £250 million,[18] which the UK should spend on body armour and maternity wards. As with Vote Leave's NHS claim, this figure was questionable – it included the £90 million cost of holding the referendum itself, which would be spent no matter what the result, and the one-off £130 million cost of buying new voting machines. More broadly, claiming the UK could not afford the £130 million outlay wasn't accurate – though £130 million seems like (and is) a lot of money, it would be less than 0.03 per cent of a single year of government spending, or £1 in £3,333. Cost simply was not the major issue in the AV debate – but any pro-AV supporter trying to quibble with the figures was left looking as though they preferred voting machines to body armour or incubators.

The AV referendum was likely unwinnable for the Yes side, but its activists nonetheless ran into No2AV's trap. Five years later, Remain did just the same all over again. Having made sure there were few vectors under which their own campaign could be attacked, Leave then managed a further innovation – neutralising their opponent's strengths. Remain's advantage was that it represented the status quo and expert opinion – in telling people, largely truthfully, that leaving would be a risk. This tactic ignored the fact that many people felt sufficiently left behind that they were happy to take a risk, but Leave also took active steps to blunt this attack.

These were not, by and large, based on a mastery of specifics: rather than trying to take on too prominently the economic forecasts by engaging with the small print therein, or offering rebuttal on the risks of failing to secure trade deals, Leave seized on the 'Project Fear' line – the broader narrative that Remain was simply using scare tactics. They also made much of a now-infamous line from Michael Gove. Faced with a challenge to name the economists backing Leave, after many prominent economists had publicly supported Remain, Gove simply dismissed the question: 'People in this country have had enough of experts.' This tapped into a current sense of disillusionment with the political and media establishments, turning a weakness into a strength.

Leave (or its supporters) also did much the same by quite effectively running their own counter-campaign to offset the idea that remaining in the EU was the safe status quo. This included implying that the referendum was the only way to prevent changes such as unfettered immigration from Turkey or an emergent EU army, and even positioning the EU as a threat to the existence of the NHS itself – the most shared Brexit-related story in the run-up to the vote was a short *Daily Express* piece titled 'Major leak from Brussels reveals NHS will be "KILLED OFF" if Britain remains in the EU'.[19] Such stories may not have broken through everywhere, but they reached thousands or millions of voters, some of who may otherwise have been persuaded by Remain's messages not to take a gamble.

None of this is to say that the Stronger In campaign never tried to deploy tactics of a similar sort. Perhaps the most significant – if unsuccessful – was a late campaign effort spearheaded by then Chancellor George Osborne to set out what a post-Leave vote emergency Brexit Budget might look like. The move saw Osborne brief a series of front pages the Treasury would usually do anything to avoid, warning of a 2p rise in the basic rate of income tax, a 3p rise in higher rates and cuts to education, defence and policing.[20] The move, in many ways, was Osborne burning his own leadership prospects to try to secure a Remain win.

This had no more basis than any of Vote Leave's claims, and worked in much the same way. There was a truthful core that could be used to defend the figures Osborne gave: *if* Brexit slowed the economy and created a £30 billion hole in public finances, and Osborne refused to change his fiscal rules, the mooted cuts would represent one way he could plug that gap. In reality, though, the Bank of England would likely stimulate the economy to offset any slowdown, a Chancellor would likely relax rules on deficit reduction to slow the pace of cuts, and if money needed to be found it would not come from anything so obvious as income tax hikes (the first two of which describe post-Brexit events as they have transpired).

This approach did not work nearly so well for Osborne as it

did for Vote Leave – largely because, as the serving Chancellor, Osborne ostensibly would be tied down to actually delivering on his threats. Even before Osborne delivered his speech, the Leave camp phoned Conservative MPs asking them if they would vote in favour of a Budget hiking income tax and cutting various Conservative spending priorities. Naturally, dozens said no, making it clear that Osborne's doom-mongering Budget would never be a reality. It was too simple and too fast to call Osborne's bluff – something Remain never managed to do to those on the Leave side. As journalist Tim Shipman notes in *All Out War*,[21] the move may even have been counterproductive – by issuing such an easily falsifiable economic threat, Osborne hurt the credibility of the other warnings issued by the Remain camp.

Clearly, Leave won the referendum – by 52 per cent to 48 per cent, a winning margin of around 1.3 million votes. The question that remains is whether the referendum outcome was inevitable given the UK's long-standing immigration concerns, social divisions, and people's settled views – or whether the outcome might have been different if each side had campaigned differently.

This is a question impossible to answer definitively, but there are signs the Leave campaign cut through to voters: by the final week of the contest, despite weeks of attacks on the claim's credibility, 78 per cent of people polled had heard Leave's assertion that the EU cost £350 million a week, and 47 per cent believed it to be true (39 per cent said false), according to an Ipsos MORI poll,[22] while 45 per cent believed Turkey would be fast-tracked into the EU. Meanwhile, only 17 per cent believed the core Remain claim that voting to leave would eventually leave every household £4,300 poorer, and only 21 per cent thought Brexit posed a risk to Northern Ireland's stability. Leave's claims had clear cut-through with a large segment of the public and were taken far more seriously than claims even from serious international organisations.

More evidence on who voted for Brexit and why – and why that may have meant that different campaigns could have changed the outcome – comes from post-referendum analysis by the social research organisation NatCen. The study found that people who thought Britain had changed for the worse over the past decade voted for Leave, as did those who thought things had got much worse for them personally than for others. People in social housing and those who said they were struggling to get by or just about managing also supported Leave. NatCen took this and other metrics to break down EU referendum voters into five distinct groups.[23]

There were two large pro-Remain groups: middle-class liberals, who supported remain by 92 per cent to 8 per cent, and younger working-class Labour voters, who backed Remain by 61 per cent to 39 per cent. These two groups just slightly outweighed the two larger Brexit groups: affluent Eurosceptics (the rural and suburban middle classes), who backed Leave by 75 per cent to 25 per cent, and older working classes, 73 per cent of whom supported Leave.

The most interesting group, though, is the final one, described by NatCen as 'economically deprived, anti-immigration' voters – making up 12 per cent of the population – who overwhelmingly backed Brexit, by a factor of 95 per cent to 5 per cent. Significantly, the research found that around one in three people in this group who turned up and voted in the EU referendum did not vote in the 2015 general election. This represented more than 1.3

million voters – Leave's whole margin of victory. If these unlikely voters had not been inspired to turn out and vote for Leave, Remain would have won: Leave turned out unlikely voters far more effectively than Remain did.

It's worth thinking about which messages may have connected with this group of voters – sometimes referred to (mildly insultingly) as 'low-information voters', a term for people not overly interested in or engaged with politics. Engagement with this group proved to be a running frustration for No. 10 communications director and former BBC staffer Craig Oliver, who wrote of his concern that the way the broadcast media covered Leave and Remain messages inadvertently favoured the former.

Oliver notes that the BBC tried to challenge Leave's claims in its 'more discursive' programmes, but was 'more concerned about … the mass-market short bulletins and website images that end up being seen by tens of millions', which he said got less effort and oversight from editors than the flagship shows, but reached bigger audiences.

'Serious journalism is struggling to hold to account those who are prepared to go beyond standard campaign hyperbole and stray into straightforward lies,' he concluded in his book *Unleashing Demons*.[24] 'If a campaign has been officially designated as the lead advocate for one side of the debate and so much of their core message is untrue – how do you report it in straightforward news terms?'

In a standard electoral campaign, many of these issues fix themselves: if a party runs on one manifesto and then does something else entirely, voters have the opportunity to throw them out of office a few years later. This is perhaps part of the reason that – despite huge public distrust in politics – British governments generally tend to deliver what's in their manifestos. Research discussed by Nicholas Allen in *More Sex, Lies and the Ballot Box* suggests that UK governments holding office for at least four years tended to deliver around 80 per cent of their testable manifesto commitments, though he did note that quite a lot of manifesto promises are too vague to test.[25] This probably doesn't naturally tally with your view of government – perhaps because it's the promises that aren't kept which are the easiest to remember. If asked to name a 2010 Liberal Democrat manifesto promise, I would guess most people would jump to the promise to scrap tuition fees. This promise was not so much missed as reversed: Liberal Democrats voted through a proposal to triple the maximum fee level – and the party lost all but eight of its seats at the following election, though it would be unfair to cite this as the sole reason for the collapse.

There is no such way to hold Vote Leave accountable for any pledges it made, and every sign suggests the campaign had very little intention of ever being made accountable. Within days of the election result, the campaign website was wiped of content and replaced with a simple victory missive.[26] Even on the morning of the referendum result, Leave supporters rapidly backed down from key campaign claims, with Nigel Farage saying, 'I would never have made that claim' of Vote Leave's £350 million-a-week NHS pledge.[27] The pledges were carefully defined – to insiders, they were never promises in the sense of a manifesto, as only a potential government could make those. To the public, they could easily appear as firm pledges.

'Leave wasn't a political party with a manifesto. This fell well short of the definition of a pledge. "Let's" meant "we could"; not "we will", journalist Isabel Oakeshott tweeted by means of explanation.

This defence assumes a huge degree of sophistication on the part of the average voter: assuming someone will see a poster ·with a one-sentence slogan, or a snatch of an interview with a Cabinet minister, and correctly deduce that this isn't a pledge or a promise but instead a vague and unactionable suggestion. It's perhaps no wonder voters become cynical and mistrustful of political processes.

That Brexit was won on these particular terms could be a peripheral issue, but for the fact that the vote has subsequently become defined as an absolute mandate for a particular type of Brexit and a particular set of policies. Many on the Leave side, before the vote, suggested that details such as the single market, customs union and Northern Ireland arrangements were not matters to be decided before an EU vote, but instead debated after. After the vote, ardent Brexiters then treated these issues as decided matters – by voting for Brexit, the country had voted to leave the single market, and saying anything else was a betrayal of democracy. Leavers could also point towards warnings from Remain politicians that leaving the EU would mean leaving the single market, despite the evidence we saw earlier that these warnings were broadly disregarded at the time, particularly by Leave voters.

It would be dishonest to say that in the months after the Brexit vote, the country has had huge regrets: polling generally shows people would by and large vote the same way in an EU referendum today as they did on 23 June 2016[28] – most voters don't feel misled. Polling also shows a far stronger lead for holding no second referendum, and very little support for blocking Brexit: even Remain supporters have accepted the result.

Similarly, though, it would be dishonest to hide that Brexit has huge degrees of complexity which were not hammered out before the vote. The UK could face a one-off bill of up to £60 billion to pay off its future EU commitments. It will need some form of agreement on regulations, customs checks and border arrangements – especially for Northern Ireland. Lots of legislation will need re-writing, and new regulators will need to be established if the UK is no longer to be party to EU arrangements. And, crucially, under the Article 50 process, there's only a two-year timetable to sort these first details – and the UK triggered Article 50 in March 2017, ahead of elections in France, Germany and the Netherlands, all of which could delay talks. This isn't straightforward.

This is the paradox that a campaign based on generalities has left us with. Theresa May and her government routinely accuse anyone of asking for clarity or checks on the Brexit process of attempting to block the will of the British public. This means that before the vote was not the right time to ask questions about this once-in-a-generation decision – that's for the government of the time to answer – and after the vote is not the time for questions either, because that's just a bid to block Brexit.

To take one example of how little some of the key issues around Brexit were publicly discussed before the vote, we can take a sample of 3 million tweets sent over the months before and after the vote. Twitter is not a representative sample of the public, of course, but is a rare chance to see at volume what actually gets discussed. The sample collected by researchers at the University of Sheffield and published by BuzzFeed News[29] showed that just 753 tweets from Leave and Remain partisans between 1 and 23 June 2016 discussed Article 50, the sole legal mechanism to actually achieve Brexit. On 3 November alone, there were more than 50,000 on the topic. This is just one example, but it does suggest that there were significant issues tied to Brexit not discussed ahead of time.

There are two consequences to the way the Brexit vote was won. One was to hand virtually all control of a once-in-a-generation process to Theresa May – who had never stood as party leader at a general election and initially refused to do so – and her ministers. The second, a consequence of the first, is to risk further public alienation from the political mainstream: people were sold a package of goods based on the pledges of Vote Leave, and without as much discussion of the roadblocks along the way as they wanted. If the trade-offs of Brexit are bigger than they expect, or the process longer and more difficult, there is every risk of further political alienation and polarisation of the sort seen elsewhere across the Western world in 2016 and 2017.

The Brexit campaign may not have been as lurid as Trump's, but its consequences in the long term could easily be even more significant. The campaign period showed how an ecosystem of official campaigns, outriders, friendly press and social media can work together to amplify messages to groups receptive to them, and how if a central campaign strategically distorts the truth it can serve as a huge advantage.

But, just as significantly, it showed the inability of mainstream politicians and media outlets to respond to the challenge. Norms of serious and impartial journalism struggled to get fair information across to certain voters. Meanwhile, Remain's instinct to build coalitions of senior figures from different political parties alongside experts appeared to backfire – appearing to some not as a rare gathering of respected figures more usually in opposition to one another, but rather as a sign that the political establishment were indeed all the same: an elite acting to preserve their own interests.

Between the Trump and Brexit campaigns, we see the ecosystem of bullshit: the combination of campaigns, media, technologies and more that come together to spread questionable information and struggle to combat it. In the next section, we'll tackle each in turn and try to explain how things have got like this.

PART II

WHO'S SPREADING THE SHIT?

CHAPTER THREE

POLITICIANS

To say that politicians have a role in the rise of bullshit carries very little risk of backlash – they're not exactly a hard target. Our trust in politicians is low, political scandals and corruption regularly lead the newspapers, and politicians of virtually every stripe are more than happy to tell you their opponents are corrupt, incompetent or worse. In many ways, these long-standing low expectations have become part of the problem: faith in politicians and the political system is so low that anything coming from outside the mainstream seems refreshing.

It's tempting to believe that low confidence in politicians and government is new, but the evidence on both sides of the Atlantic has shown consistently terrible trust figures for decades. In the UK, polling data since 1983 has consistently shown that just one in five British voters say they trust either government ministers or 'politicians generally', with no real difference between the two.[1] Even the huge Labour electoral surge of Tony Blair's 1997 landslide victory – and the high hopes accompanying it – made no dent in the numbers. Figures from the US show a similar deeply grained cynicism: asked if they trust the federal government to do the right thing, only around one in five Americans say yes (though this saw a huge spike around the time of the September 11 attacks).[2]

This kind of cynicism, if sustained for long enough, eventually breeds apathy, reflected in falling turnout and low youth engagement in the political process. These trends begin to fuel cycles: rather than trying to reach out to non-voters or floating voters, campaigns may try to ensure enough of their own base turns out – presenting their rival as a threat to core issues for their base, be it 'taking your guns' or 'ending a woman's right to choose' and suggesting this election is the last chance to save it. It's an atmosphere that favours the outsider over experience, and promises over accomplishments – leading to the rise of unlikely candidates, be it Jeremy Corbyn, catapulted to party leader after thirty-two years as an undistinguished left-wing backbencher, or Trump's rise from joke candidate to President. Outsider politicians campaign on changing the system – whether 'straight talking, honest politics' or 'drain the swamp' – and through novelty, shifting the debate from experience or issues to their own strengths.

No politician has proven better at playing this game than Donald Trump and his inner circle – whether through luck, natural gift, or experience honed through years of playing the gossipy New York media scene to fuel his real estate and hotel empire. One such example saw Trump use the media's obsession with Prince Charles and Princess Diana in 1994 to plant stories about apartments in Trump Tower and his club Mar-a-Lago.[3]

'I handled the applications myself,' Trump said of the royal couple's imaginary application for Mar-a-Lago membership. Or, as Trump set out in his book when gaining PR for his new building:

I call the society editor [of a New York tabloid] and tell them that Princess Diana and Prince Charles are going to purchase an apartment in Trump Tower. And they, in turn, investigate the source, call Buckingham Palace. And the comment is, 'no comment.' Which means that it appears to the public that Princess Di and Prince Charles are going to purchase an apartment in the Trump Tower.

Trump's approach in selling his club memberships and Trump Tower apartments deviated well away from the usual sales tactics, to pure and simple – if relatively harmless – fakery. He shifted away from the relative merits of the product he was offering to whatever garnered headlines and publicity, and left the rest to take care of itself. And in his presidential campaign, Trump demonstrated a similar ability to crowd out the media landscape with his own running dramas, rather than the traditional issues you might expect to dominate a presidential year.

One way to track this is by looking at the combined number of TV minutes devoted to issues – defined by the Tyndall Report, who track such coverage, as 'the attempt by television news to establish a political agenda that is driven by the perceived problems that the country faces rather than those talking points that the candidates select to promote their own causes'.[4] The Tyndall Report had looked at the total number of minutes per night devoted to such coverage across the three main networks, ABC, CBS and NBC, since 1988. In all the elections before 2016, this had bounced between a low of ninety-eight minutes in 1996 to a maximum of 220 minutes in 2008. In 2016, there was just a combined thirty-two minutes per evening on issues coverage – more than an hour a night less than in any previous election.

'This year's absence of issues is an accurate portrayal of the turf on which the election is being played out. It has turned into a referendum on the candidates' fitness for office,' the site concluded.

With just two weeks to go, issues coverage this year has been virtually non-existent. Of the 32 minutes total, terrorism (17 mins) and foreign policy (7 mins) towards the Middle East (Israel-ISIS-Syria-Iraq) have attracted some attention. Gay rights, immigration and policing have been mentioned in passing. No trade, no healthcare, no climate change, no drugs, no poverty, no guns, no infrastructure, no deficits.

David Plouffe, the Democratic strategist and campaign manager of Obama's 2008 campaign, weighed this as one of the factors contributing to the Donald Trump victory he failed to predict. 'Mrs. Clinton talked about what she wanted to do from a policy perspective every day, but this campaign was not the Lincoln–Douglas debates, it was *Mad Max: Fury Road*,' he wrote in the *New York Times*.[5] 'The race turned into *The Jerry Springer Show*, and that was the kind of campaign Mr. Trump was most comfortable with – and I'm sure the ugliness had the added effect of suppressing turnout.'

Trump's approach relied on exploiting weaknesses within the operation of most mainstream media: the deep-rooted cultural goal of objectivity held by many US papers and network outlets, the long-running assumption that anything said by a major candidate is intrinsically news, and a media so used to forensically digging through evasions, spin and small lies that they're virtually wrong-footed by untruth.

Such a skill is not unique to Trump. In his foreword to Robert Hutton's book *Would They Lie to You?*[6] the UK political commentator and former Conservative MP Matthew Parris recounted a media training session he attended for televised debates.

'I was once asked to play the part of a corrupt Third-World despot, with whom a Tory hopeful did battle in our mocked-up TV studio. He came equipped with all the evidence, all the facts and figures, to prove my villainy,' Parris wrote.

> But my strategy defeated him. I decided simply to lie. I did not fudge or hedge, attempt explanations, downplay the horrors, or make excuses. I just flatly denied every accusation he threw at me … He longed for a half-truth or a something-short-of-the-truth or a not-quite-the-truth to expose; but I gave him only the Lie Simple. I never gave him his 'Aha!' moment.

There is a startling historical parallel to one of Trump's more distinctive media traits – his ability to create news simply by promising news at a future date. Time and again Trump showed his ability to spin almost nothing into headlines. This trait began in multiple 2012 tweets from Trump during his running bid to discredit Obama, claiming alleged new evidence, from an unspecified 'extremely credible source'[7] that Obama's birth certificate was faked, to a 'confidential source'[8] on the US's debt situation, to claiming a convicted fraudster had helped the President with a house purchase.[9] Trump used this promise of, or allusion to, information just as deftly when on the defensive.

During his campaign Trump held press conferences promising to release tax information at some future date – taking the sting out of attacks that he hadn't disclosed anything, while not actually addressing any substantive points. This trick was repeated with announcements of future announcements about conflicts of interest and trust arrangements for Trump's business empire during his presidency: month after month, Trump promised disclosures on this 'soon' (it was regularly delayed), eventually holding an event taking steps falling far short of a blind trust.

This is a technique which comes almost entirely from the playbook of Senator Joseph McCarthy,[10] best known for his relentless and high-profile pursuit of alleged communists inside the US government, Hollywood and elsewhere. McCarthy constantly sought – and got – headlines on the thinnest of material: promises of new allegations to come, numbers plucked out of the air, and vicious smears of anyone who tried to curb his crackdowns.

McCarthy's ability to create headlines – described as 'pseudo events' – is described in the essay 'The Image: A Guide to Pseudo Events in America' by Daniel Boorstin.[11] Describing McCarthy as a 'natural genius at creating reportable happenings that had an interestingly ambiguous relation to underlying reality', Boorstin explains how McCarthy managed to co-opt even media outlets hostile to his witch-hunts in service of his mission.

'He knew how to get into the news even on those rare occasions when invention failed him and he had no facts to give out,' Boorstin quotes Richard Rovere, a reporter from the era, as saying.

For example, he invented the morning press conference called for the purpose of announcing an afternoon press conference. The reporters would come in ... and McCarthy would say that he just wanted to give them the word that he expected to be ready with a shattering announcement later in the day, for use in the papers the following morning. This would gain him a headline in the afternoon papers: 'New McCarthy Revelations Awaited in Capital.'

McCarthy consistently generated headlines, and if even one reporter attempted to ignore one of his thinly sourced attack lines, he would face questions as to why he'd missed the story everyone else was running.

'They stood astonished that he could make so much news from such meagre raw material. Many hated him; all helped him. They were victims of what one of them called their "indiscriminate objectivity". In other words, McCarthy and the newsmen both thrived on the same synthetic commodity,' Boorstin continued.

> Senator McCarthy's political fortunes were promoted almost as much by newsmen who considered themselves his enemies as by those few who were his friends ... Newspapermen were his most potent allies, for they were his co-manufacturers of pseudo-events. They were caught in their own web. Honest newsmen and the unscrupulous Senator McCarthy were in separate branches of the same business.

Plus ça change, plus c'est la même chose – the media has just the same vulnerabilities now as it did then, and they've been exploited just as deftly. But the parallels between McCarthy and Trump may be more than just coincidence – the two are connected by a string of advisors and confidants.

Since the mid-1970s, Donald Trump knew and was represented

in legal cases by notorious New York lawyer and fixer Roy Cohn, who had served as McCarthy's chief counsel during the red scare, helping to pursue alleged sympathisers and – despite his own homosexuality – lead a campaign of persecution against gay federal employees. Cohn, who was disbarred for unethical conduct shortly before his death, served as a mentor figure to Trump.

'People who knew Cohn and know Trump – people who have watched and studied both men – say they see in Trump today unmistakable signs of the enduring influence of Cohn,' Politico noted in 2016.[12] 'The frank belligerence. The undisguised disregard for niceties and convention. The media manipulation clotted with an abiding belief in the potent currency of celebrity.'

The connections between Cohn and Trump's 2016 campaign go further than mere mentorship. Cohn had once helped Roger Stone, then a political operative for Ronald Reagan, manipulate a primary election in ethically questionable ways.[13] Cohn introduced Trump and Stone to one another, and Stone went on to serve as a semi-official advisor and confidant to Trump and his presidential campaign. A flamboyant figure often on the fringes of Republican politics, Stone claimed to have 'back-channel communications'[14] with Julian Assange during the presidential campaign, and appeared to be behind a bizarre claim from Trump that the father of primary rival Ted Cruz had been involved in the assassination of JFK.[15]

Trump's aggression, bullshit and media bombardment is often referred to as a new phenomenon the media could not have been expected to be able to immediately handle – and an entirely new challenge they would have to learn how to deal with. Some aspects, such as 24-hour news channels, social media and the proliferation of hyper-partisan websites, are indeed new challenges. But much of Trump's approach comes from his own tactics in New York in the 1990s, echoes those of McCarthy in the 1950s, or simply brings tactics routine in the political fringes to centre stage. There is a lot that Trump's political opponents – and the media – could have seen coming.

Just as the Trump candidacy and its playbook have a long hinterland, the battlefield for the UK's Brexit vote was also shaped over the course of decades. Some of these factors are substantive: tensions in areas with relatively high levels of immigration, especially when these were believed to be responsible for pressure on local services; left-behind communities feeling they had little to lose in triggering a big political change; and a country which had simply never had a great deal of love for the European Union. Each of these has been subject to acres of analysis, and merits still more, but they aren't really the concern of a book looking at how miscommunication and misconception have shaped the world, and how much of it grows out of where politics meets the media. These are fields that could become sprawling and abstract, but in the UK – especially when it comes to EU myth-making – there is one man in whom all of these fields coalesce: Boris Johnson.

There is a short version of the story: Johnson rose from Conservative MP to become a popular two-term Mayor of London, building his public profile further through a successful London Olympic Games. After his term as mayor, Johnson joined the political Cabinet of David Cameron – an old Eton school friend and university associate – before taking the decision to join the Leave campaign, becoming its highest-profile champion. Following the vote to leave and May's elevation as Prime Minister, Johnson became Foreign Secretary and one of the most senior figures in executing the UK's decision to leave the European Union.

We're going to go with the longer (and more telling) version of the story, which shows Johnson as the epitome of a certain kind of apolitical, conviction-free politics of bullshit – of comments which may or may not be serious, of personal advancement, and where telling a good story is more important than fretting over whether it's true.

This version of the tale begins shortly after Johnson's graduation from Oxford – where he had been a member of the exclusive and upper-class Bullingdon Club – in his short-lived career as a journalist at *The Times*. It's a tale Johnson told in his own words in an article for *The Independent* in 2002, describing his 'biggest cock-up'.[16]

The cock-up was connected to a front-page story on the find of the Rose Palace of Edward II. Johnson explains having a vague awareness of Edward II having a same-sex lover (or 'catamite'), Piers Gaveston.

'I was desperate to get hold of a historian who could help me, but the only one I knew was my godfather Colin Lucas, a very distinguished man who is now vice-chancellor of Oxford University,' Johnson explained.

I rang him and he obligingly gave me some quotes about Edward II. The trouble was that somewhere in my copy I managed to attribute to Colin the view that Edward II and Piers Gaveston would have been cavorting together in the Rose Palace. Unfortunately, some linkside don at a provincial university spotted that by the time the Rose Palace was built, Piers Gaveston would long have been murdered. It was very nasty. Colin hadn't quite said that, and now his academic reputation was on the line.

It was extremely difficult, and I had absolutely no idea what to do. I was 23, overcome with guilt and shame that this error – this howler of mine attributed to Colin – had crept on to the front page of *The Times*, which was holy territory for me. So I made matters worse. I wrote a further story saying that the mystery had deepened about the date of the castle.

Even in the confession of his error, Johnson is vague and light: the quote, which was the grabbiest and catchiest of the article, 'somehow' got attributed – note the passive phrasing, implying no one is to blame – to Johnson's source, who had not said it. Johnson refers dismissively to the person who spotted his fabrication – 'some linkside don at a provincial university' – and then mentions that rather than confess his error (or fabrication), he instead doubled-down with a whole new story.

Let's be clear: fabrication is the original sin of journalism. For anyone less connected and influential than Johnson, a mistake of this magnitude would mean never working in the industry again. Johnson was indeed fired – and did note that his article may have cost his godfather a shot at becoming master of Balliol College, Oxford. The story and fabrication may have been inconsequential, but Johnson had shown himself an unreliable reporter at the beginning of his career, and even years later seemed largely unconcerned.

Part of the reason for his lack of concern may have been that the incident barely caused a blip in his journalistic career. Johnson was almost immediately brought onto the leader-writing team of the *Daily Telegraph*, a prestigious role, and by 1989 had been promoted to be the paper's Brussels correspondent – reporting on the European Union.

His presence soon became regarded as a menace and a threat by the officials whose work he covered, as *The Independent*'s then Brussels correspondent wrote in 1995, shortly after the end of Johnson's five-year stint in the city ended.

'It's all Boris's fault. That's what many say in Brussels,' her piece begins.

> A young journalist called Boris Johnson came to town one day as Brussels correspondent of the *Daily Telegraph*, and single-handedly launched the tide of Euro-phobia in Britain. He made things up, they claim, and his writings fed the far-right with material to launch their crusade against the Brussels plot to rule the world.

Johnson certainly challenged the collegiate and insider-ish approach expected by officials at the time, but significantly he was credited with the creation of the 'Euro-myth', writing stories about how Brussels was threatening the British sausage, cheese, and more – and sparking imitators across the UK media. By 1992, the European Commission had launched its own 'Euromyths' debunking effort (still available online today), comprehensively listing and trying to counter (in vain) a tirade of stories, almost universally from the UK.

The headlines on the EU myth-busting site from its launch in 1992 are exhausting: 'Commission to force fishermen to wear hairnets', 'EC closes butchers shops', 'Charity shops banned from selling second hand toys', 'EU bans wooden oars for stirring the Christmas pudding', 'Fishing boats obliged to carry condoms' and 'Scores of foreign boats to invade Essex coast'.[17]

All of the stories emanated from the UK, all were untrue (some ridiculous), and EC officials had clearly and publicly said so. By 1995, the team was busting two myths a week, but to no effect: while the misleading stories reached millions, none of the blogs in the examples above have reached even 1,000 hits twenty-five years after publication. Generations of Brits grew up on a media diet showing the EU as ridiculous and pernicious, and Johnson is broadly credited for creating the phenomenon.

Johnson himself took credit for changing the course of European history, with a splash story titled 'Delors [then EC president] plans to rule Europe', a hyped-up though not untrue account of a briefing which fuelled anti-EU sentiment in Denmark during a referendum on an EU treaty. 'The aftershocks were felt across Europe, and above all in Britain,' Johnson noted.[18]

Though a Eurosceptic by instinct, Johnson was noted to have a complicated relationship with the union – his father had been a senior EC official, correspondents at the time stated he'd made a run for the European Parliament, and Johnson was a noted internationalist. Johnson rose to become editor of *The Spectator* and then a Conservative MP.

Through his career, Johnson managed to shrug off comments that would have killed off the career of almost any politician through an odd kind of anti-establishmentarianism. Just as Trump managed to seem anti-establishment while being a New York billionaire, Johnson came from the core of Britain's establishment but managed to dismiss comments wildly outside the norm by dismissing them as jokes. Johnson has described black people as 'piccaninnies', referred to 'watermelon smiles', said Africa's problem is that 'we are not in charge any more', claimed Obama had an 'ancestral dislike' of the UK due to his part-Kenyan heritage and referred to the President of Turkey as a 'wankerer'.[19] Johnson's career also survived multiple affairs, one of which he publicly denied (as a shadow minister) until he was caught out. Through it, his rise continued unabated.

By the time the EU referendum was called, Johnson was an instrumental figure: it was believed he could swing the result in either direction – and it was widely believed it was Johnson's ambition that would swing the decision: which would best help him become Prime Minister? Johnson's team briefed that the Prime Minister had offered him any job in the Cabinet (except Chancellor) to back Remain, while supporting Leave would boost him among backbenchers.[20]

In the event, Johnson decided to announce his decision in the next edition of his *Telegraph* column – for which he was paid in excess of £250,000 a year – and spent a weekend writing two versions, one for Remain and one for Leave; it was the second of the two which was eventually published.

'There are some big questions that the "out" side need to answer. Almost everyone expects there to be some sort of economic shock as a result of a Brexit. How big would it be?' Johnson asked in the Remain version of the piece, which emerged weeks later.[21] In a column which expressed many reservations about the EU, Johnson noted Brexit could also threaten the union if Scotland pushed for independence, could boost Putin by making the political climate less stable, and stated that the EU 'is a market on our doorstep, ready for further exploitation by British firms: the membership fee seems rather small for all that access'.

Johnson did not focus his campaigning efforts on addressing the issues he posed – being among the most willing to ride on the '£350 million-a-week' battle bus, and ceremonially burning a cheque containing the misleading figure. Johnson, who is of Turkish heritage, also reversed his long-standing position supporting the country's membership of the European Union, stating during the campaign:[22] 'I am very pro-Turkish but what I certainly can't imagine is a situation in which 77 million of my fellow Turks and those of Turkish origin can come here without any checks at all. That is really mad.'

By September 2016, the job done, Johnson had reverted to his original position, and despite the UK's plans to exit the EU, offered the country's assistance in helping Turkey with its bid for EU membership. Rather than refuse to toe a campaign line he didn't support, Johnson simply set out a position he didn't believe – while continuing to poll better than any other politician on trustworthiness during the Brexit debate.[23]

Johnson's career could be characterised as the politician-as-nihilist: a genteel version of Donald Trump's post-truth politics, reliant on charm to get away with an approach to the truth which could be set out as flexible. But now Johnson, like other leading Brexiteers, has a formal role in actually delivering the deal. As Foreign Secretary, Johnson routinely has to deal with the foreign politicians he had previously been able to swipe at with impunity – and has to share stages with people whose views he has contradicted in the most lurid of terms. In many ways the role is Johnson's first serious political one (much of the London mayor's role is symbolic and easily delegated) – and it seems set to pose a challenge.

As Foreign Secretary, Johnson told a Czech media outlet that it was 'bollocks' to suggest free movement of people was a core principle of the EU – in open contradiction to both EU treaties and other national leaders.[24] Johnson also endured a difficult press conference with his German counterpart who declared himself 'not amused' by Johnson's support of Brexit or his attempts to make light of their differences.[25] He also faced booing at his first public speech, at the French embassy in London,[26] and, ahead of Britain's negotiations to exit the EU, has faced public rebukes from senior ministers.

'I think he's offering to the British people options that are really not available,' Dutch finance minister Jeroen Dijsselbloem told the BBC's *Newsnight*.[27] 'He's saying things that are intellectually impossible, politically unavailable. So I think he is not offering the fair approach that gives the British people a fair view of what is ahead, of what is available and what can be achieved in these negotiations.'

Humiliatingly, Johnson was even likened by the Prime Minister in a public speech to a dog which was 'put down ... when its master didn't need it any more'.[28]

Johnson's early career shows both the strength and the weakness of the type of politics that led to his rise: taking a casual approach to the truth has helped advance Johnson's causes and himself, as has treating anything to which people take offence as a joke. But the risk of rising by this route is that eventually you want some people to take you seriously, and no one is used to doing so. The change of gear is proving difficult for the Foreign Secretary, and it remains to be seen how he settles in the role.

We've seen parallels – as well as significant differences – in the media approaches of Johnson and Trump. Both can grab a headline, push a narrative with thin material, and have used the 'it was a joke' defence to escape controversial remarks. Both came into public life with long hinterlands. Johnson's first steps on the world stage have shown him to falter when forced by overseas politicians to abandon levity as a defence. The question for those who would have challenged him sooner is whether anyone else could have done that on the way up, while campaigning. Both men – and Senator McCarthy – also demonstrate how neither the media nor politics act in isolation, and how even outlets which regard themselves as opposing a candidate can serve to boost them.

The question for politicians who wish to take on such candidates is how to move beyond saying such approaches are bad and damaging, and shift instead to either adopting some of the same tactics, or learning counter-measures against them. It is crucial that they learn what doesn't work: when countering a politician like Johnson, who can publicly U-turn on a policy twice in six months, noting inconsistency simply doesn't land as an attack.

There is a broader question too, though not one that will easily be addressed: it serves the interest of almost any individual politician to attack 'the system', 'the establishment' or 'the elite', but the collective effect is to reduce the faith in mainstream politicians all round. The result is a political arms race – any side which drops such attacks unilaterally could easily find itself losing, fast – which benefits only those on the fringes. De-escalating the situation won't come in one step, but would benefit almost all concerned.

Politics has never been and will never be a forum of pure and earnest debate on public policy issues – but there are safe and dangerous levels of disengagement and cynicism, and some approaches have more potential for harm than others. When political actors can create feedback loops with the media to fuel agendas with the flimsiest of evidence or truth, this erosion accelerates. This chapter handled the political side of such loops – the next chapter looks at the media side of the same equation.

CHAPTER FOUR

OLD MEDIA

The fourth estate may be a maligned institution, but for most of us it's our window to what's going on with the world. Despite its battles to compete in a new media era in which search and social dominate, old, or traditional, media – TV, radio, and newspapers – still reaches the largest audiences for the most time, and takes the most revenue doing it.

As such, traditional media plays a key role in shaping our view of world events, even for people who view 'mainstream media' (or the MSM) with scepticism or even derision. Despite talks of disintermediation – skipping the old media gatekeepers who pick the headlines – much of alternative media relies on riffing off or against information first published by old media outlets. And any politician ignoring such outlets will miss most of the electorate. For now, there is no bypassing them.

With that in mind, there is no way bullshit can be on the rise without major media outlets playing a role in it – though with the culture, economics and practices of different outlets varying so much, there any many factors at play. Often, outlets propagate bullshit despite their efforts to do the opposite – outlets focused on objectivity can struggle to deal with politicians and campaigns not wedded to the truth (as laid out in the previous chapter), or to communicate in a way that reaches modern audiences. Other outlets, whether due to their political agendas or their own economics – the two often run together – play an active role in propagating stories and narratives they know to be dubious. All of these are long-term issues, but alongside this backdrop, outlets are having to deal with a new phenomenon where candidates and campaigns – whether Jeremy Corbyn in the UK or Donald Trump in the USA – prefer to treat the media as just another political opponent to fight, rather than a messenger or a non-partisan institution. The result? A fourth estate left juggling a revenue crisis, an industry-wide collapse in trust, a swathe of new breeds of competitors and a political climate well outside what it's familiar with.

The narrative a lot of mainstream outlets would like to believe – and would like the public to believe too – is that we have respectable fact-based mainstream media, and the brand-new phenomenon of 'fake news' from hoaxers, fraudsters and even from Russia or other governments trying to disrupt elections. If governments and/or social networks tackle those actors, the problem is solved. Among other problems this narrative ignores is a particularly stark one: for a variety of reasons, mainstream outlets make fake news – or things similar to it – too.

The *Daily Express* – which has a daily audience of 392,000 in print and 1.5 million online – is particularly notable in this regard. Though not taken especially seriously in the Westminster bubble, the paper's audience is larger than most broadsheets, and it was one of the most ardent supporters of Brexit. But alongside its usual diet of Eurosceptic and anti-immigration news, it serves up headlines including 'SHOCK CLAIM: Chemtrails "will wipe out humans" causing biblical-style floods, says expert',[1] 'Illuminati card game that "foretold 9/11 and Diana's death" predicts "Trump assassination"',[2] and 'NASA'S "SECRET UFO": Truth about "flying saucer found" at space lab on Google Earth'.[3] Though a very careful observer will find the stories filed under a 'weird' section of the site, the stories are presented identically to the site's real news offering. The paper is not the only one of the major UK outlets to work in this way.

In its 'tech and science' section, *The Sun*, the country's largest newspaper, offers up stories like 'CLOSE ENCOUNTER: Google Earth satellite pictures show moment Brit was "punched in the face by a grey alien" before he was abducted'[4] and 'FLESH EATERS: Millions of humans doomed to become CANNIBALS as drought and famine sweep the world, expert warns'.[5]

For sites looking for easy traffic, these kinds of conspiratorial stories are a cheap way to draw in the numbers – and to many people it's possible stories like the above are so obviously fake as to be harmless (though to conspiracy theorists, any kind of mainstream pick-up can be taken as a form of validation). In other cases, the strange-but-true stories tack far closer to real political coverage.

To UK newspaper readers, the *Daily Mail* is known as a mid-market paper with a right-wing and highly socially conservative agenda. Online, it's the world's biggest news website, with a massive US audience, though is better known for its celebrity coverage than for its hard news. The site ruthlessly and rapidly churns out stories to garner its huge readership, and these sometimes venture into the blatantly untrue.

The outlet carefully skirts a line in how it does this in a bid to avoid openly pushing false stories. One classic example of this was the way it picked up a niche online conspiracy theory speculating that a secret service agent at Trump's inauguration had worn prosthetic hands in order to hold a handgun under his coat – a theory easily disproven by watching video footage (rather than a still image) for just a few seconds.

The *Mail* ran the story with early headlines of 'Trump's Secret Service bodyguard "wore prosthetic hands"' and 'Did Donald Trump's bodyguard wear FAKE hands during inauguration so he could hold a gun under his coat?'[6] – despite noting in a bullet point very near the top of the story that he definitely had not. The story was the most visited on the site for most of the day – insiders said it did more than twice as much traffic as the second-most visited[7] – before changing hours later (with no note of the previous headline) to a headline debunking and ridiculing the story: 'Sorry folks, they WERE his real hands: Footage emerges disproving bizarre theory Trump's bodyguard had fake arms so he could hold a gun under his coat'.[8]

This habit of running a story quickly to grab the traffic, then just invisibly changing it – sometimes to the opposite – isn't a one-off, and isn't exclusive to the *Mail*. One such story it ran un-checked was 'Advisor says Elton John will play Donald Trump's inauguration'. Less than twenty minutes later, it was changed to 'Elton John DENIES he'll play inauguration concert for Trump'.[9] *The Independent* – once a broadsheet newspaper, now on-line-only – ran a headline claiming '20 million Muslims march against ISIS'.[10] In reality, the photos and videos showed photos of an annual religious pilgrimage, rather than any form of protest. Upon realising this, the site – again with no note or correction – changed it to the somewhat weaselly: 'Millions of Muslims take part in mass pilgrimage of Arbaeen – in spite of Isis'.[11] Another example of the phenomenon of publishing without checking, and changing without ever acknowledging an error, can be found at the *Daily Mirror*. On Boxing Day, the site ran "'Britney Spears is dead", according to Sony Music',[12] based solely on a badly phrased tweet from a hacked Sony Twitter account ('britney spears is dead by accident!'). Soon afterwards, the headline inevitably became: 'Britney Spears is NOT dead: Sony Music's Twitter account is hacked and trolls post sick hoax'.[13]

These rapid-fire and sometimes just downright dumb stories aren't something news sites do for kicks: they're a response to the strange incentives of the internet. Any story which ranks near the top of Google News will get more traffic and attention than one that doesn't, and the search engine's algorithm has traditionally favoured sites which are first to the story. Facebook favours partisan and would-you-believe stories over down-the-line reporting because it's simply more shareable. And traffic, of course, means revenue for the sites. Running a story early then simply reversing the headline gets traffic: waiting and checking it out, then running nothing, gets none.

The price that's paid is the audience's trust: if newspapers don't differentiate the stories that they've put time and reporting resources into from those they run based on a single tweet, why should readers give any more credence to one than another? Even when looking at the quick turnaround ones, if sites change headlines – or entirely reverse a story – without anything flagging that they've done so, how are readers expected to know where they are in the process? By running nonsense alongside decent reporting, making no difference between the two, and almost never acknowledging when they've screwed up, outlets propagate the culture of bullshit – what's true barely matters, if it's entertaining.

In UK newspapers, and US cable news, there are also issues around the political biases of outlets influencing their willingness to spin stories with some core of truth at the centre of them. Sometimes such stories are trivial, other times they're serious, but these distortions often work in the direction of polarising politics or of further marginalising or othering already vulnerable groups.

Sometimes it's seemingly trivial things that can set off these reactions. One such example was tracked by BuzzFeed News,[14] who had noticed Twitter users complaining about Muslims trying to ban a beloved household institution: Peppa Pig (a cartoon for under-fives). 'Muslims are now outraged by Peppa Pig, muslims really will never be part of Western society', said one. 'I saw Peppa Pig trending and knew straight away that it had something to do with offended Muslims. This multiculturalism is an epic failure,' said another. The story, which had originated from a questionable headline in an Australian paper, was picked up by *The Sun*, the *Daily Express* and the BBC.

One problem: the imam who had supposedly called Peppa Pig a 'corrupting influence' said he'd never heard of the show in his life. Though he had been encouraging people to watch Muslim-friendly cartoons, he said he had no issue with pigs in TV: 'I've patted pigs, I've watched *Babe*, we just don't eat them,' he said. The sole source for any such story was a Facebook post by a different programme on the TV channel the imam had promoted which used the phrase 'our Peppa Pig alternative'. The post contained no criticism of that cartoon, or any other.

Peppa Pig-gate was just the most trivial end of a running series of distorted and exaggerated reports on Muslims in the UK media – one which prompted Miqdaad Versi, assistant general secretary of the Muslim Council of Britain, to launch a one-man mission to try to secure corrections.[15] Stories amended after complaints by Versi included one from *The Sun* headlined 'SUPERMARKET TERROR: Gunman "screaming Allahu Akbar" opens fire in Spanish supermarket while "carrying bag filled with petrol and gunpowder"', which was altered to remove 'screaming Allahu Akbar', when both police and the supermarket concerned said this had not been chanted. *The Sun* also initially incorrectly claimed a gunman who killed six people in an attack on a mosque in Canada cried 'Allahu Akbar'.[16] The *Daily Express* was among a group of newspapers which ran headlines such as 'Some Muslims so isolated in UK they believe country is 75 per cent ISLAMIC, says shock report'.[17] The headline was based on a passing reference in a government report to a study which had suggested pupils in one school had said they thought 50 per cent to 90 per cent of the UK was Asian. The story, despite later being retracted, was picked up and spread by far-right groups including the English Defence League and Britain First.

Not all stories that are polarising are false, of course. UK newspapers don't have a culture of objectivity: though they operate in different ways, almost every paper in the country has an overt political bias. On issues such as Brexit, this politicisation can get intense. On 3 November, the UK Supreme Court ruled that Parliament must have a say before Theresa May launched the process to exit the European Union, in response to a case brought by a group of campaigners. On 4 November, the *Daily Mail* ran a front page with pictures of three of the judges above the headline 'ENEMIES OF THE PEOPLE' and the caption 'Fury over "out of touch" judges who defied 17.4m Brexit voters and could trigger constitutional crisis'. The accompanying article slammed the 'unelected' judges, mentioning that one was a 'committed Europhile'.[18]

The ruling was not made because the judges wanted to make it – they judged a case which was brought in front of them, as is their responsibility – but it also didn't serve to block Brexit, instead stating that by law Theresa May would need Parliament's permission to begin the process. But the article was perhaps the most blatant of many painting a narrative that anyone raising any questions over the Brexit vote was anti-democratic, was trying to block the whole process, and was an elitist. It also provoked an aggressive and not-too-accurate backlash, likening the article to a pro-Nazi front page from the mid-1930s, which, it was claimed, pictured a group of judges and called them 'enemies of the people'. The comparison was untrue: the headline translated as 'traitors to the people' and referred to a group of German exiles who had their citizenship revoked.[19] The political left believe the right has reached a milestone set by the Nazi Party, while the political right believes the left are trying to reverse the will of the people through undemocratic means. Neither view has much basis in reality.

US newspaper culture is very different – but its cable TV news is not, and partisans on either side of the divide don't watch one another's news: Fox News has net favourable ratings among conservatives of 69 per cent, but -61 per cent from liberals. The reverse is true for MSNBC, of which liberals have a 36 per cent positive view, while conservatives have -65 per cent.[20] The two channels' primetime broadcasts have consistently given an entirely different view of America and its top stories each night. Even outside of election years, the two partisan networks devote their time to radically different stories: the two had very different takes (and devoted very different amounts of airtime) to Obamacare and Benghazi, for example.

We've talked about how the media can be played by politicians and campaigns happy to exploit their habits, but it's clear that media outlets also have their own agendas and their own economic reasons for occasionally pushing either false or distorted stories. There is nothing wrong with a partisan media: indeed, when 'view from nowhere', down-the-middle journalism can seem bloodless, partisan media has the potential to connect with audiences that other reporting would miss. The risk can come when the desire to attract and fire up a partisan audience comes at the price of scepticism. One of the most shocking historical examples of this was perhaps *The Sun*'s coverage of the 1989 Hillsborough football disaster, in which ninety-six football fans were crushed to death.

The Sun at the time was relentlessly pro-police and anti-football hooliganism, and so ran (on the basis of uncorroborated testimony from police) a front page reading: 'THE TRUTH', claiming fans had picked the pockets of victims, attacked police as they administered CPR, and even urinated on police. The claims were untrue, and wildly offensive to fans who had seen friends and families injured or killed in an accident that was eventually found to have been caused by a series of police blunders, with officers then smearing the victims to deflect blame. The story – which would certainly be called 'fake news' – came not through fabrication from *The Sun*, but from their readiness to accept sensational claims that suited their long-standing agenda from a source of whom they should have been far more wary. As the story began to unravel, rather than row back, the paper doubled down – and as a result is still reviled (and not sold) in Liverpool today, more than twenty-five years later.

In the current environment, those leaning left in the US will leap on any action by Donald Trump as a sign that he's corrupt, a Russian stooge, or insane; those leaning right are just as ready to gun for the left as anti-free speech, embroiled in fake news, and unpatriotic. The UK is in similarly high dudgeon over Brexit. We – and our media – are all ready to believe the worst about each other. That's the environment in which sketchy stories thrive.

It's tempting when looking at the examples above to assume that bullshit is a question of bad outlets versus good outlets – but in practice it's more complicated than that. It's easy to assume bad faith: that outlets care only about ratings, or profits, or furthering the political agenda of their corporate parent or billionaire owner. There are, though, many reasons less sinister that news output may be less than perfect – journalism is referred to as a first draft of history partly because it's hard if not impossible to always get a definitive version of events within the space of mere hours, especially when there are virulently different versions of events.

This gets particularly difficult when almost every outlet is having to produce more journalism more quickly with fewer resources. In the UK, the main source of revenue for most papers remains print advertising, which is falling at a rate of around 15 per cent a year,[21] draining around £155 million a year out of papers' coffers.[22] This follows more than a decade of dramatically plunging print circulations, affecting broadsheet and tabloids, left-leaning and right-leaning alike. *The Sun* sold 3 million copies in 2006 and just 1.6 million in 2016; the *Mail* saw sales slip from 2.3 million to 1.5 million; the *Telegraph* dropped from 900,000 to 460,000; and *The Guardian* plunged from 366,000 to 161,000.[23] All of these outlets have huge and still-growing online audiences – which dwarf by an order of magnitude their print readerships

– but hopes that digital advertising revenues would offset print declines have been stymied: digital advertising has grown, but this is slowing as Facebook and Google take the overwhelming majority of the pie (more on this in Chapter Ten). All of these trends are mirrored across US papers.

TV news on both sides of the Atlantic faces similar challenges – the decline in viewing figures may be less dramatic, but a collection of statistics gathered by former *Guardian* editor Peter Preston show TV faces fewer people, watching for less time, and with an ageing audience.[24] Preston's figures show UK viewing time dropped 10 per cent between 2012 and 2015, while in the US the drop was 15 per cent. The average age of the BBC One audience rose from fifty-two in 2009 to fifty-nine in 2014, while in the US the average viewing age for CNN was sixty-two, MSNBC sixty-three, and Fox News sixty-seven. Younger audiences are watching dramatically less TV news than average adults: audiences aged sixteen to twenty-four watch around twenty-five hours a year of news, versus an average of 108 hours for all adults.

The result of these trends is fewer journalists: the landmark census of newsrooms conducted by the American Society of News Editors showed a drop in the number of full-time journalists from 54,100 in 2005 to 32,900 a decade later[25] – a drop of 40 per cent. And where print journalists would once just produce written stories for a printed publication, newspaper newsrooms now produce text, video, web content, chat, material for social platforms, and more. This means less time per story, and fewer resources to spend finding news first-hand.

What are the consequences of these pressures for audiences? Generally, low-resource newsrooms play it safe: if you have an inexperienced recent graduate reporting on a political row, the simplest way to do it is simply to report what a candidate says, and then have a rival disagreeing – making no attempt to verify the contents of the message. This is something of a caricature, but often reporting follows similar lines, especially as such a piece would satisfy many outlets' standards of neutrality or objectivity – even if one candidate was brazenly lying. Well-resourced newsrooms with experienced staff have the ability and confidence to challenge political claims. Poorly staffed ones struggle.

One innovation that aimed to serve as a counterweight to this kind of he-said she-said coverage was the creation of the fact-check blog (discussed at length in Chapter Twelve). A specialist journalist, or a small team of them, would dig into contentious claims made by prominent politicians and judge whether or not they could be fairly described as true. Fact-checking bloggers now sit in mainstream newsrooms including the *Washington Post*, the BBC, *The Guardian* and *Channel 4 News*, as well as a number of independent fact-check-only organisations. Many of these blogs do fantastic work, but on their own they cannot remotely stem the tide, and arguably could even make things worse. By shifting the responsibility to say whether or not politicians are telling the truth onto a particular blog, it may serve to remove that responsibility from political and other reporters – it's OK if they just report the row, as another team will take responsibility for the facts. For now, we might also want to question whether the kind of person who enjoys reading fact-check columns is typical of the general voter. For one: when's the last time you searched for a fact-check of a political claim you believed and supported?

A final trend to note: trust in mass media is falling. The pollster Gallup has asked Americans annually since 1997 how much confidence they have in newspapers, TV and radio. Between 1997 and 2005, around 50 per cent said they had a great deal or a fair amount of trust in the mass media, before the beginning of a decade-long slump in trust, which hit an all-time low of 32 per cent in 2016.[26] Perhaps even more worrying, the broken-down figures showed just how polarised America has become: only 14 per cent of Republican voters expressed confidence in mass media. In the UK, trust in print journalists has been at a low level for decades. Since 1983, only around one in four people expressed trust in journalists – less than estate agents or bankers, and markedly less than a 'person in the street'.[27] TV newsreaders, though, score highly in trust – perhaps a signal of the ongoing esteem in which the BBC in particular is held in the UK public mind. Falling trust could be seen as either a cause of the drop in audience time and attention, or a consequence of it – as fewer people engage with mainstream publications, they have less experience of them in which to gain confidence.

For centuries, the media has held the role of holding government and politicians to account – the 'fourth estate' description of the media grew up in the nineteenth century as a formalisation of the media's role in keeping power in check. If the media is losing reach and losing trust, its ability to hold power to account becomes weaker. The media can't fix its economic problems overnight, but that may not be the only barrier standing in the way of its work.

There's an old (and often misattributed) adage that 'laws are like sausages – it's better not to see them being made'. The same may be true of journalism, but journalists no longer have the benefit of obscurity: hackers target journalists to see their emails, campaigns launch attacks on journalists and their methods and motivations, and journalists – in particular at partisan sites defending a candidate – form themselves into a circular firing squad attacking each other's stories. This means much of the process of journalism is there on the surface for a wide audience who have little reason to understand it.

Looking at the way White House reporters refer to Donald Trump, and the way liberal audiences react to that, is an example of this issue. On the first Monday of Trump's presidency, Sean Spicer gave his first official press conference. The event came after a bizarre statement the previous Saturday in which Spicer had berated the press for (accurately) stating that Trump's inauguration had drawn a smaller crowd than Obama's. Unlike in his Saturday briefing, Spicer took questions from outlets and made some conciliatory noises, quickly garnering praise. The White House Correspondents' Association called the event a 'positive step' and 'encouraging',[28] while *Washington Post* correspondent Karen Tumulty praised Spicer's 'solid, professional job', branding the conference a 'reboot'.[29]

This rapid reconciliation drew criticism: from the podium, Spicer had repeated untrue claims about Trump's record inauguration crowd and had arguably endorsed a war crime – by suggesting seizing Iraq's oil in exchange for providing military support.[30] Similarly, the conference did not contain any apologies for Trump's repeated attacks on media outlets. To many Trump critics among the public, this behaviour may appear craven – but that view ignores the fact that in order to find any stories, reporters need to cultivate sources within the administration to find out what's actually going on. Correspondents shouting at Trump may be reassuring to his critics, but it won't help them find any real news – but that's not an easy message to get across.

This is just one of a range of media habits that those of us in the industry assume the audience understands, which they may in reality not. Stories in many outlets tend to include a statement from the subject of the story, which in the case of investigative or critical pieces often means the bottom of a written article is a lengthy quote saying everything above it is wrong. These are included because industry codes (in the UK) and norms (in the US) say it's good practice, and because it helps grant a story extra legal protections. UK broadcasters are required by their legal regulator to include these kinds of statements. Journalists tend to assume the audience knows this. It's entirely possible they don't.

In January, the *New York Times* ran a headline which at a casual glance looks fairly standard for the organisation's style: 'Meeting with Top Lawmakers, Trump Repeats an Election Lie'.[31] The headline provoked a major row in media circles, as the *NYT* had done something well outside the norm. It had called the President-elect a liar. The headline referred to a statement by Trump that no mainstream outlet would ever claim to be true – that there were three million fraudulent votes in the US election. Why, then, is it a big deal to call something untrue a lie?

In the UK, this largely relates to legal risk: to call someone a liar is defamatory, and means they could sue for damages. Even if a claim is patently untrue, this may still not lead to a libel victory, as to show in court that someone is a liar isn't sufficient; the publication is then left trying to prove that the person saying it *knew* it was untrue when they said it. It's pretty impossible to prove what's going on inside someone's head. Outlets in America are less constrained on this front, but face huge cultural barriers to using the word. Among a cavalcade of coverage,

UK commentator John Rentoul called the use of 'lie' in head-lines a 'mistake' which 'undermined the *NYT*'s reputation as a news organisation.'[32]

Such is the culture at the 'respectable' end of journalism that calling a manifestly untrue and dangerous statement a lie is enough to provoke an ethics row. Such caution with language might be commendable, but we don't live in the rarefied universe where everyone is following that kind of careful standard. The President of the USA is happy to call news outlets 'fake', 'frauds', 'dishonest', 'phony', 'disgusting', 'dumb', 'garbage' and 'terrible' – and that's just CNN.[33] Social media users are more than happy to throw around direct and clear accusations. A new breed of hyper-partisan web-sites are happy to tap into the same blunt new world. Detached, objective and balanced is the gold standard of traditional journal-ism – but is it still the best way to hold power to account?

This question becomes much more urgent as the media is pulled into politics as if it were just another political opponent – a practice Donald Trump has honed into an art through his cam-paign and early presidency. A candidate who merely dislikes the press (or a particular outlet) simply boycotts it – as Jeremy Corbyn effectively does in the UK. Not so for Trump: he embraces it, ap-pearing on networks even as he castigates them. For a post-truth candidate, the media needs to be treated not as a service trying to put out the first draft of the truth, but as just another player with their own agenda. That way, if they challenge a claim we needn't get into rows over details and facts, but instead just dismiss the outlet out of hand. This is exactly the playbook Trump deployed at his rallies, where reporters in the press booths faced jeers, boos and insults – indirectly egged on by Trump.

'The establishment and their media neighbors wield control

over this nation through means that are very well known,' Trump told a rally crowd in Florida, the *New York Times* reported.[34]

> Anyone who challenges their control is deemed a sexist, a racist, a xenophobe and morally deformed. They will attack you. They will slander you. They will seek to destroy your career and your family. They will seek to destroy everything about you including your reputation. They will lie, lie, lie, and then again, they will do worse than that. They will do whatever's necessary.

Trump picked fights online and on TV with reporters who challenged him. When Fox News anchor Megyn Kelly asked Trump a tough question on his view of women – noting that he'd called 'women you don't like fat pigs, dogs, slobs and disgusting animals'. Trump launched a months-long vendetta against the anchor, at first saying she'd 'bombed', then saying she'd had 'blood coming out of her whatever' – taken by many to be a derogatory reference claiming she was on her period – and praised a surrogate who claimed she was 'fascinated by sex'.[35]

The behaviour didn't stop when he won his election race: at virtually every opportunity, Trump makes the media the villain. When he faced leaks from CNN and BuzzFeed News alleging ties to Russia, he branded the former 'fake news' and the latter a 'failing pile of garbage'.[36] When his then national security advisor General Michael Flynn was shown to have misled Vice-President Mike Pence – leading to Flynn's resignation – Trump nonetheless called the story 'a fake news, fabricated deal to try to make up for the loss of the Democrats', telling reporters at the same event: 'The public doesn't believe you people anymore'.[37]

This leaves a media which is much more comfortable sitting

on the sidelines working out how to respond to being dragged centre-field: it has to work out how to deal with a presidency that will not only plainly and repeatedly lie, but will strategically treat them as an enemy. Margaret Sullivan, the former public editor of the *New York Times* and now a media columnist at the *Washington Post*, sets out one possible response.

'White House press briefings are "access journalism," in which official statements – achieved by closeness to the source – are taken at face value and breathlessly reported as news. And that is over. Dead,' she writes.[38]

> Journalists shouldn't rise to the bait and decide to treat Trump as an enemy. Recalling at all times that their mission is truth-telling and holding public officials accountable, they should dig in, paying far more attention to actions than to sensational tweets or briefing-room lies – while still being willing to call out falsehoods clearly when they happen.

Greg Sargent noticed much the same: '[W]hat Trump and his advisers are doing *is explicitly stating their contempt for the press' institutional role as a credo*' (emphasis his).[39]

Journalism professor Jay Rosen took this to its furthest logical extent: news outlets should only send interns to the White House briefing room. 'When I say #sendtheinterns I mean it literally: take a bold decision to put your most junior people in the briefing room,' he urges.[40] 'Recognize that the real story is elsewhere, and most likely hidden. That's why the experienced reporters need to be taken out of the White House, and put on other assignments … they can't visit culture war upon you if they don't know where you are.'

That's not what's happening. Other than the smallest of baby steps – the *New York Times* occasionally using the word 'lie' in a headline; CNN carrying one press conference on time delay (then going back to airing them live) – it's business as usual for the media. Outlets are sending the same journalists to press conferences as ever they did, despite relentlessly reporting that all that comes out is misinformation. Fox News has reverted to a primetime line-up entirely composed of partially or enthusiastically pro-Trump anchors. The response to the Trump presidency in its early days has been to carry on unchanged.

Part of the reason for this is that while Trump may prove a threat to trust in the media, and to the journalism it produces, he is great for business. For the networks, Trump has proved fantastic for ratings, and therefore good for revenue. Beyond that, having a President whose TV viewing habits are so easy to discern – he often tweets about what's on TV and regularly picks the shows he appears on – means that ad rates for those shows are set to be hiked. Want to reach the President? Advertise on *Morning Joe* or the *O'Reilly Factor*. 'Instead of lobbying through the usual channels, it's like speaking directly into the president's ear,' a consultant told Politico.[41] Trump is proving similarly good for print outlets he refers to as his enemies: for all he maintains that the *New York Times* is 'failing', it now has more than three million subscribers,[42] and in the days immediately after the elections it won new subs at ten times the normal rate.[43]

For some outlets, this creates a dilemma: carrying on with coverage-as-usual may be ineffective in countering Trump's bullshit or in holding this new type of President to account – though as Trump transitions from campaigner to commander-in-chief, this remains an open question – but it's great for the bottom line.

In such situations, expect whatever's best for the bottom line to win out, and the status quo is working.

Those of us in the media tend to overplay our own role in events. Had fewer than 100,000 people in three key states voted differently, Hillary Clinton would be President now, and the months after her victory would have seen media think pieces on how dogged reporting on Trump's taxes in the *New York Times* and on Trump's charitable foundation in the *Washington Post* stalled the Republican candidate and contributed to Clinton's win.[44] Fake news would be a non-story, though the challenges of trust, reach and economics facing the outlets would be the same. Brexit served as a wake-up call to the Westminster bubble for issues that had grown over decades. Trump played the same role for the US.

Some of those challenges have been with us for a long time. Others are far newer. The internet and new media could be described as either for traditional outlets – the changes to working practices and revenues have been the media story of the decade. What's newer is the rise of hyper-partisan news for a mass audience, and it's this that's the focus of the next chapter.

CHAPTER FIVE

NEW MEDIA

By the time of the electoral contests of 2016, the internet was hardly a novelty and had long since passed being a bolt-on for the traditional media. Most people who read *The Guardian* or the *New York Times* read them online, and increasingly broadcasters are reliant on the internet too. With that in mind, the distinction between old and new media in terms of their role in bullshit is not as dramatic as once it might have been. Both face similar pressures in terms of reaching audiences, in terms of trust, and (often) in terms of advertising models – and a lot of the pressures from the way social networks operate, and crowding out from fake news, hold just as much for online-only outfits as for old media.

That said, the last decade has already seen a number of generations of online-only outfits. The mid-2000s saw the launch of the Huffington Post, BuzzFeed, Politico and the Daily Beast, among others. The early 2010s saw a boom of explanatory journalism, much of it based on a newfound (and what now looks potentially short-lived) reverence for statistical journalism in the wake of Nate Silver's almost uncanny prediction in the *New York Times* of the 2012 presidential election. This success netted

Silver his own site, FiveThirtyEight, for ESPN, and also saw the launch of explanatory journalism site Vox.

More recently, though, we've seen the rise of the hyper-partisan site: Breitbart, though founded in 2007, has risen to world prominence alongside Trump – as well as expanding internationally – while the UK has seen a rise of hyper-partisan journalism of the left in the form of The Canary, a left-leaning site whose adulation of Jeremy Corbyn is matched only by its animus towards the mainstream media. When it comes to the dawn of the era of bullshit, it's this second group that's most relevant to this chapter, but we'll get the first out of the way first.

If we were going to be completely blunt, all that separates some old media and new media outlets is that the latter have much lower overheads. This is especially true for US magazines, where long-running legacy costs mean some struggled to be sustainable at a print circulation of one million. By starting up a new business without inherited debt, leases and other measures, smaller staff and no print sites, magazine-style sites such as Slate or The Daily Beast have a lower cost base – it's easier to live off the relatively smaller revenue of digital advertising (and sometimes a measure of digital subscription revenue) if you've not spent decades on print revenues. Though the sites still face many of the same pressures in terms of needing to attract big traffic to get any form of manageable revenue, and still face the squeeze from Facebook and Google's dominance of digital advertising, they're arguably better positioned than old media to do so.

Other sites operate business models not reliant on either display advertising – banner adverts and similar appearing around content – or subscription. BuzzFeed (to repeat my conflict declaration: BuzzFeed is my current employer) shows no display advertising whatsoever. Instead, its revenue comes from sponsored posts, which are made by the company's commercial team – not their editorial staff. The advertising, whether a post on the site or a standalone video, is always bespoke, and uses the insights on what types of editorial content is currently going viral to help it create its content. Though the posts are all marked as sponsored content, some commentators have expressed concerns that it may trick readers who are only used to display advertising. Such concerns haven't stopped the model being added to the mix by a variety of sites, and newspapers also run similarly supported sections in print.

But a site operating without any display advertising whatsoever has an additional advantage: it loses the economic incentive to run stories purely because they will attract clicks from search engines (see previous chapter for a fuller discussion on this) – instead publishing only stories that will genuinely satisfy an audience, so that the formula can be repeated, whether that's a celebrity piece, a quiz, a tweet round-up or investigative reporting.

Another liberating factor for outlets without printed papers is that they can focus only on reporting stories and issues which will connect with their audience: however digitally minded an organisation with a printed newspaper, it does need enough stories in the 400–800 words range to fill its news pages. Such stories are often commodity news – rewrites of wire pieces, or pick-ups of reports. These are often referred to as 'death zone' stories – articles which just don't interest online readers. As Quartz editor Kevin Delaney puts it: 'Too much reporting is 700-word articles that everyone else has got.'[1] A final advantage for newer online-only outlets is that as newer organisations, they've been able to hire only digital natives, people who are able to work across multiple platforms, often across both text and videos, and who are comfortable doing much of their own production work – building in headlines, captions and photos ⁺hemselves. This is work and training that traditional organisations have had to spend a great deal of time and funding to do, often against stiff resistance from newsroom staff. Newer outlets may lack the institutional reputation of their traditional rivals, often have smaller staffs, and may have shallower pockets – but they've got no shortage of advantages too. Overall, for many of these outlets, their overall philosophy is the same – the mix of reporting to comment to analysis may vary, but all the outlets named so far this chapter have much more in common than distinct, and face the same commercial and trust challenges as each other. The same is absolutely not true of the outlets we'll discuss in the rest of the chapter, who built and defined their brands in opposition to the mainstream media, old and new alike.

The UK's most prominent home-grown hyper-partisan news site is The Canary, a left-leaning website founded in October 2015, shortly after Jeremy Corbyn became the shock winner of the Labour leadership contest following a surge of support from a new wave of anti-establishment left wingers, many of whom had never been involved in politics or a primary before. Many were furious with the mainstream media – including and especially left-wing and centrist outlets – for what they felt was unfair treatment with Corbyn, and were looking for a fairer alternative.

Kerry-anne Mendoza launched The Canary with this goal in mind: a handful of individuals control our mainstream media. 'Mass media coverage is largely conservative,' says the site's mission statement.[2] 'We want to create a counterpoint. An online media outlet that has a global outlook and reach.' The site claims to be politically independent: 'We're not actually ostensibly left-wing,' Mendoza told BuzzFeed News.[3] The site's top-performing stories tell a different story. Among its most shared pieces are: 'The UK's youngest MP just demolished the Tories, in her most scathing attack yet', 'This is the bombshell dropped by Theresa May's government while the media whined on about Traingate', 'The sorry facts which show the BBC has moved beyond bias, into pure propaganda' and 'Osborne distracts Britain with his Budget, then drops this utter bombshell'.[4] The site's sweet spot is headlines which combine the 'bombshell' of a Conservative minister doing something bad, ideally combined with the allegation that other media outlets aren't reporting that wrongdoing.

The site has faced regular accusations of exaggeration or encouraging conspiratorial thinking. One story that drew controversy was a piece run a week before the US election claiming: 'A major media outlet just revealed who won the US election… a week in advance'. The piece was based on a screen grab of a table of apparent election results on a local affiliate of NBC – but was simply showing dummy data sent out by AP (who supply results on the night) to help sites make sure their websites are displaying it properly.

The Canary thought differently. '[M]any have suggested the election is rigged. In October, the BBC and *The Guardian* both ran stories questioning the veracity of the election results,' it stated. '… After all, Clinton has suggested rigging elections in the past.'[5]

Months later, the story remains live and unchanged on the site, despite multiple attempts to notify its editors that it had simply made a mistake. Other controversies include The Canary pushing a conspiracy theory around a leadership challenge to Jeremy Corbyn, claiming the lobbying company Portland Communication had orchestrated the effort – prompting death threats to some of those involved.[6] In another instance, the site ran a story titled 'A junior doctor has killed herself, leaving a message to Jeremy Hunt in her suicide note'. The piece failed to follow multiple ethical guidelines set out by the Samaritans, including not attributing suicide to a single source and not basing news stories on the contents of suicide notes.

The Canary runs exaggerated and occasionally conspiratorial stories which routinely suggest that the government is acting maliciously and that the media – including the BBC – are willing accomplices in the plot. But the reason for these partisan and grabby headlines isn't just ideological: the site's writers are paid by the click. While some writers get a small flat monthly fee from the site, most are paid through a revenue share. The site shares ad revenue – after running costs – from every piece, giving the writer 50 per cent, the piece's editor 10 per cent, senior management 20 per cent, and the company takes the final 20 per cent. In practice, this can mean 40 per cent for some of the site's senior editors – The Canary is registered as a for-profit company, with Mendoza and fellow senior manager Drew Rose being its joint shareholders.

This is a business model that can only serve to promote bullshit. Any writer on the site knows that a piece is much more likely to go viral and get shared if it suits the political expectations of its readers, if it hypes a story to its limits, and if it suggests someone else is trying to keep it secret. A measured take trying to stick to the facts will take the writer much more effort, and make them much less money. So everything is 'shocking', 'disturbing', or a 'bombshell'. Even the left-leaning *New Statesman* gets exposed for telling 'porkies', *The Guardian* runs 'fake news' and the BBC's reputation is 'in tatters'. If Trump is the perfect post-truth politician, The Canary is a strong contender for the perfect post-truth outlet: it claims to have the one true narrative, it claims to be free of bias and politics (and ignores all evidence to the contrary), it spreads its own bullshit, and it attacks anyone offering a different narrative as insincere or controlled by vested interests.

The Canary is not the hyper-partisan website with several of its staff working just yards away from the Oval Office, though. That honour goes to Breitbart, for many years a fringe and largely ignored right-wing blog that tapped into the resurgence of the right – and the rise of what's now known as the alt-right – to hit a mass audience, and to hit political power. By the end of the presidential campaign, the site was reaching 20 million unique users a month, had opened a London office with close ties to UKIP (its UK editor-in-chief even ran an ill-fated attempt to become Nigel Farage's successor as the party's leader, announcing his campaign on the site he ran),[7] with plans in place to open more across Europe.

Breitbart's executive chairman until the summer of 2016 was Steve Bannon – a combative, right-wing ideologue who championed the motto 'honey badger don't give a shit' – named for the notoriously aggressive mammal, which has become a staple of internet subculture – for the site, framing starkly its combative tone.[8] Most famously, he once referred to himself as a 'Leninist' whose goal was to 'destroy the state'[9]. Bannon has risen to one of the most powerful posts in the White House as Trump's chief strategist, with a seat on the National Security Council – leading him to be described as possibly the 'second most powerful man in the world'.[10] Two other Breitbart staffers also quickly took up senior posts in the Trump White House: Stephen Miller, a senior advisor notable for being the alleged architect of Trump's highly controversial travel ban, and Sebastian Gorka, a national security advisor.

But despite their proximity to power, none of the three would be the right figurehead for the rise of bullshit: Bannon may hold views objectionable to many, but few doubt he's an ideologue. He's not trolling people for kicks; he's working to advance an agenda. If anyone at Breitbart embodies and typifies the rise of bullshit, it's not any of the employees who have made their way to the White House: it's Milo Yiannopoulos.

Such is the myth-making around Yiannopoulos, to many on the left in the US Yiannopoulos is a dangerous and offensive firebrand, barely short of a four-headed fire-breathing monster, a man in the process of trying to change his name into a brand: MILO,[11] a Madonna clone with a stuck-down caps lock key. Yiannopoulos built a huge online following – and a slew of coverage – through a trail of wildly and needlessly provocative comments, speeches and articles aimed at virtually any racial group, sexual orientation, trans group, or liberal. This in turn led to a self-promoting nationwide speaking tour across the USA's university campuses, on a huge tour bus festooned with his photo, provoking counter-protests which pushed him into the headlines yet again. The result: a media machine and a \$250,000 book deal from Simon & Schuster provoking a row all of its own,[12] as booksellers faced calls not to stock the title and other authors left their publisher rather than share it with Yiannopoulos.[13]

Those who've been anywhere near London's journalism scene over the past decade may well have a very different picture of

Yiannopoulos, though. Yiannopoulos has jumped from respectability to controversy, left failure after failure in his wake, launched attacks on those he's wronged, and been caught in lie after lie. Such the string of serial bullshit left behind Yiannopoulos that everything right down to his age, nationality, religion and even name are tied up in interweaving falsehoods, told to suit whatever story Yiannopoulos was trying to tell the world at the time. Here, then, is a rough history of a man with as good a case as any to be the archetypal bullshit merchant.

Yiannopoulos was born Milo Hanrahan in October 1984 in Chatham, a small town in Kent about sixty miles from London. Yiannopoulos's father, a Greek immigrant who opted to use his mother's maiden name of Hanrahan, had a modest but comfortable income running nightclub security across the town. Yiannopoulos had a somewhat tumultuous childhood, with his parents separating when he was young and Yiannopoulos himself living on occasion with his paternal grandmother instead of either parent.[14] Despite this, Yiannopoulos eventually obtained good A-level grades and started degrees – dropping out both times – at Manchester and Cambridge Universities.

By 2006, Yiannopoulos – now going by the name Milo Andreas Wagner – was advertising himself as a jobbing web designer, running a podcast, launching a fan club and soliciting donations 'for the cause', with the 'cause' left unspecified.[15] Milo Andreas Wagner also published two volumes of poetry, *A Swarm Of Wasps* and *Eskimo Papoose*,[16] a book which was later found to have used Tori Amos song lyrics without attribution[17] and which was later dismissed by Yiannopoulos as a 'joke book'. Amazon and Waterstones both list an additional work due to have been published in 2009, titled *Petrol and Matches*.

It was as Milo Andreas Wagner that Yiannopoulos started to make his first inroads into the journalistic mainstream, ironically through working on a book about conspiracy theories and misinformation. The 2008 book, *Counterknowledge*, by Damian Thompson, presciently notes on its jacket how 'unproven theories and spurious claims are … helped by the media, internet bloggers, and even the publishing industry' to create 'a global generation of misguided adherent who repeat these untruths and lend them credence'.

'Wagner' created a website for the blog and helped manage a team blog updating content around it – including authoring a post warning of the dangers of people using the internet to spread misinformation. 'Access to computers, and therefore to the Internet, raises another, decidedly more sinister, possibility,' he wrote.

> Burgeoning access to the internet in South Africa is having at least one disastrous effect: the ill-educated are being mercilessly exposed to horrifically pernicious AIDS denialism … the spread of the internet in South Africa is fuelling the spread of lies and misinformation about the fatal disease. [18]

Yiannopoulos's phase as Milo Andreas Wagner was accompanied by his first discernible attempts to alter his age and place of birth. One remaining sign of this comes from a Wikipedia user page from the time. It's impossible to confirm whether the profile was Yiannopoulos, but it linked to his website of the time, stated information he quoted in other places, and was built in 2007 – long before Yiannopoulos had any significant public profile. The profile – which only ever edited its own user page and a series of wiki entries on Mariah Carey – claimed that 'Wagner' had been born in 1983 in Athens, claiming also fluency in German and expertise in multiple musical instruments.[19]

Yiannopoulos, as 'Wagner', also worked as an assistant and speechwriter to the actress and activist Bianca Jagger, taking an email address with a charity which she then chaired.[20] The role ended acrimoniously after a relatively short period.

It was Yiannopoulos's work for *Counterknowledge* which netted him his first high-profile platform, though, bringing him to the attention of then editor of the *Telegraph*, Will Lewis, who hired him as a technology blogger – where Yiannopoulos (now writing under the name 'Milo Yiannopoulos') was already writing in what's now known as his typical inflammatory style – until, as may become familiar, his staff contract with the paper was ended in favour of a freelance arrangement.

The *Telegraph* did offer Yiannopoulos a second chance of sorts by allowing an events company he'd founded to put their name to a new 'Start-Up 100' award he launched for tech companies in 2011. The awards quickly descended into chaos, with the chair of the judging panel discovering when he announced the top winner that his decision had been switched without his knowledge,[21] while a series of sponsors for the event promised by Yiannopoulos failed to materialise, leaving the *Telegraph* seriously out of pocket on the event[22] – and Yiannopoulos firmly in the doghouse.

By this point, Yiannopoulos had launched multiple companies in the UK. In March 2009, he'd created a company, of which he was sole shareholder, named Counterknowledge Ltd – named for Thompson's book – giving a date of birth in 1983. Six months later he launched Wrong Agency Limited – the events company he used for the Start-Up 100 – this time giving a 1984 birth date.

Neither company ever filed a set of accounts or any other doc-umentation, and were struck off after missing filing deadlines. Yiannopoulos – who has never changed his name by deed poll – also declined to give any former names on official company register documentation.

. None of this stopped Yiannopoulos launching his third start-up, a tech news site called The Kernel, which quickly hired a team and began generating articles and exclusives which were relatively well-regarded, even if they hadn't abandoned Yian-nopoulos's trademark aggressive tone entirely. During this period Yiannopoulos courted others in the tech press – in-cluding various left-wing liberals and feminist writers – trying to sort regular drinks, noting he had 'admired from afar' and wanted to meet them – 'first round on The Kernel!' he promised. Having built a reputation as something of a controversialist, this was Yiannopoulos at his most emollient. It did not last.

By the autumn of 2012, it was clear Yiannopoulos's company had hired people and offered them salaries it simply couldn't afford to pay. Having been regularly frustrated by polite efforts to get their back pay, writers who had quit while still being owed thousands finally sued The Kernel for their wages. Yiannopou-los's response was to go nuclear on any writers he suspected had talked to the media about The Kernel's internal woes, threaten-ing to ruin those who had crossed him.

'You've already made yourself permanently unemployable in London with your hysterical, brainless tweeting, by behaving like a common prostitute and after starting a war with me, as perhaps you are now discovering,' he warned in one email.

He followed this up to the same former writer – to whom he owed thousands in back pay – 'You've not only torpedoed your chances of ever having a career in journalism in London, but you're rapidly losing my sympathy as well,' he opened, before threatening to tell lurid tales and publish photographs of the writer's alleged behaviour.

By 2012, Yiannopoulos had a reputation as someone whom people would prefer not to cross: to anger him was to provoke a series of tweetstorms, menacing emails, threats to publish previous correspondence or photographs, and the like. As Yiannopoulos has gained an ever larger following of ever more aggressive right-wing supporters willing to pile in on his behalf on anyone who crosses him, people have got warier still. Even A-listers aren't immune: joining in the attack on an all-female remake of *Ghostbusters*, Yiannopoulos launched a tirade of tweets against Hollywood actress Leslie Jones. Jones complained, leading Yiannopoulos to be permanently banned from Twitter – but the resulting torrent of threats from his supporters in its wake drove her, too, off the social network for a time.[23] For these reasons, it's worth noting here, everyone interviewed for this section of this chapter spoke only on the condition of anonymity.

Yiannopoulos's threats were not enough to prevent the lawsuits against The Kernel: a court ruled it must pay contributors £16,853 in back pay.[24] Just days after Yiannopoulos insisted – in typically ebullient fashion – that the site was perfectly solvent, the company admitted it couldn't pay the amount, and the site was shut down and eventually closed, becoming yet another Yiannopoulos business which never filed accounts and was thus shuttered. He later added two more to the list: Hipster Ventures Ltd and Caligula Ltd. Because of their rapid collapse and failure to ever file documentation, there's no way to know how much (if any) money flowed through any of the businesses.

It's not just Yiannopoulos's companies that have faced court orders to pay up. Yiannopoulos has similarly rung up at least seven charges against him personally, dated between November 2012 and January 2016 – for £403, £75, £225, £660, £1,935, £2,165 and £535. All seven show on the official register as 'unsatisfied', meaning the court has no record that the amount due was paid – though sometimes fines are paid but not recorded on the register.

Yiannopoulos's serial business failures and exaggerations did little to curb his public bravado – or total lack of consistency. In 2012, as the UK was on the verge of passing the right to marry for same-sex couples, Yiannopoulos became one of the country's most visible opponents of the move – doing numerous TV interviews on the topic as a gay man opposed to gay marriage. Lest anyone think this was a position from principle, or faith – Yiannopoulos tended to profess his Catholicism at the time – by 2013, just a few months later and once the bill had passed, Yiannopoulos reversed his position, not only becoming a supporter of gay marriage, but also announcing he was engaged to be married himself.

If any one event represented a climax of Yiannopoulos's mixture of bullshit and self-aggrandisement, it was the birthday party he held that year, which he said would also mark his engagement, at a private members' club near the Old Street roundabout.

'As you all know,' his invitation began, 'I'm turning 27 this year.' 2013, in fact, marked Yiannopoulos's 29th birthday. He declared the event would double as a charity fundraiser and so he would sell tickets to his birthday guests. Prices started at £55, rising to £275 – not including booking fees. Guests were promised food, champagne and 'a trayful of expertly engineered cosmopolitans'. Several attendees said they suspected no one had paid – 'everyone was on the guest list' – and said the room was half full, the alcohol ran out quickly, and the room was decorated with four cheap pop-art canvas portraits of none other than Milo Yiannopoulos, one of which was stolen by a guest.

Even this tale got wildly exaggerated in Yiannopoulos's retelling. In one of a series of emails complaining about a journalist writing stories he didn't like (and trying to get her sacked), he complained about 'attention-seeking staff who gatecrash my parties, drink my booze and then complain about me on the internet' before going on to suggest that 'they stole at least one picture, which cost over £100 … I didn't bother mentioning it at the time because the total bill was ten grand'. The canvas print bounced around several London journalist flatshares for a few months before eventually being unceremoniously tossed in a dumpster. There is no UK record that Yiannopoulos, under any of his names, ever got married.

Not long after this came Yiannopoulos's big break: GamerGate. This was an online insurgency, supposedly about 'ethics in games journalism', in which a group of predominantly angry young men sought for boycotts, asking advertisers to withdraw their support from a number of video game sites over their apparently liberal 'social justice warrior' agendas. The movement, which in reality was often viciously sexist, began as one man's angry revenge on his games journalist ex-girlfriend and spiralled into an internet hate campaign against female technology writers and their supporters. In 2013, Yiannopoulos had written far more derisively about gamers than the female targets of GamerGate ever had. '[T]here's something a bit tragic, isn't there, about men in their thirties hunched over a controller whacking a helmeted extraterrestrial?' he wrote in The Kernel.[25] 'I'm in my late twenties, and even I find it sad. And yet there are so many of them – enough to support a multi-billion dollar video games industry. That's an awful lot of unemployed saddos living in their parents' basements.'

As ever, vitriol outweighed consistency. Yiannopoulos's gift for extravagant rudeness, and his willingness to casually engage in cruelty against virtual strangers, made him the perfect cheerleader of a movement he barely understood and as a man who couldn't name even three video games[26] surely can't have cared a great deal about.

Still, such was the size of the movement that Yiannopoulos said he was going to write the book of it. As he said in his post on Breitbart:

GamerGate is the biggest internet storm in a decade – a battle that has spawned an unprecedented four-and-a-half million tweets, death threats, a front-page story in the *New York Times*, a segment on *The Colbert Report*, cost Gawker Media over a million dollars, left hundreds of journalists angry and humiliated and precipitated a huge, unending wave of bitchy insults, bitter recriminations and online controversy.[27]

That post was written in December 2015, fifteen months after Yiannopoulos's first involvement in GamerGate. He was 'well into the writing process', he promised and hoped to 'have a completed manuscript by February [2016]'. The book never materialised and has no listing and no scheduled publication date.

GamerGate expanded and metastasised into the movement that became known as the alt-right, a new and brash version of the far right for the internet era, often racist, anti-Semitic and nationalistic, and wildly pro-Trump. The movement has expanded offline, and now stages conferences in Washington DC and elsewhere – but has still provided an angry and energetic portion of Trump's online base. Yiannopoulos happily became its darling, while denying that he himself is of the alt-right, and played up a Jewish identity to serve as a defence against accusations that the movement was anti-Semitic.

As with so much else, Yiannopoulos has shown willingness to be flexible about his stated religious identity: for much of his early career, he presented as a relatively devout Catholic – telling friends he'd converted as an adult (he does not appear on the Church's records of such converts) – and then later made more of a Jewish identity, though was not in any sense raised in that faith. When being hostile to the LGBT movement, Yiannopoulos stresses that he's gay; when surrounded by people with anti-Semitic views, he stresses his Jewishness. Yiannopoulos is never near to the core of a movement: not only is he not ensconced in a White House role, unlike several of his Breitbart colleagues, he's barely had a few fleeting photo-ops on rope lines with Trump. Yiannopoulos is at best tolerated by those at the top, because he's admired by parts of the fandom. His reward was a $250,000 book deal, revealed late in December 2016 with a publication date of March 2017 – an astonishingly tight turnaround which would usually suggest the book was written and the manuscript finalised. But by February, that date had been pushed back to June 2017 – apparently to allow the book to be expanded and revised to bring in news of student protests against the book itself.[28]

And then, predictably, things fell apart once again – shortly before he was meant to speak at the influential conservative activist conference CPAC, footage of Yiannopoulos appearing to endorse sex between adult men and teenage boys resurfaced.[29] While some fans rallied to his defence, the lukewarm support he'd had from those nearer the establishment melted away. The $250,000 book deal was scrapped.[30] The speaking invitation for CPAC evaporated. He's out from Breitbart with plans to create his own new venture. The cycle repeats.

Critics of Yiannopoulos paint him as a provocateur, an extremist, a dangerous, polarising figure. A longer history reveals something different: a man who has over the course of a decade told needless untruth after needless untruth, in ways that would inevitably be found out and which are often nearly as destructive to himself as to anyone else – a string of failed jobs, businesses and allegiances, left as detritus on a path which seems to lead to nowhere. Other than attention, what is it Yiannopoulos even wants?

Someone being insincere is not enough to make them harmless. And the hey-I-was-just-joking defence can work just as well, and for just as long, for some in the media as it does for some in politics. Yiannopoulos isn't a leader of anything, but he serves as a lesson in how a serial bullshitter can wreak havoc for year after year: calling someone out once is not enough.

CHAPTER SIX

FAKE MEDIA

If there's a pantomime villain in the tale of post-truth, it can only be 'fake news', an apparently new phenomenon which has risen in the social media era to threaten first our media and then democracy itself. Within months of first entering popular usage, 'fake news' has become routinely thrown around by social media users to dismiss negative stories about politicians they support; from fringe outlets attempting to write off the mainstream news; to political leaders – including Jeremy Corbyn and Donald Trump – attacking reporting or outlets to which they objected. Social networks are publicly working on ways to tackle the spread of fake news, advertisers are looking for ways to block fake news sites, and the UK Parliament is even holding an inquiry into the rise of fake news.

When we discuss fake news in this chapter, we're going to use the original and very tight definition of stories that have been wholly fabricated, usually in a bid to try to reach a large audience for any one of a variety of purposes. Unlike some overzealous bids to tackle fake news – one of which listed the *New Yorker* and *Private Eye* alongside fake sites as both outlets run satire[1] – we're also going to exclude deliberate parody from established outlets, even though on occasion such pieces are read as serious when some internet users (often those outside the outlet's typical audience) miss the joke. This is about the hoaxers, the pranksters, those trying to fire up polarised bases, or just making up a piece for their own amusement – and how they became one of the most talked-about topics of the mainstream media.

A ranking of the top fifty fake news stories of 2016[2] was compiled by Craig Silverman, the media editor of BuzzFeed News, and a crusader for several years against hoax images, spoof copies of reputable websites, and fake news. The top performing stories list shows how fake news ranges from the harmless to the deeply dangerous: from dubious and colourful 'true crime' tales to stories playing on racial tensions amid Black Lives Matter protests; from fake promises of political concerts to claims of secret political murders – many naming celebrities in their headlines for an extra viral boost.

Examples include 'Obama Signs Executive Order Banning The Pledge Of Allegiance In Schools Nationwide' (#1), 'Trump Offering Free One-Way Tickets to Africa & Mexico for Those Who Wanna Leave America' (#4), 'Florida man dies in meth-lab explosion after lighting farts on fire' (#6), 'Police Find 19 White Female Bodies In Freezers With "Black Lives Matter" Carved Into Skin' (#9), 'Donald Trump Protester Speaks Out: "I Was Paid $3,500 To Protest Trump's Rally"' (#15), 'Rupaul claims Trump touched him inappropriately in the 1990s' (#28), and 'Atlanta Officer Kills Black Woman, Injures Child, Following Breastfeeding Argument' (#44).

Illustrating how the ecosystem feeds off what works on one site before trying it on another, some of the top fifty stories had almost identical headlines, albeit with a small but very significant tweak. No. 47 on the list is a piece first seen in July titled 'Pope Francis Shocks World, Endorses Hillary Clinton for President, Releases Statement'. Up in third place, ostensibly from an entirely different website, comes the October headline 'Pope Francis Shocks World, Endorses Donald Trump for President, Releases Statement'. The second headline, which appeared nearer election day when more people are interested in politics, attracted more than four times as many social media shares as the first.

It's impossible to prove, but it's hard to believe that everyone sharing these stories is in on any joke – many of the stories are mocked up to look like authentic news. The leading fake news stories often use web addresses which appear to a casual user as if they're those of established news sites. One of the most frequent to appear is 'abcnews.com.co' – a spoof of the ABC network, whose real address is 'abcnews.go.com'. Another site making a frequent appearance was 'tmzhiphop.com', a play on the hugely popular celebrity gossip site TMZ.com. Others simply used sites which plausibly sounded like they *might* be real news outlets – the Boston Tribune, the Valley Report, the Empire Herald and the Baltimore Gazette, named after a short-lived nineteenth-century Baltimore paper, which brazenly claims to be the city's 'oldest news source and one of the longest running daily newspapers published in the United States'.[3] If imitation is the best form of flattery, mainstream outlets should be blushing fairly hard by now.

Some elements of the story around fake news and the 2016 US election are stranger than anything the hoaxers could ever concoct, and perhaps the strangest of all is the origin of much of the pro-Trump fake news which became so prolific in the last months of the election campaign – a tiny town in the Balkan republic of Macedonia named Veles. Despite having a population of just 45,000, residents of the town launched at least 140 different fake news websites as part of a bizarre online version of the gold rush era: in Veles, it quickly became known that faking it was easy money. Teenagers in the town – who didn't care a great deal either way about Donald Trump or US politics – created sites, invented fake news stories, or stole them from other sites, and attempted to cash in, as Craig Silverman and Lawrence Alexander reported.[4]

'I started the site for a easy way to make money,' one teenager operating a fake news site told the pair. 'In Macedonia the economy is very weak and teenagers are not allowed to work, so we need to find creative ways to make some money. I'm a musician but I can't afford music gear. Here in Macedonia the revenue from a small site is enough to afford many things.'

Those who got on the fake news bandwagon early could make up to around $5,000 a month from their sites, BuzzFeed News heard – good money anywhere, but a fortune in Macedonia, where average salaries are only around $400 a month. However, as with real-life gold rushes, as more people in Veles and elsewhere churned out pro-Trump stories – the stories with the best chance of hitting huge traffic – the odds of success, and the subsequent revenue, dwindled. Stories published by teens in the town reached huge audiences. One, inventing a claim that Clinton had said in 2013 that Trump should run for President, was shared 400,000 times on Facebook – more than twice as many shares as the *New York Times*' huge election scoop on Trump's 1995 tax return.

Veles saw an influx of journalists from around the world keen to interview the townspeople and ask if they were morally conflicted over their possible role in swinging the US election. One sixteen-year-old behind one site explained to *Channel 4 News* how he was just feeding a demand.[5] 'They are thirsty for the articles, that's all I have to say about them, they want to hear news about Donald Trump,' he said in an often monosyllabic interview. 'I dunno how to put this, there isn't much to do around here. A lot of kids don't go out. We're doing this out of boredom.' The teenager said he felt 'bad' about untrue stories, but said he'd continue with the site.

'Do you think if your kid had made 30,000 euros a month you'd make a problem?' another teen told a BBC journalist,[6] having been asked if his parents would object to his fake site. 'There's no dirty money in Veles,' the town's mayor told the same reporter.

The attitude of the Veles locals has a striking parallel: that of locals in countries used by the ultra-rich, oligarchs and companies – not to mention criminals and money-launderers – across the world as tax havens. In such places, locals can pick up hundreds or thousands of dollars a year acting as puppet directors for companies involved in the offshore trade – potentially depriving governments overseas of millions or billions.

On a reporting trip to the tiny Caribbean island of Nevis (average income just over $1,000 a month) in 2012, I asked the spokesman of the country's Prime Minister – who was based in a disused hotel across the road from a broken-down petrol station. 'The offshores are one of the reasons Nevis and St Kitts are doing well,' she told me.[7] 'Is it locals complaining, or those from overseas? It's not the locals! If Britain is crying about its tax dollars, that's not really a problem for us.'

It's hardly a surprise relatively poor countries are none too fussed when their nationals find safe and easy ways to boost their incomes, and have little desire to become the front line of defending the interests of countries much larger and richer than themselves, whether the mechanism is through aiding tax avoidance or fuelling misinformation. But it does mean it would not only be unreasonable to hope such governments would lead the charge on fake news, but it would also be doomed to failure.

The business model operated by the Veles teens was about as simple as they come, and a mirror of much of the mainstream media's financial approach: the teens wanted stories to go mega-viral and hit an audience of millions, each of whom would see a collection of low-value banner adverts on the site. Each view may generate only fractions of a cent, but if these can be accu-mulated in the hundreds of thousands or even millions, this quickly becomes a significant source of income, especially when the content is acquired for free through being either made up or stolen, meaning hosting the site – and the time taken to design something that looks roughly credible – is virtually the only cost.

But display adverts are far from the only way that fake news merchants can make themselves richer, and the rewards from other means often merit going to much greater lengths to make a sophisticated fake. One of the most lucrative business models for fake news is based on convincing people to sign up to casino sites, or sites offering ultra-high-risk 'binary option' invest-ments. Such sites offer generous fees to anyone who signs up new members, whether a flat fee or a percentage share of what can be thousands of pounds wagered on the sites.

One particularly elaborate example, first reported in BuzzFeed News,[8] featured a convincing replica of the CNN site – which popped up as an advert behind other windows – with the head-line 'Stephen Hawking Develops a Computer Code Unlike Any Other', with a picture byline of 'Eric Brauer', a non-existent CNN staffer with a stolen photo, but one for whom the fakers had built a Facebook page to enhance his credibility.

The article claimed the legendary physicist Stephen Hawk-ing had managed to develop a new trading algorithm which consistently beat the market with zero risk, and had decided to release it for free to the public in the hope that within a decade it would create a world where 'there will be no significant lower and upper class and the wealth will be evenly distributed be-tween hard working people'. The article was even accompanied by fake Facebook comments – some of them sceptical – and phony share and like counts. Anyone who clicked through a link from the 'CNN' article was greeted with a video with a faked synthesised voice, almost but not quite identical to Hawking's, introducing the scheme.

Those who had bought into the sophisticated fake news system would have signed up to an ultra-high-risk trading site with every danger of losing all of the money they invested in it. UK residents have reported losing hundreds of thousands of pounds through such binary option sites.

After their debunking by BuzzFeed News, the Hawking Code website and CNN clone were both deleted from the internet – but several other fake stories, some imitating celebrity news, some imitating business sites, pushing to similar schemes were still present on the same servers. To take down fake news schemes one at a time is to begin a game of whack-a-mole that will never end. What's significant to note is that even in the unlikely event that the major banner advertising networks managed to comprehensively cut off fake sites, we still wouldn't see the end of fake news: there will always be some gambling sites, questionable investments, alternative medicine providers, or others more than happy to pay generous affiliate fees to anyone who drives sign-ups to them, with few questions asked. Even respectable players in the industry such as William Hill have had affiliates attempting to use fake news sites (the 'Evening Post')[9] to push would-be punters their way – in exchange for a flat referral fee, or even a percentage of stakes, depending on the scheme. Often such behaviour can happen without any knowledge or approval on behalf of the site being pushed, in the case of affiliate schemes which don't do much checking. For as long as fake news can help persuade people to sign up to news sites, and they're happy to pay for it, people will keep making it.

Not everyone who makes a fake news website makes it for money, though. Those who aren't motivated by money, broadly speaking, can be divided into two groups: one group is made up of hoaxers and pranksters, making fake news for the thrill, for attention, or to enjoy the 'stupidity' of groups they dislike. The other type is the partisan who invents news which they think will help the cause or the candidate they've decided to champion. There is a huge risk in terms of trying to get people in either group to tell you what they've been doing, how they feel about it, or what the fallout has been – both groups are full of people who are, by definition, bullshitters. If they weren't good at sounding plausible, their fakery would never have caught on and been believed, so it's important to remember when reading their rationales and their interviews ahead in this chapter that while it's possible those concerned got caught in a rare moment of candour, it's also just as likely that they're engaged in a wind-up of their interviewer for their own obscure reasons. As the *New Yorker* put it, 'on the internet, nobody knows you're a dog'.[10]

Even with that in mind, the *Washington Post*'s interview with Paul Horner – who has for several years made his income from his fake news and hoaxes – remains fascinating. Horner, who authored several of the stories in the fake news top fifty, repeatedly states that he invented pro-Trump stories to show up Trump supporters as dumb, though also acknowledges that he may have helped him get elected.

'Honestly, people are definitely dumber. They just keep passing stuff around. Nobody fact-checks anything anymore' he told the newspaper. 'My sites were picked up by Trump supporters all the time. I think Trump is in the White House because of me. His followers don't fact-check anything – they'll post everything, believe anything. His campaign manager posted my story about a protester getting paid \$3,500 as fact.'

'I just wanted to make fun of that insane belief', he says of the story (not deleted), which gained hundreds of thousands of shares. Horner said he preferred his fake stories – which were shared as true by millions over the year – to be regarded alongside the satirical site *The Onion*: 'The stuff I do – I spend more time on it. There's purpose and meaning behind it. I don't just write fake news just to write it,' he said.[11]

When I visited it months later in researching this book, Horner's ABC News spoof still carried his fake 'paid protesters' story with a fake byline of a supposed ABC News reporter. It launched an advert claiming my computer had a 'critical alert' from a site pretending to be Apple Support, telling me I needed to phone a number and give my credit card details to stop scammers stealing my details – a common but convincing scam which every year tricks thousands of people into handing over their details to criminals.

The article, which is written in news rather than satirical style, present screenshots of 'evidence' of the adverts for anti-Trump protesters. Nothing on the page – or on the site, that I could find – gave any indication that the site was intended as satire or a joke. If it is this that propels Horner, he has a cruel sense of humour, and one that could leave his site's unwitting visitors at risk from the unscrupulous people who advertise with him.

When it comes to partisans pushing outright fake news – and fake sites – it's perhaps Italy that offers up the most blatant and extraordinary example in the Western world. Italy's politics are currently dominated by a populist party, the Five Star Movement. A deep-dive led by BuzzFeed News Europe editor Alberto Nardelli[12] – an Italian citizen himself – discovered a network of supposedly 'independent' news sites operated by party leadership: as if Jeremy Corbyn owned The Canary, or Trump owned Breitbart – but made no mention of the fact.

'Under lurid, all-capped headline phrases such as "THE TRUTH THEY ARE TRYING TO HIDE FROM US", the party's blogs … and other sites in the network have cross-posted scores of fake stories,' the story reveals. 'These include claims that the US is secretly funding traffickers bringing migrants from North Africa to Italy, and that Barack Obama wants to topple the Syrian regime to create instability across the region so China cannot get access to its oil.'

Such behaviour is a step beyond even Donald Trump's occasional habit of retweeting a supporter linking to a fake news site: institutions directly connected to political players are pushing out openly fake and supposedly 'independent' news to further their agenda. The fix for that behaviour will be different to that which would tackle hoaxers, or those in it for the money – further proof if it were still needed that hopes of an easy or quick technological fix to fake news or to bullshit are in vain.

But it's not, of course, Italy that people worry about when talking about politicians and states playing a role in fake news: the bear in this particular room could only be Russia. How much of a role do Putin and the Russian state play in the dissemination of fake news? There are two main Western-facing outlets connected to the Russian state that act overtly: one, the TV channel and website Russia Today (or RT) may spin stories and pick its news to suit a very particular agenda, but generally stops shy of outright fakery. Its sister site Sputnik, on the other hand, runs a combination of wire re-writes, comment pieces and the odd very questionably sourced piece that could qualify as fake – though an analysis of a month of traffic at the site found the overwhelming majority of pieces failed to muster even 1,000 hits.[13] If Sputnik is Russia's vehicle for spreading fake news, it's not doing terribly well – though other sites do occasionally pick up and run with its stories, while Russia Today's occasionally hyper-partisan segments often catch hold of a substantial online audience.

Inevitably, Russia has more tricks up its sleeve. Reporters have for several years uncovered 'troll factories' connected to the Russian state, where paid staff work feverishly each day to make pro-Putin and pro-Russian comments across the internet, as well as attacking the credibility of any negative story – and often the person reporting it – creating the illusion of a huge organic groundswell of support for the country.[14] Given the involvement of Russian hacking in the US election, it shouldn't come as a surprise that German spies and officials are keeping a wary eye on Russia ahead of their November ballot, warning of a risk of Russian-backed fake news to swing the election.[15]

They are almost certainly wise to be wary: Russia has repeatedly shown itself able and willing to play the troublemaker in the West's media and its elections. However, there's a risk of creating a fake narrative about fake news itself. The proliferation of pro-Trump fake news could be seen as a sign that Russia – who also intervened in the US election in his favour in other ways – was behind fake news. This theory, though, ignores the straightforward explanation that pro-Trump content got the biggest audience and so served every type of player in the fake news world best. Fake news has existed for many years, even if it drew less attention, and is made for many reasons – and while we shouldn't ignore Russia, we also shouldn't jump to conclusions that every hoax is part of Putin's master plan.

We've seen that political fake news exists, that it can reach huge audiences, and that there are a whole host of different reasons it gets made. It's time to turn to a much more open question: is it actually having any impact on the political process? The only way to have an absolutely definitive answer on this would be to somehow re-run the 2016 election with all else being identical, but in a world without fake news – which is sadly impossible. So what we're left with is trying to use other information to come to an educated guess.

If we look only at the very most successful fake and real news stories, it looks as if fake news has a dramatic effect. A study by Craig Silverman[16] – yep, him again – examined the total shares of the twenty most popular real political stories of the US election versus the top twenty fake stories of the election. From February through to July, real news comfortably outweighed fake in total shares, but in the final months of the election, this changed – between August and November, the twenty most shared real stories gained a total of 7.3 million shares. The top twenty fakes got 8.7 million – and seventeen of the twenty were either overtly pro-Trump or anti-Clinton. This clearly shows such stories had the potential to be influential.

Broader studies using different methodology offer something of a contrasting picture. Research published in the *Columbia Journalism Review*, using an aggressive definition of 'fake news' which included sites such as Breitbart, suggested the total reach of real news sites was dramatically larger than that of fake ones, even immediately before the election.[17] These two studies need not be contradictory: large mainstream outlets publish hundreds of stories each day while fake news sites only publish one or two – so while the best-performing articles may battle toe-to-toe, overall traffic and shares will always lean towards the mainstream. Another study covered by Poynter offered more assurance to the 'fake news isn't a problem' camp, by asking voters where they got their news and which stories about candidates they recalled – eventually concluding that each fake news story would need to have the same impact on voters as thirty-six TV adverts to have altered the election result.[18]

So far, so reassuring. But journalist and fake news expert Alastair Reid, the former editor of First Draft News, said judging the impact of fake news by what people remembered would always understate its effect.

'A lot of the studies on "fake news" and its effect, especially around the election, all focus on the effect of made-up stories about the candidates. So that's one specific medium by which misinformation is travelling, and one topic,' he said.[19]

But both online misinformation and elections are much more complex than that, and the studies are ignoring the heaving mass of memes, pictures and videos about the issues surrounding the election...

If you look at some of the private Facebook groups or Twitter accounts which are most active in the political space, they are full of memes, pictures and videos. Attendees to the Inauguration Deploraball boasted, on tape, about 'meme-ing [Trump] into the presidency' and that they 'directed the culture' on social media. To focus only on web articles ignores a huge part of the misinformation ecosystem.

It's the amplifying effect of social media and our loved ones (see the next two chapters) that makes fake news dangerous, Reid warns, and it's these factors that are the most difficult to quantify: in essence, researchers risk looking only at the bit of the iceberg above water and gauging it's not too much of a threat.

'It's like advertising,' Reid concludes.

We don't watch television to find out what products we want to buy, but do those adverts influence our shopping habits? Decades of research show that they do. It would be naive to think information on social media works differently. And when it's false or misleading information shared by friends or family we are more likely to believe it than other sources.

This comes to a central issue, what Reid called a 'misinformation ecosystem': people who encounter fake news don't come across it in a vacuum. It comes in searches and social feeds alongside partisan news, juxtaposed with direct appeals from campaigns, news from mainstream outlets, and comments, photos and memes made by friends and families. To look at fake news in isolation is to miss the real problem entirely.

This fact hasn't escaped experts in digital journalism. Blogger and journalism professor Jeff Jarvis noted: 'Fake news didn't come just in Facebook. It came from Fox and CNN and, yes, newspapers. Bullshit news.'[20] And Emily Bell, director of the Tow Center for Digital Journalism at Columbia University explained that panic over fake news serves as a proxy for a broader crisis.

'Fake news is a proxy for a host of concerns over the obscure power of our emerging news ecosystem,' she said.

> As a term it just represents ideas or facts you might not like – as well as fabricated nonsense. The real crisis in journalism is its loss of control and influence to larger-platform companies [such as Facebook or Twitter]. The 'fake news' issue is real but the disproportionate outrage over it speaks to a profound anxiety over what sort of news ecosystem and public sphere we want.[21]

This is perhaps best illustrated by a quick look at the UK, which may also help to explain why this chapter features so many US examples and nothing of UK politics whatsoever. There's a good reason for that: it's very hard to find any evidence of fake news on UK politics which reaches any form of mass audience, as a study by Jim Waterson for BuzzFeed News revealed.

'Out of the hundred most shared links relating to the new prime minister, there was only one overtly fake article which appears to have hoodwinked a large number of people,' he concluded.[22] 'A piece published by the site *Mook News* entitled "Tony Blair Ready To Take Over From Theresa May."'

This isn't to say the rest of the list was all high-quality and entirely accurate journalism – but partisan and hyper-partisan articles appeared to have all but crowded out the outright fake. This was echoed in a separate analysis of the far-right Britain First group on Facebook, which found the most-shared stories were distorted or partisan versions of real events, with little or no completely fake articles in the mix.[23]

This is proving a headache for Parliament's Culture, Media and Sport committee, which launched an inquiry into fake news in January and decided to restrict its scope solely to the strict definition of fake news, and how such material is disseminated on Facebook and other social networks. What the committee is getting in some volume – and what it does not want – is a number of campaigns encouraging people to send examples of their concerns about reporting in more mainstream outlets.[24] The committee has been left to attempt (likely in vain) to convince them to contact the newspapers' regulatory body, IPSO, instead.

'Fake news' arguably started out as a scapegoat, and rapidly became nothing more than an insult for disliked coverage. It's a good villain: few people will try to defend outright fakery and, even better for most mainstream outlets, this was an issue that Facebook, the internet, and the hoaxers were responsible for – leaving traditional media ostensibly blameless (though, as Chapter Ten will show, this isn't strictly true). If we turn the screws on Facebook, and we turn the screws on advertising networks, the theory goes, we will fix public discourse. Perhaps both steps would be positive – but as is hopefully apparent by now, when every other media actor is also spreading bullshit, we need to set our sights a bit wider.

Through this chapter – and many of the chapters before it

– we've been taking social networks as a given. Without them, most of these fake news sites and stories would have withered on the vine with under a thousand hits: social sharing – not Google search – is the lifeblood of fake news, just as it is of hyper-partisan news, and increasingly of mainstream outlets too. Facebook brings sites, niche and mainstream alike, their traffic while simultaneously competing with them for their audience's attention and for their advertisers' dollars. Facebook, and its smaller rivals, are involved in the news ecosystem – and the bullshit ecosystem – at every stage of the food chain. It's time to take a closer look at exactly how that chain works.

CHAPTER SEVEN

SOCIAL MEDIA...

Social networks have been a common thread through every other chapter in Part I. Political campaigns make smart and sophisticated use of Facebook advertising. Mainstream and partisan media court social networks to grow their audience. Fake news relies on social sharing to survive. While Facebook and Twitter may insist they're technology companies, not media companies, they're an integral part of the media ecosystem – and a big part of how bullshit information spreads.

As Facebook is by far the biggest player in the social network world, it will be the main focus of this chapter. We all know Facebook is big, but its sheer scale compared to almost any other player in the media industry is staggering. BBC's flagship *News at Ten* show reaches 4.5 million people a night.[1] ABC and CBS's nightly newscasts each reach around 9 million viewers.[2] The MailOnline – the world's largest news website – reaches nearly 15 million users a day.[3] Facebook, meanwhile, reaches 1.2 billion users each day – eighty times as many as the *Mail*.[4]

Its financial clout is also on a different scale to any of the other players in this industry. Macedonia's fake news purveyors were thrilled to net $5,000 a month. The *Washington Post* sold for just

$250 million in 2013,[5] while the *New York Times* is worth around $2.4 billion. On a bigger scale, Time Warner – which owns among other things CNN, HBO, Warner Bros and New Line Cinema – is worth $74 billion. Facebook is worth more than five times more even than Time Warner – $387 billion.

Facebook's financial scale and sheer reach would make it significant enough on their own, but Facebook also shapes the format in which publishers create news and competes with them for advertising dollars. A change to Facebook's algorithm can make or break publishers, as making posts or shares a little bit more or less vulnerable can mean thousands or millions more – or fewer – clicks. Similarly, Facebook's various decisions to boost video, live broadcasting or longer-form videos prompt immediate changes in newsrooms across the world. Its power is undeniable; its reach is unmatchable by anyone but Google, and it is the platform by which most fake news and bullshit is shared. After a decade acting as if it's not a player in the media industry, Facebook is facing unprecedented demands to use its market power for good.

It's worth starting by looking into Facebook's strange and complex relationship with the news media. Before the rise of Facebook, news online was all about search: the main way anyone found their content was through Google search, and so inevitably newsrooms altered their behaviour to attract search traffic. Headlines were (and still are) tailored to do well on Google's algorithm, and to top Google News. Some stories were written just to pick up traffic through Google. One popular trick is to churn out hundreds of (largely pointless) stories on TV shows headlined 'What time is [x]?'. *The Independent* has written around 6,500 such pieces, and the *Telegraph* has produced 13,000.[6] News sites respond to whatever will give them traffic.

Search, though, is no longer the only show in town. Measuring traffic to websites, and where it comes from, is not a straightforward task, but by 2015 there was solid evidence that, at least by some methodologies, traffic to news sites from Facebook had overtaken traffic from Google – meaning what people share is as important as how the world's largest search engine treats the site.[7]

Tailoring content to suit search engines generally encouraged sites to make the signposting on their articles clear and straightforward. The incentives on social are different: one approach is to be relatable and conversational, rather than formal. Another is to encourage partisan headlines that people will share through outrage – as we saw time and again in earlier chapters. One recent study suggested that fake and hyper-partisan sites got around three times more of their traffic through Facebook than did through what it called 'real' news sites.[8] Social sharing is essential for such sites, and seems to serve them better than it does most of the mainstream.

Facebook's algorithm drives many trends in mainstream, partisan and fake news alike, but is entirely opaque. The site does not show you every post each of your friends make, and shows you only a small percentage of posts from pages you follow – and the order in which they appear is not chronological, but again determined by the site. This algorithm is often tweaked, with dramatic results. In late 2015, news sites had enjoyed a traffic boom from Facebook. In early 2016, that ended: Facebook made some adjustments that reduced how many people saw posts from publishers, causing a 42 per cent drop in publishers' reach on the network.[9] These tweaks can also significantly affect traffic to the actual websites – and thus the revenue publishers get from advertising. One change later in 2016 caused traffic from Facebook to a host of publishers to drop by between 20 per cent and 50 per cent.[10]

Publishers have a rather one-sided relationship with Facebook: they are hugely reliant on it for traffic, but Facebook – despite regularly promising to be a friend of journalism – doesn't really reciprocate that need. There are times when what Facebook wants and what news outlets want are directly opposed to one another. In June, Facebook changed how its main news feed worked, to reduce the priority of content from publishers – because it wanted people to see more information about their friends' real lives instead (think wedding and baby photos).

Facebook's shift increased the prominence of new posts from friends and families, reducing the visibility of what publishers posted. 'To help make sure you don't miss the friends and family posts you are likely to care about, we put those posts toward the top of your News Feed,' said the site's VP Adam Mosseri in a post explaining the move.[11] BuzzFeed News's Charlie Warzel was blunter: 'Facebook just issued its own referendum on news in its News Feed. Put simply, the users have spoken and news lost.'[12]

This is an example of Facebook's interests being different from those of publishers. The social network is battling its own problem – that its users are sharing fewer posts about themselves and their families than they used to. Facebook began with people sharing news about themselves, photos of themselves, and pictures of themselves, their kids, and (of course) their pets. Last year, these kinds of posts had dropped by around 21 per cent,[13] leading Fortune to note: 'Personal updates – including the half-based opinions, but also the baby photos, engagement announcements, and vacation photos – are what keep people coming back to Facebook … Without the personal updates, Facebook becomes a glorified, $327 billion content recommendation engine.' Personal content is a unique asset, not only keeping users logging into the site to check what their friends are up to, but keeping them attached to it as a place with years of their own history. The more of it Facebook has, the more difficult it would be to get a user to switch to some new network – and prioritising personal posts gives the social network more information about its users – making advert targeting more successful.

Facebook's business model is in some senses similar to that of news sites: it wants a user's attention for as long as it can manage so that it can show them targeted adverts. If showing news content helps keep users on Facebook, that's what it'll show them. If entertainment does better, then it'll do that – and if personal content is what works, Facebook will prioritise that. That does, of course, mean that Facebook is also a commercial rival to publishers: last year its digital advertising revenues rose 43 per cent year-on-year, while the rest of the industry actually fell over the same period – Facebook and Google are taking virtually all of the new money from online advertising which publishers were desperately hoping would go to them.[14] When it comes to advertising, Facebook is if anything a direct competitor to news sites, exacerbating the financial difficulties of newsrooms which in many cases were already struggling.

Sometimes, Facebook's interests do coincide with those of publishers: Facebook wants content, publishers want to reach new audiences. But it should be clear that's not always the case. When it comes to promoting news content, Facebook changes direction regularly, sometimes becoming publishers' best friends, but giving and taking away with little warning in ways that are sometimes inexplicable to industry players. And on fake news, overblown stories and bullshit, Facebook has been patchy at best.

News has consistently proven a headache for Facebook. In 2014, the site added a feature to users' home pages, referred to as 'trending' – a collection of topics, mainly news stories, which were taking off on the site. Each topic was given a terse description and a link to an authoritative source writing about it. Being chosen in the list would mean a big traffic boost for whichever site was picked. The trending topics were picked by a small group of journalists hired as contractors by Facebook, instructed to spot topics highlighted by the site's algorithms and write the short descriptions. The operation was run under the requirements of strict confidentiality – everyone involved was required to sign non-disclosure agreements. They didn't work. Facebook was mired in bad publicity as the trending news team began to leak details of how the team operated and what powers the curators had, which included the ability to 'blacklist' topics and prevent them appearing in the trending list under rules which weren't public or, according to some former employees, all that clear.[15]

There was worse news to come for Facebook after a former curator with conservative political views said other curators at the site were blacklisting – either deliberately or subconsciously – right-wing topics. 'I'd come on shift and I'd discover that CPAC or Mitt Romney or Glenn Beck or popular conservative topics wouldn't be trending because either the curator didn't recognise the news topic or it was like they had a bias against Ted Cruz,' the individual told Gizmodo.[16] 'I believe it had a chilling effect on conservative news.'

Topics which had been omitted from the trending list, in the former curator's view, also included 'former IRS official Lois Lerner, who was accused by Republicans of inappropriately scrutinising conservative groups; Wisconsin Gov. Scott Walker; [and] popular conservative news aggregator the Drudge Report'. The allegation – which Facebook denied – proved explosive, forcing the site to try to explain how its news selection process worked. Facebook was also left in some ways trying to explain the impossible: how it could build a story-selecting system with zero political bias – a familiar issue to many news outlets trying to convince readers of the same thing.

Not long after this row, Facebook laid off its remaining curators and replaced them with an algorithm which would automatically pick which news topics would trend – something curators had suspected had been the plan all along, with human curators used to 'train' the algorithm. The site said the shift was a planned move, unrelated to the controversy, to make trending easier to scale: 'A more algorithmically driven process allows us to scale Trending to cover more topics and make it available to more people globally over time,' it stated.[17]

The algorithm not only failed to prevent fake news, it began in some cases to actively promote it to tens or hundreds of millions of users. 'BREAKING: Fox News Exposes Traitor Megyn Kelly, Kicks Her Out For Backing Hillary' one headline pushed by the new trending algorithm stated. Kelly had neither endorsed Clinton nor been fired. Another falsely claimed: 'SNL Star Calls Ann Coulter a Racist C*nt'.[18] The algorithm at one point even managed to highlight a 9/11 conspiracy theory claiming that the World Trade Center collapsed after a 'controlled explosion'.[19] And, infamously, on one day in August Facebook's algorithm decided that a man's decision to have sex with a McChicken sandwich was the news the world most needed to hear.

Facebook was left on the horns of a dilemma: if it has human curators to pick its trending topics, it's open to just the same allegations of bias as any other journalism outlet. But its attempts to automate topic selection have on occasions backfired badly – leading the world's biggest social network to actively promote (and risk appearing to endorse) partisan and fake news stories. This is an issue Facebook cannot ignore.

Tackling fake news is not the only issue around the bullshit ecosystem with which Facebook is contending: the other is what's come to be referred to as the 'filter bubble': our friends tend to have fairly similar political views to our own, and so are likely to share stories we would agree with. If we get most – or even a sizeable chunk – of our news from our Facebook feed, we can be left with the impression that almost everyone agrees with us. This factor can be exaggerated – more people report getting news from TV and other sources than Facebook – but that doesn't mean that the effect is trivial.

Eli Pariser, who wrote the book *The Filter Bubble* and is sometimes credited with coining the term, said the effect was subtle. 'It's much easier than it's ever been to live in an information environment that is several standard deviations from normal,' he told The Verge.[20] 'It changes the cultural conversation for everyone … Millions of people believe what they hear from many outlets less than they otherwise would and are more willing to believe some pretty far-out ideas than they otherwise would thanks to social media.'

It's an easy and common mistake for people to assume that filter bubbles are a new phenomenon of the internet era. This forgets a time when people would buy and read only one news-paper – which in the UK carry an open political bias – creating a bubble of its own. Similarly, people's class, profession, and location all create a real-life bubble of shared interests.

Posting to these kind of politicised bubbles becomes an act of performance as well as an act of simply sharing interesting links. Sharing a post that your bubble may disagree with risks provoking a backlash, and not just a backlash from strangers on the internet but rather from your own friends and relatives. Sharing a post that your bubble will agree with offers affirmation through likes. That desire to share only a particular set of our views creates a feedback effect, and can push polarisation even further. When these effects combine with people who have joined pages supporting political parties or candidates, they become still stronger: the bubble is self-reinforcing.

The result is that even relatively straight-down-the-line news stories can become something else entirely. A report into social care, for example, was picked up by the group 'Jeremy Corbyn for PM'. 'The possibility that the cuts to health and social care are implicated in almost 30,000 excess deaths is one that needs further exploration,' the post states – before concluding: 'A horrifying form of population control?'[21]

Commenters agreed: 'IDS is guilty of murdering these people,' said one. 'Just another group in the Tory cull of what they see as 'non-contributing' members of the lower orders,' another agreed. 'Their [sic] obviously hoping the elderly will die, and they can claim back their pensions,' said a third. It's not enough for cuts to be having consequences on vulnerable groups – for people in this community, such consequences have to be part of a deliberate plan by Conservative ministers to kill off the elderly.

On the other side of divide, a photo on Britain First's Facebook page showing Labour leader Jeremy Corbyn and shadow Chancellor John McDonnell is shared with the caption 'Share if you are sick and tired of these pro-IRA losers sympathising with terrorists!', to comments of 'If i said this once i'v said it a thousand time put ther heads on trators gate,' 'There was a time when they would have been put in the Tower of London' and 'These two should be in prison with Tony Blair!'[22]

These aren't forums that are going to change the mind of someone politically undecided, but they do fire up people on one side or the other – and make it possible for bullshit to win out over reality even months after an issue should be settled. The UK's vote to leave the EU in June 2016 caused the pound to immediately plunge about 15 per cent against the dollar, making UK imports more expensive and leading to higher inflation. By February 2017, inflation had risen to 1.8 per cent from 0.5 per cent in the month of the vote[23] – with forecasters virtually unanimous that it would continue to rise.

Despite this, supporters of Brexit hear a very different version of events. Leave.EU – the unofficial campaign for Leave in the referendum – continued posting long after the race was run. 'A new report says that the average British family could save hundreds of pounds a year on the food and clothing costs, as a direct result of Brexit,' it posted.[24] 'This puts to bed another Project Fear scare story which claimed food bills would go up after we left the EU. So much for that!'

The post gained more than 1,000 shares and prompted attacks on the media. 'And yet dispatches are on tonight saying how brexit will cost us hundreds in our food bills. Typical agenda pushing bs,at least leave.eu produce the facts,' one person posted.

Another trusted the post despite an actual price rise which had already taken place: 'Ha ha ha ha, so where does this leave those idiotic Toblerone makers who are reducing the size of "British" Toblerone bars due to Brexit increased costs ??'

This is the power of bullshit: people become so ready to hear what they want to believe that a Facebook post is believed not only over experts, but also over events which have already happened. This was not a case of trusting experts warning of price rises versus politicians saying they wouldn't – this was a case of simply denying increases that had already happened, and then blaming the mainstream media for accurately reporting them. The filter bubble fuels the post-truth society by making it easier for people to ignore reality.

This isn't just exploited by people at the grassroots of politics: campaigns now routinely make use of Facebook's highly specific advertising targeting to send messages only to specific groups open to them – these can be used to dissuade likely Sanders supporters or other groups from turning out to vote for Hillary Clinton,[25] for example, or to send tailored messages to different groups likely to support Brexit. Messages need no longer withstand the scrutiny of the general public or the media – they can be tailored ever-more closely to different groups, out of sight.[26]

When groups with different views do engage online, it doesn't tend to be constructive. It's Twitter – a social network with 300 million active users, rather than Facebook's 1.8 billion – that has the particular issue with this, as almost all posts on Twitter are public and easily shared to other users. This can lead to pile-ons, especially when exploited by users with large numbers of followers. Someone with 200 or 300 followers on the site who upsets or offends someone with far more followers can suddenly find

themselves facing thousands or tens of thousands of aggressive
and unpleasant comments from total strangers.

One of the best-known and nastiest cases of such a pile-on
happened to Leslie Jones, a famous Twitter user with thousands
of her own followers. She became the target of the right-wing
(and often racist and sexist) GamerGate and alt-right movement
by the simple virtue of being one of the stars of an all-female
remake of *Ghostbusters*. As the abuse started, Jones chose
to highlight the vile racial slurs she was receiving to her own
followers in a bid to bring the extent of online hatred to light.
Jones blocked accounts that sent her abuse, spoke out against
the bullying, and tried to use every advantage of her own profile
to withstand the torrent. But still it came, exacerbated further
by accounts 'retweeting' faked tweets from Jones which
further fuelled the anger of those attacking her.

In a long series of tweets, Jones wrote:

> Most of these comments sound like they are from ignorant
> children. 'I'm the source of AIDS?!' WTF!! These people hate
> themselves. You have to hate yourself to put out that type of
> hate. I mean, on my worst day I can't think of this type of hate to
> put out. I don't know how to feel. I'm numb…
>
> I used to wonder why some celebs don't have Twitter accts.
> Now I know. You can't be nice and communicate with fans 'cause
> people crazy … I just am saddened today. Twitter, I understand
> you got free speech. I get it. But there has to be some guidelines
> when you let [hate] spread like that.[27]

Twitter has often faced criticism for slow and inadequate responses to online abuse, but in this instance banned multiple

accounts for the racist abuse they sent. However, when faced with tens of thousands of accounts – some of them newly created only to send abuse – closing individual accounts is like bailing out a boat with a thimble. Twitter's ability to fuel mobs is a consequence of the way the system is built, with any user able to talk to any other, and unless a user has deliberately set their account to be private, their tweets can be made visible to anyone. For any topic with enough people having strong views one way or the other, stepping into the conversation comes with the risk of attracting an online mob – which makes any kind of attempt to reach across the fence an unappealing prospect.

The architecture of social media leaves us open to lines of deliberate attack from those trying to deceive or discourage us: we believe we're in groups of like-minded people, and this leaves us open to be exploited by malicious actors – potentially including Russia, or others seeking to manipulate elections. The *New Yorker* showed how this happened in pro-Bernie Sanders groups, and suggested (though was not certain) that the Kremlin may have been involved in these and similar activities.

'John Mattes, a Bernie Sanders organizer who ran a Facebook page for supporters in San Diego, noticed a surge of new adherents with false profiles. One "Oliver Mitov" had almost no friends or photographs but belonged to sixteen pro-Sanders groups,' the article explained.[28]

On September 25th, Mitov posted to several pro-Sanders pages: 'NEW LEAK: Here Is Who Ordered Hillary To Leave The Four Men In Benghazi!—USAPoliticsNow.' It was a baseless story alleging that Clinton had received millions of dollars from Saudi royals. Mattes said, 'The fake news depressed and discouraged

some percentage of Bernie voters. When I realised it, I said, "We
are being played.'"

Social media weaponises bullshit: when people see something
on their social feeds, they're not seeing information from a fake
news or hyper-partisan site, they're seeing information from
their friends or relatives. Because we like and trust our friends,
we're more inclined to like and trust what they share on social
media. Unless we deliberately make ourselves step back, we're
not generally dispassionately analysing the source of information – we're judging it as OK because it comes from our friends.

'People want information that makes them feel better,' Claire
Wardle, research director of First Draft News, told *The Guardian*.[29] 'We're living in a time where there is so much fear and
concern mapped onto social technology … if one of your peers
sends something, you already trust them. So you are much less
likely to be critical.'

Almost half of Americans routinely get news from Facebook,[30]
elevating friends and family – often themselves lacking in media
literacy – to information sources on an equal footing to major
media outlets. 'People are turning to alternative sources of news,
or, more commonly, to the news their peers are sharing,' says
Leah Selig Chauhan of the think tank Demos.[31] 'If an individual
"trusts" the outlet they are following then it is completely plausible that they would feel no need to double check these validity of
the stories anyway. This is even more likely when news is shared
by friends or family.'

Given that even accurate or fair stories can be shared on
Facebook with messages making them much stronger – or
over-interpreting what they're actually saying – no solution to

fake news or low-quality stories that polarise audiences will stick if it doesn't involve changes to either Facebook or its users. The reality of the Facebook format puts content from the *New York Times* on an equal footing to content from Breitbart and to the entirely fake news site the Boston Tribune. Facebook is too intrinsic to the rise of the problem of bullshit to not play a part in any solution.

In the days after the US election result, Facebook founder and CEO Mark Zuckerberg publicly dismissed any idea that Facebook or fake news had influenced the election. 'I think the idea that fake news on Facebook – of which it's a very small amount of the content – influenced the election in any way is a pretty crazy idea,' he said.[32] 'There have been hoaxes on the Internet, there were hoaxes before … we do our best to make it so that people can report that, and as I said before, we can show people the most meaningful content we can.'

Despite this defensive initial response, Facebook has changed its mission statement, announcing the shift in a more than 5,000-word statement from Zuckerberg, which despite its length avoided specific references to either Trump or Brexit – and skirted details on many issues it touched on. Facebook previously had a mission to 'connect the world'. It has not made its statement more nuanced.

'In times like these, the most important thing we at Facebook can do is develop the social infrastructure to give people the power to build a global community that works for all of us,' says Zuckerberg in his letter.[33] 'Our job at Facebook is to help people make the greatest positive impact while mitigating areas where technology and social media can contribute to divisiveness and isolation.'

Zuckerberg also acknowledged that the issues with content online and on Facebook go far beyond what's generally meant by 'fake news'.

> The two most discussed concerns this past year were about diversity of viewpoints we see (filter bubbles) and accuracy of information (fake news). I worry about these and we have studied them extensively, but I also worry there are even more powerful effects we must mitigate around sensationalism and polarization leading to a loss of common understanding.

This was followed by restating a position long held at Facebook that views expressed through the site are more diverse than getting news from 'the same two or three TV networks' or 'newspapers with their consistent editorial views', but said Facebook could do more to tackle such issues, building in fact-checkers' views and trying to de-prioritise sensational headlines in the News Feed – but otherwise the statement largely dealt in sentiment and broad-brush strokes rather than in details.

One criticism of the Zuckerberg statement is that it's so idealistic as to be virtually meaningless – its general emphasis on 'supportive communities' and the 'global community' risked bogging it down entirely, rather than addressing the real challenges in front of the network. Charlie Beckett, the director of the Polis think tank at the London School of Economics, said Facebook was essentially still in denial – thinking it could continue to act as if it were apolitical.

'I don't think that in any real or helpful sense there can be such a thing as a "global community". As the United Nations soon discovered, there are only competing national or regional interests,' he wrote. 'Insisting on a "community" rather than recognising these often conflicting forces can often make things worse not better … Trying to pretend that Facebook can be all things to all people might sound lovely in general. But what happens in practice? For example, in China?'[34]

Adrienne LaFrance, a staff writer at the *Atlantic* magazine, said Zuckerberg's plan amounted to requiring its 1.8 billion users 'to act as unpaid editors, volunteering to teach Facebook's algorithmic editors how and when to surface the content Facebook does not pay for … building a global newsroom run by robot editors and its own readers'.[35]

Zuckerberg's address, she argued, was not short of praise for the role of journalism, or recognition of the need for quality journalism, and acknowledged that journalism provided much of the content Facebook needed – but signalled that Facebook would do nothing to save it.

'Lip service to the crucial function of the Fourth Estate is not enough to sustain it,' she concluded.

> All of this is the news industry's problem; not Zuckerberg's. But it's also a problem for anyone who believes in and relies on quality journalism to make sense of the world. Zuckerberg doesn't want Facebook to kill journalism as we know it. He really, really doesn't. But that doesn't mean he won't.

Facebook helps drive huge audience numbers to both real and fake news, while also posing an existential threat to the revenues of the former. A minor change in its algorithms can reshape the focus of news organisations across the world. Facebook's power represents an opportunity to tackle the rise of bullshit: the company and its founder have had to acknowledge their role in the industry and their responsibility to help tackle polarisation and fake news – and governments across the world (especially in Europe) are looking at what they could do through legislation to make Facebook take more responsibility for material on its network. Facebook's scale and power across the information ecosystem is a source of concern for many – but that same scale and power means any positive change Facebook makes (or is forced to make) will have ricochet effects across the industry and across the world.

So far, we've looked at almost every type of organisation con-tributing to the rise of bullshit: political campaigns, old media, new media, fake news and the social networks where they come together. We've left out one fundamental part of the system, though: the audiences of each. The last significant player with a role in the bullshit puzzle is, dear reader, you. Yes, you.

CHAPTER EIGHT

...AND YOU

Previous chapters have tended to treat the public as passive consumers of news and misinformation, victims of the malice or mistakes of other actors. That's not entirely fair: we're not all passive consumers of everything we receive. Just as we choose who we vote for, we also choose what we read, what we watch and what we share – though we're not always entirely honest about it. Even a decade ago, when a 2007 Pew research poll asked the US public about news coverage, 87 per cent complained there was too much celebrity news, and 54 per cent of those blamed the news media for providing too much of it. The public also, as they often do in such surveys, complained the media don't provide enough good news.[1]

Sometimes news organisations take this kind of research seriously. In 2016, a UK newspaper publisher decided to launch a new paper, *New Day*, which would have a more 'positive' outlook and avoid partisanship, offering instead 'balanced opinion'. The paper, with the motto 'Life is short, live it well', was launched after extensive polling of what the public said they wanted.[2] Just two months after it launched, it was shut down due to poor sales.[3] Meanwhile, the *Daily Mail* went from being a newspaper with virtually no website to speak of to the world's biggest news-paper site[4] – in large part thanks to a relentless focus on celebrity news. What we actually read and what we claim to want to read are radically different things.

In many ways, we get the media we deserve: outlets and hoax-ers alike produce material that finds an audience. Politicians do what they think will attract voters. And social networks just put us in touch with each other. So if bullshit is in the ascendency, and trust in reliable information is at a low, we as consumers, paying customers and voters play a role in that too – and in this era when we can all create and share on a near-equal footing to traditional news outlets, that's becoming all the more significant.

One place to start is by looking at what we currently believe: if our perceptions going into an election, or even before reading an article, are wrong then what we decide or believe afterwards will be wrong too. And, as a whole, we as a public are wrong about a lot of things central to public policy making. Immigra-tion is consistently named in polls as one of the top three issues facing the UK,[5] detailing concerns ranging from the country being 'full', to pressures on local services, to some people worry-ing about the religious or ethnic mix of the country drastically changing. The issue is given as something voters care about a great deal – but we're not well informed about it: on average, the UK public estimates 31 per cent of the population is made up of immigrants; in reality it is only 13 per cent.[6] People estimate that 30 per cent of the population are black or Asian, while the real figure is only 11 per cent. And, most dramatically, people estimate that around 24 per cent of the country are Muslims, whereas the true figure is just 5 per cent – less than a quarter of the esti-mated value. Conversely, people believe the country's Christian population has dropped to 34 per cent, whereas in reality it's 59 per cent.

These perceptions matter. If people think the scale of immigration is more than twice its real level, that the country is much more Islamic than it is, and that the pace of societal change is much faster than it really is, this is likely to have an impact on their views on whether or not immigration is too high. This isn't the same as saying anyone concerned about immigration is wrong – but these inaccurate pre-existing beliefs provide a significant hurdle to anyone who would want to advocate a change in policy.

This is just one of a range of major issues the British public is – on average – wrong about. Crime fell by more than half between 1995 and 2013, but 58 per cent of the public don't believe the figures. We believe one in six underage teenage girls become pregnant, while the real figure is nearer one in 165. And one in three people think the government spends as much on unemployed people as it does on pensioners, while in fact pensions cost fifteen times as much as unemployment benefits.

We could just choose to read this as a public who has been misinformed for various reasons by the politicians and the media, but in reality the picture may be more complicated – and tackling the issue won't be easy. 'We need to avoid dismissing public opinion,' Ipsos MORI's research director Bobby Duffy said as the research was published.

Everyone has a vote, misperceptions have always been with us and they may reflect concerns – that is, people may overestimate issues because they are worried about them, not the other way round. A lack of trust in government information is also very evident in other questions in the survey – so 'myth-busting' is likely to prove a challenge on many of these issues.

Whatever the reason for the public's views diverging from reality, it is an issue that needs tackling: people are more likely to believe new information which accords with their current beliefs, and more likely to share it – and when commenting or posting online, people's existing beliefs become all the more significant. 'Public priorities may well be different if we had a clearer view of the scale of immigration, how much would be saved by different changes to benefits, how much is spent on foreign aid and the real incidence of teenage pregnancy,' Duffy noted.

Such misconceptions build over time, are shaped by political and media narratives, and then come to fuel those narratives in turn – and these mistaken beliefs aren't restricted to the UK. In the USA, where a debate over the size of the federal government and the generosity of social programmes has raged for decades, people are even unsure about facts as they relate to themselves. One survey cited in a book on the New Deal by Jefferson Cowie[7] showed 57 per cent of Americans said they received no support from any government programmes. But when actually presented by the researchers with a list of twenty-one different social programmes, 94 per cent of these people revealed they had actually benefited from at least one programme, with an average benefiting from four. Even when thinking about our personal situation, our political views – or our first impressions – can lead us astray.

This was serious enough when we were passive consumers of information and were generally only involved in the political process every few years at the ballot box. But now we're all much more involved day-to-day, particularly on the internet. The combination of political polarisation, our filter bubbles, our propensity to believe material shared by our friends and family, and our shared misconceptions can lead to bullshit material reaching huge audiences without the involvement of any major political players or outlets – we make our own.

There is a vocabulary to these kinds of political memes: a quote, sometimes with a short snippet of comment, overlaid on a photo of a political idol or opponent, shared into social groups of like-minded followers, generally with no sourcing, evidence or back-up for what's said therein. Some are just partisan, some are misleading and some are outright false – and many of the most successful also attack the mainstream media.

Supporters of Jeremy Corbyn are among the most prolific users of such graphics. One, in the wake of local election results, listed: '1995: Blair's first local elections. 46 per cent councillors won. "Landslide for Labour". 2006: Cameron's first local elections. 41 per cent councillors won. "Best Tory result for years." 2016: Corbyn's first local elections. 47 per cent councillors won. "Disaster for Corbyn."'

To people inclined to support Corbyn and without a detailed knowledge of how elections work, the meme serves to suggest the Labour leader had been more successful in his first elections than the previous two election-winning Prime Ministers, and that the media was hiding this fact. In reality, the areas being challenged in each contest were very different: Blair's contest was in marginal seats; Corbyn's, the Labour heartlands. Blair's first contest led to a net gain of 1,800 councillors, Cameron had gains of 300, while Corbyn's middling performance in Labour heartlands led to a net loss of eighteen council seats.[8]

That second message, though, doesn't easily fit on a small image on social media, and wouldn't be shared nearly as enthusiastically to nearly so many people. Other viral images spread around the result, noticed by Vice, carried the same theme: 'Labour wins the London mayor election, gets a higher percentage of the vote than the Conservatives, and gets 1,270 councillors elected to 726 for Conservatives ... but we at the BBC have decided this is a disaster for Jeremy Corbyn' said one. Another showed a photoshopped picture of BBC political editor Laura Kuenssberg: 'Please help. This is Laura Kuenssberg. She has been kidnapped by the Conservative party & is being forced to deliver their propaganda on the BBC.'

Another post stated 'Some things you won't hear on the BBC and MSM. Labour is the most popular party and @jeremycorbyn has a huge mandate'. The post was accompanied with graphs produced by the BBC – and all polling evidence showed that nationally, Labour was nowhere near being the most popular party.

Other fan-created memes focus on attacks. When Owen Smith challenged Jeremy Corbyn for the Labour leadership in the summer of 2016, social networks were flooded with information – often exaggerated or lacking in content rather than outright made up – on Smith. One showed Smith next to a series of claimed character flaws, including: 'Plotting for last six months', 'Cant make his mind up whether he supported Iraq war or not', 'Cant say where his magic £200billion [Smith had pledged a £200 billion investment fund; Corbyn in response pledged £500 billion] will come from', and 'Would Nuke millions of innocent people'.[9] Another said Smith was not the 'soft left' because he 'described Tony Blair as "a socialist"', 'attended an arms trade annual dinner' and had been 'plotting this coup since January'.[10]

On occasion, the attacks target Conservatives – one pictured Theresa May, then the Home Secretary, with her husband. 'Mr & Mrs,' it began.[11] 'She controls the budget for the police force and prisons. He is a major shareholder in [private security contractor] G4S. I'll just leave this here.'

Theresa May did not, in fact, control the prison budget as Home Secretary – but, much more significantly, her husband was not a shareholder (major or minor) in G4S. This has been repeatedly debunked by multiple media outlets,[12] and still persists as a meme, resurfacing every few months and being shared anew, usually accompanied by outrage at the mainstream media for covering up the scandal.

In the US, this stuff is amped up to eleven. Republicans share photos of Barack Obama saying: 'My legacy will be an America brought down to the level of the rest of the world'[13] and Hillary Clinton saying things such as: 'I will get the NRA shut down for good if I become President. If we can ban handguns we will do it' or 'The average Democrat voter is just plain stupid.'[14] Liberals share quotes suggesting Sarah Palin said Alaska has 'all sorts of Eskimos and other foreigners',[15] or Trump claiming: 'If black lives don't matter here go back to Africa.'[16] All of the quotes are false.

The phenomenon reached its nadir in a saga eventually referred to as 'pizzagate', when Twitter and Facebook users began believing that hacked emails from Clinton associate John Podesta contained evidence of a paedophile ring at the heart of the Washington DC establishment. The early messages fuelled further such posts on conspiracy message boards, and then on fake news sites. Eventually a user – seemingly as a wind-up – suggested that innocuous words in emails were a code: pizza meant a girl, pasta meant a boy, sauce meant orgy, and so on.[17] Despite the ridiculousness of the claims and the total lack of evidence, the online 'detective' work eventually led to a particular pizza shop in Washington DC – into which an armed man stormed days later, to 'self-investigate' the conspiracy.[18] Thankfully, no one was injured.

Even when the results are not so blatantly dangerous, these kinds of messages are a perfect vector for bullshit: they reach an audience predisposed to believe and share them and similarly predisposed to mistrust mainstream outlets giving contradictory information – and they come from people we trust and largely agree with. Talking about images and memes, rather than links to sites, might seem like a niche issue, but evidence suggests they are far more likely to be shared. An analysis of posts on Facebook by Breitbart showed only one in twenty posts were images – but these made up half of the page's total shares.[19] While we all look at links and sites, the fake news ecosystem has moved on. We've all seen images like these on our feed, and most of us have shared them – and when it's something we agree with, we often don't check first: how often do you look for a fact-check on something you agree with versus something you don't? We're all part of the problem.

Many of us have another bad habit that can help spread bullshit: lots of us share articles on social media without ever actually reading them – or even ever opening the story at all. A study published in the summer of 2016 analysed thousands of links posted using the service bit.ly, which displays statistics on how many users have ever clicked – and for 59 per cent of those links, not a single person had ever clicked through, meaning that of those people who shared or commented on the attached Facebook or Twitter post, the majority had read nothing except the headline. This removes any chance of a discussion including nuance or caveat, and can – perhaps counterintuitively – actually reinforce mainstream media power, by making the choice of headline far more decisive in terms of deciding how a narrative is formed. 'This is typical of modern information consumption,' said study co-author Arnaud Legout.[20] 'People form an opinion based on a summary, or summary of summaries, without making the effort to go deeper.'

This social media habit has knock-on effects for editors when considering headlines, especially when many outlets are accustomed to using headlines to summarise the key claims of a politician's speech or press conference, leaving tackling the factual basis of those claims to further down the article. In the Trump era, this means even a well-written and accurate article can spread misleading information to the large audience of non-clickers, simply due to a timid headline.

The Washingtonian noted this effect in the aftermath of Trump's untrue claims that he had only lost the popular vote due to millions of illegal voters. *USA Today* ran an article which did challenge this claim, but featured the headline: 'Trump: Clinton won popular vote because millions "voted illegally"'.

'This *USA Today* headline [is a] textbook example of how journalists and news organizations are used to handling statements from politicians and public figures,' the Washingtonian piece explained.[21] 'The first sentence of their story immediately clarifies that what Trump said is an "unsubstantiated claim." The problem is, most people will never read that far.'

Other outlets tried alternative headline formulation which tried to inject scepticism right from the outset: one tried '… but offers no evidence', another referred to a Trump claim as 'bogus', and a third went further still, stating that Trump was 'caught in a ridiculous lie'.

Greg Sargent of the *Washington Post* noted another example,[22] in which Donald Trump announced after a phone call with the communications company Sprint that he had created 5,000 new jobs – despite the new roles having been part of a plan that pre-dated the election. Sargent's story flags other issues, including companies happy to give the President a good if not wholly true headline, and a President happy to take credit where he hasn't earned it, but for now we'll focus on the headlines. Some injected a slight note of scepticism by referring to Trump's statement as a 'claim', while others didn't manage even that. CNN ran 'Trump declares victory: Sprint will create 5,000 U.S. jobs'. AP offered 'Trump takes credit for 8,000 jobs from Japanese mogul'. The *Washington Post* opted for 'Trump touts thousands of new jobs in deal with Softbank CEO', while ABC chose 'Trump claims Sprint to create 5,000 jobs "because of me"'.

Sargent cautioned that for stories such as these, the early scepticism of the headlines was crucial, as it was in almost no one else's interest to try to clarify the real story afterwards. 'It's obvious that Trump has adopted a strategy of actively trying to game such headlines in his favour,' he wrote.

> When Trump falsely takes credit for a company's decision to keep or move jobs here, why would that company want to set the record straight, when so doing could incur the wrath of the new administration, and when allowing Trump's self-serving tale to stand could conceivably lead the new administration to view it favorably? The full story will be even harder to come by in these situations – making it more important that headlines

inform readers and viewers when Trump's claim is unverified or suspect.

The headline issue is certainly one for media outlets to consider and act on, but we should also ask ourselves how often we scan a headline and take it at face value, or even share it without doing the same – it's on us, too.

There is an underlying factor around what we trust that we tend to underestimate: conspiracy theories – and conspiratorial thinking – is far more widespread than we think. We tend to think of conspiracy theories as something right on the fringes of political thinking, left to small groups of obsessives. They're not. A recent survey by Chapman University showed a sample of people a list of topics and asked if they thought the government was concealing what they knew about them. Fifty-four per cent believed information was being concealed on 9/11, 43 per cent on aliens, 42 per cent on global warming, 33 per cent thought plans for a one-world government were being covered up, while 30 per cent believed the government was hiding information on the origin of Aids.[23]

Only one in four Americans strongly disagreed with all nine conspiracy theories on the list, meaning a majority had a degree of belief in at least one – and half believed three or more. Belief in these conspiracies correlated with other effects, too. 'Conspiracy theorists tend to be more pessimistic about the near future, more fearful of government, less trusting of other people in their lives and more likely to engage in actions due to their fears, such as purchasing a gun,' the analysis stated.

While the Chapman University focused on the government concealing information, a different study conducted by PPP was more direct. It found that 37 per cent of Americans believe global warming is a hoax, 28 per cent believe a 'secretive power elite with a globalist agenda is conspiring to eventually rule the world through an authoritarian world government, or New World Order', and 13 per cent said they believed Obama to be the Antichrist.[24]

We might believe this widespread streak of conspiratorial thinking to be a new development, something created in recent years as the post-truth phenomenon took off, but history suggests otherwise. In *The United States of Paranoia*, Jesse Walker argues:

> Conspiracy theories played major roles in conflicts from the Indian wars of the seventeenth century to the labor battles of the Gilded Age, from the Civil War to the Cold War, from the American Revolution to the War on Terror ... they have been popular not just with dissenters and nonconformists but with individuals and institutions at the center of power. They are not simply a colorful historical byway. They are at the country's core.

The British public, incidentally, were markedly less inclined to believe in conspiracy theories, but were not totally immune. Forty-one per cent believe the government is covering up the true number of immigrants in the country, 13 per cent believe in a secret cabal in charge of the world regardless of election outcomes, 9 per cent think global warming is a hoax and 4 per cent believe Aids was either created or spread deliberately.[25]

Politicians and media outlets willing to tap into post-truth (or bullshit) are tapping into something arguably ingrained in our psyche – an underlying tendency in many of us to trust elaborate theories more than the institutions at the core of our nations. Such reasoning taken to extremes can be unspeakably danger- ous – conspiratorial thinking was at the core of witch-hunts, of lynchings, and even of the Holocaust. Most of what we have now is conspiracy-lite: Trump, Brexiteers and other populists suggest that existing 'elites' and institutions are corrupt and against regu- lar people, while on the other side of the divide, elaborate online theories explaining Trump's supposed brilliant master plan rou- tinely spread like wildfire on social media.[26]

'No matter what measures we take, fake news will persist because human nature persists,' concludes Politico columnist Jack Shafer on this kind of thinking.[27] 'People throw their money away on get-rich schemes, play three-card monte, correspond with Nigerian scamsters and get fleeced, even though they know better. Deep in the brain exists a hungry lobe that loves to be deceived.'

Part of trying to deal with bullshit, with a decline in trust in institutions, and with a rise of populism is to acknowledge where we are now – including where public opinion is. One aspect we're forced to note is that a large portion of people have less in- terest in buttressing the media than they do in supporting strong leaders to 'save' their country. The Pew Research Center asked US voters in October 2016 whether they agreed that 'freedom of the press to criticise political leaders is essential to maintaining a strong democracy' – and while 72 per cent of Clinton voters said this was very important, only 49 per cent of Trump voters would say the same.[28] The US is far from the only place facing this com- bination of rising populism and falling trust in institutions. A huge multi-country survey by Ipsos MORI found more than 50 per cent of people in eleven countries, including France, Israel,

Italy, Australia and the UK, said they wanted a 'strong leader' willing to 'break the rules' to solve their nation's problems – just over 40 per cent of Americans said the same. The survey also found that more than half of people in nineteen countries said experts don't understand the lives of 'people like me'.

Our role as citizens and news consumers in the dissemination of bullshit brings in things that are easily fixable and things that aren't. Habits like sharing articles based purely on their headlines have relatively easy fixes – we could learn to click (and think) before we share, or sites could move share buttons to the foot of articles, for example. There are potential technological fixes for aspects of the filter bubble, too. Other issues are trickier: changing our propensity to believe and share memes we agree with, or to differentiate between real and fake news, may be about media literacy. Other issues may have no fix: if conspiracy theories are an innate part of our psyche ready to be tapped into, and we've built a global communications network to make that easier, how can we respond?

So ends our list of who plays a role in spreading bullshit, and how the different actors in each group behave. Having looked into how bullshit was deployed to change the world, and who the agents involved in the ecosystem are, it's now time to try to look into how the system works. This is a problem we'll tackle in three parts: our belief in bullshit, the business model of bullshit, and the culture that lets it thrive unchecked.

PART III

WHY BULLSHIT WORKS

CHAPTER NINE

WHY WE FALL FOR IT

We've been focusing up until now on how bullshit spreads, and some of its consequences. The remaining piece of the puzzle is to look at *why* it spreads: why we tend to believe it, why people and organisations have incentives to spread it, and why stopping or slowing it down proves difficult for others. We're tackling each in turn, and this chapter looks at the various quirks of our psychology that make us amenable to believing and spreading different types of bullshit.

These tie into quirks in how we think and act. These include, in short, that we find information more believable if it aligns with our current worldviews, and that most of us find anecdotes more convincing than statistics. When we're in a group environment – as we are on social media – how we act around each other emphasises these effects: we like to show we're part of the group, we attack people who aren't part of it, and groups which start out moderate can easily pull themselves into more extreme positions, even without anyone intending for this to happen. This chapter will focus, largely in the abstract, on the combination of psychological factors that deal with how we process and produce information – but we should keep in mind what the modern media landscape looks like as we read on. Online, we have our natural groups we create by accident (our Facebook friends and similar) as well as divisions we create deliberately, such as the political parties or causes we sign up to. We can regularly see what other members of those groups see and share, and they can see what we do too – the architecture and infrastructure of the modern internet could almost have been designed to trigger the instincts that make us most likely to believe things which aren't true.

One of the simplest things we're all inclined to do is look for and accept information which supports our current beliefs – for example, if we're against the death penalty, we're more likely to look for and share articles which seem to show that the death penalty is ineffective or cruel, and even possibly more likely to remember material in these kinds of stories (though this is contentious). This is known as 'confirmation bias': we look for and retain information that confirms our beliefs, and we struggle to accept information that goes against them.

This might seem to be just stating the obvious: no one likes admitting they're wrong about a dearly held belief, and no one wants to admit they're acting irrationally – but we act like this when there's nothing much at stake. The book *Irrationality* by Stuart Sutherland lays out how this can work[1] – here's one such case which I'd invite you to try yourself before reading on. Here's a sequence of three numbers: 2, 4, 6. The task is to work out what the underlying rule is governing that sequence. The participants in the actual experiment were invited to offer alternative three-number sequences. The researchers would then say whether or not that sequence followed the rule. Once they felt relatively sure of what the rule was, they were invited to guess it.

So – stop for a moment and consider which sequence you might guess next.

Some people offered sequences like '8, 10, 12', or '16, 18, 20' next, and were told that these followed the rule. This might lead you to conclude the sequence is 'three successive even numbers'. But in reality, you've gained no new information from those sequences versus the first one – and this isn't the rule. Others might try '8, 12, 16', and assume it's 'three ascending even numbers'. Another option would be '1, 3, 5', assuming it's 'any three numbers increasing by two each time'. Both sequences follow the rule, but neither rule is correct. Here's another sequence which follows the rule: '-1, 8, 29', and one that doesn't '5, -2, 14'. What's the rule?

In reality, the rule the researchers used was 'any three numbers in ascending order' – but rather than challenging the apparently stronger pattern we see in the example we're given, we tend to offer numbers which confirm it. But we only get to the right answer by testing contradictory sequences. Our instinct even when we're faced with abstract mathematical sequences is to look for confirmation of an obvious belief or hypothesis – and this effect seems only to get stronger for beliefs that we have an emotional connection to. One study looked at strong supporters of John Kerry and George W. Bush, showing them apparently contradictory statements made by each candidate, and some statements explaining the apparent contradiction. Predictably, partisans on each side were more likely to acquit their own candidate while feeling their rival had contradicted himself – but the study also found that in these cases an MRI scanner showed little activity in areas of the brain connected to 'cold reasoning'.[2] We're already not good at assessing information we disagree with, and when it's a strongly held opinion, we may even bypass logical assessment anyway. *Irrationality* sets out the most extreme consequences of these cognitive biases – using the example of Admiral Kimmel, the Commander-in-Chief of the US Pacific Fleet in the run-up to the attack on Pearl Harbor, who didn't cancel shore leave or increase alert efforts even after a submarine was sunk near the base.

'We have now established two ways unconsciously used to maintain beliefs – refusal to act on contradictory evidence and refusal to believe it or act on it if it is brought to one's attention,' Sutherland concluded.[3] 'Kimmel was guilty of both faults. He failed to seek evidence from Washington to clarify an ambiguous message, and he refused to believe the submarine sunk outside Pearl Harbor was Japanese.'

The US lost four battleships and 188 aircraft in the attack, and 2,403 people were killed. Kimmel was relieved of his command within a fortnight, and retired within months.

Confirmation bias alone is difficult enough to tackle, but some studies suggest there's an even stronger effect at play: when presented with evidence that contradicts one of our most closely held beliefs, it may actually serve to *reinforce* that belief rather than challenge it. This apparent effect, discovered in experiments by Brendan Nyhan and Jason Reifler at Dartmouth College, has come to be known as the 'backfire effect'. In a series of experiments, Nyhan and Reifler showed students of different political persuasions an untrue statement, and then information from a credible source correcting the error.

The first experiment, conducted in the autumn of 2005, showed participants a statement from (then) President Bush stating that Iraq had WMD, immediately followed by a correction – cited to

AP – quoting a report which said there was no evidence that Iraq had WMD. The correction reduced the likelihood of liberals and neutrals to say they believed Iraq had a WMD programme – but conservatives were actually *more* likely to say Iraq had WMD after the correction. 'If subjects simply distrusted the media, they should simply ignore the corrective information,' the researchers noted.[4] 'Instead, however, conservatives were found to have moved in the "wrong" direction – a reaction that is hard to attribute to simple distrust.'

The researchers repeated the experiment on different issues, again triggering backfire effects. Students were shown an untrue claim that President Bush's tax cuts had stimulated the economy so much that they had increased government revenues, then were immediately shown evidence that this wasn't true – but were more likely to believe the untrue claim after the correction than before it. Another study, this time on whether or not President Bush had banned stem cell research, did not itself provoke a backlash – perhaps showing that people's views on this issue are less strong than on the others – but groups opposed to Bush did still exhibit a resistance to believing the information in the correction. One important caveat, though – when another group of researchers tried to test for the backfire effect on a range of thirty-six issues, they only detected a backfire effect on one.[5] How strong and how common the backfire effect is remains a subject of debate.

The consequences of the backfire effect when it does kick in, though, could be huge. 'Just as confirmation bias shields you when you actively seek information, the backfire effect defends you when the information seeks you, when it blindsides you. Coming or going, you stick to your beliefs instead of questioning them,' an article by David McRaney concluded.[6]

What should be evident from the studies on the backfire effect is you can never win an argument online. When you start to pull out facts and figures, hyperlinks and quotes, you are actually making the opponent feel as though they are even more sure of their position than before you started the debate. As they match your fervor, the same thing happens in your skull. The backfire effect pushes both of you deeper into your original beliefs.

When we reach across the political fence online and offer up evidence supporting our arguments, it rarely goes well – we feel affronted that our political opponents are rarely convinced by our reasonable approach, and perhaps even get angry that people won't see sense. We can fire up our own base, but arguing from evidence – as the evidence, ironically enough, suggests – likely won't work.

Compounding these effects is our poor general understanding of statistics: for all sorts of reasons, we both struggle to understand statistics in news and also tend to disbelieve them if they contradict our anecdotal experience. This is compounded by journalists and others – whether due to their own poor grasp of statistics or in order to push an agenda – often distorting how statistics are presented to the public, with serious and detrimental effects. One fallacy with severe real-world consequences was to confuse correlation and causation: assuming that because something happens shortly after something else, the one caused the other. This was one of the main drivers of a huge outbreak of public concern that the vaccination for measles, mumps and rubella (MMR) was causing autism in children. This claim was not only fuelled by a fraudulent doctor, Andrew Wakefield, but also spread across the media – but it was never supported by a single piece of high-quality evidence.

However, it seemed plausible simply because the two events were correlated: children receive their first jab around the age of one, and autism generally first manifests in those children with the condition when they're toddlers[7] – shortly afterwards. The whole controversy led to thousands of parents deciding not to give their children the MMR vaccine, reducing the level below what's necessary for 'herd immunity', leading in turn to a number of outbreaks across the country. Nine years after being discredited in the UK, Wakefield is near the centre of US politics, pictured at inauguration balls,[8] with Trump apparently endorsing his baseless anti-vaccination views.[9]

When we get into stories that involve actual figures, things get even trickier. Week in, week out, we're inundated with stories that tell us various habits either raise or reduce our risk of cancer – to pick one at random, in 2015, outlets across the world warned that eating two rashers of bacon per day raises the risk of bowel cancer by 18 per cent.[10] This tells us less than it seems, though: without knowing what our risk of getting bowel cancer was if we *don't* eat bacon, we don't know how bad this is. As it turns out, over the course of their lifetime, about five in 400 people will contract bowel cancer. If every single one of those 400 people began eating two rashers of bacon per day, this would rise to six in 400.[11] This second way of looking at the numbers may be less alarming, but also shows how useless the relative figures are: let's say some other foodstuff increases the chances of a more common disease by 10 per cent, but would mean ten extra cases in 400. This 10 per cent risk sounds less bad than the 18 per cent, but would actually affect far more people. The way the media talks about statistics, and the way we generally understand them, doesn't help us understand the real world.

This problem is heightened when we're dealing with risks that scare us: statistics just don't really reassure us. A sizeable portion of us are afraid to fly,[12] whereas fear of driving is much lower. This is despite the fact that flying is by far the safest mode of transport: only one in 3,000,000 flights have a crash that results in fatalities (and almost every plane crash with fatalities has some survivors). Mile-for-mile, travelling by train is twice as deadly as flying; travelling by car is 100 times more deadly than flying; and taking a motorbike is 3,000 times more deadly than flying.[13] And what's vastly more likely than any of the above to kill you is either heart disease or cancer – but even knowing this, planes remain scarier than, say, obesity.

If we're talking about things that scare us, terrorism comes incredibly high on the list, and is used by the media for headlines and by politicians to push through political agendas and win elections – Trump's promise of a hardline position on terror has served as justification for his travel ban from seven countries, and more. But our fear of terror is beyond all proportion with its risk. Michael Rothschild, emeritus professor at the University of Wisconsin, calculated an extreme scenario to illustrate this risk. He imagined a world in which terrorists successfully hijacked and destroyed one plane every month in the US – dramatically worse than any real-world scenario in any country in the world. Someone who took four flights each month in this world would have a one in 540,000 chance of being killed in any given year. Someone who only took one flight a year would have a risk of dying of less than one in 6,000,000. By contrast, the chances of dying in a car accident on any given year is one in 7,000, of cancer is one in 600, and heart disease is one in 400.[14] Even if terror attacks got unimaginably worse than they are, it would be a much smaller risk than just going about our everyday lives. Our fears, and our inbuilt resistance to being reassured by evidence, makes us susceptible to bullshit.

So far, we've only looked at factors which affect us as individuals, able to assess and react to information on our own – but of course none of us live in total isolation, and in the online era we see our news alongside our social groups. We see the news our friends share, and we know what our friends think of particular speeches or candidates. For those of us who strongly identify with a political cause or campaign – something which gives us a sense of group identity – this becomes an even bigger factor, and all of these influences affect how we judge and share information, and so shape what we believe.

Generally, we like to fit in with our friends and colleagues. This kind of conformity doesn't easily fit into how we think about ourselves, but a majority of us will act to fit in with a group even when it's a group full of strangers and the question at hand is simple and entirely apolitical. In her book *Wilful Blindness*, Margaret Heffernan sets out a study showing how dramatic this effect can be. Students were brought into a room with a group of fellow students apparently participating in the same experiment and were asked to say which out of three vertical black lines was the same length as a fourth line on the whiteboard. The task was not difficult: the lines were clearly very different in length, and the correct answer was obvious. However, in each room only one student was an actual subject: every other student in the room had been told in advance to choose the same wrong answer, with the actual test subject answering last. Even in a case like this, with the group comprising total strangers and the question at hand being both obvious and uncontroversial, 40 per cent of subjects chose the obviously wrong answer given by everyone else rather than trusting the simple evidence of their own eyes. The experiment was repeated with different variations, and found that under one condition or another, 58 per cent of people would confirm the popular answer in at least one of the tests given.[15]

This kind of conformity isn't about obeying a leader or following instructions – this is just something many of us do to ourselves, choosing to go with the flow rather than make our own assessments. When a majority of us will choose conformity over truth in such simple conditions, it's not hard to see how this habit can affect us in our lives: becoming embroiled in bad corporate cultures, not speaking out against practices we disagree with, reflexively defending politicians or simply not stating that we don't share a particular opinion of a group we generally agree with.

Conformity is little more than a desire to be polite or to fit in – but arguably it can even in its own right be dangerous. Heffernan warns that conformity can serve to explain why many of us believe climate change is real but take very little real action.

> We live with people like ourselves, and sharing consumption habits blinds us to their cost … we're obedient consumers and we might change if we were told to, but we're not. We conform to the consumption patterns we see all around us as we all become bystanders, hoping someone else somewhere will intervene. Our governments and corporations grow too complex to communicate or to change and we are just left where we do not want to be.[16]

There's evidence that we'll act to show our belonging inside a group, so it's worth thinking about how that works in practice on social media. If one of our concerns is how a group we like and want to feel part of will react, what kind of story will we share? If we're a Trump supporter and have read two articles, one questioning whether his team could have executed his order banning travellers from majority-Muslim countries better, and another attacking the media for misreporting Trump's presidency, we might share the second because we know for sure it'll get a good reaction from our group.

This kind of sharing behaviour, particularly when carried out by those on the left, was given the slightly derisory name 'virtue signalling' – the right-leaning *Spectator* magazine gives itself credit for coining the phrase, which has rapidly become a term of abuse used by those on the right against the left. 'People say or write things to indicate that they are virtuous,' James Bartholomew wrote in the magazine.[17] 'Sometimes it is quite subtle. By saying that they hate the *Daily Mail* or Ukip, they are really telling you that they are admirably non-racist, left-wing or open-minded.'

The way 'virtue signalling' is used as a term almost exclusively relates to the right, but signalling behaviour – people trying to send cues that they're still part of a group – occurs on both sides of the political divide, with tropes such as disliking political correctness, supporting free speech or attacking metropolitan elites working as signalling devices of the political right. One consequence of this kind of signalling can be to convince partisans that public support for their position is much broader than it really is, especially if it's something few people would want to publicly oppose.

Signalling, argued Helen Lewis in the *New Statesman*, 'had many social media users convinced that Ed Miliband could squeak the election; after all, their friends seemed to be lapping up the mansion tax and the action against non-doms. No one seemed enthused about taking £12bn off the benefit bill, or reducing the help given to disabled people'.[18] Ed Miliband's Labour Party lost the 2015 election, which polls had suggested they'd narrowly win. The combination of the filter bubble and signalling within it can give us false expectations of people's views – who on the centre or left would want to express reservations on the deficit or support for austerity? Many stayed quiet, then voted Tory. Our instincts on conformity fuel a desire toward 'virtue signalling', and distort what all of us see.

When we're talking with people we largely agree with, though, our views actually change. Imagine taking a group of people who by-and-large agree on a topic, but with differing degrees of intensity, and having them discuss that topic for a few minutes. You might imagine that the consensus opinion of the group would settle somewhere around the middle point of the individual pre-discussion opinions. That's not what happens.

The academics Cass Sunstein and Reid Hastie gathered groups from two cities, the relatively liberal city of Boulder and the relatively conservative city of Colorado Springs. Participants were asked to privately give their views (on a scale) on three issues beforehand: climate change, affirmative action and same-sex marriage. People were then matched in groups with other people from their own city (so that the participants in each group were somewhat in agreement with each other before the discussion) and asked to debate each issue, then asked for their opinion – both privately and as a group – on the issues once more.

The results were stark. The Boulder groups became more liberal on all three issues, and the Colorado Springs groups more conservative – not only in terms of the group verdicts, but also in the views the participants expressed privately: the discussion made each individual stronger in their opinions than before. Equally, the groups became much more similar: before the short discussions, there had been a fairly wide range of opinions on each issue – after even a short chat, opinions in the groups had become much more homogenous. Finally, the Boulder and Colorado groups had polarised: where before the discussions there was overlap between the groups, afterwards the liberals and conservatives were much more divided.[19]

These effects were noticed in groups of relatively like-minded people over a period of just a few minutes. With people who interact day after day and month after month, without a lot of outside interaction it's not difficult to see how substantial this shift can become. The effect persists across countries and cultures, and affects even professionals whom we might expect to be alert for such influences. People will polarise in their group assessments on questions of judgement as well as on questions of opinion: studies of business people asked to predict the likelihood that a sales team would sell a certain number of units showed that a group discussion resulted in a much more confident opinion than the average guesses of participants before the chat began – people polarised their factual assessments. Perhaps most dramatically, the effect even extends to federal appellate judges, who sit on panels of three. One study found that while you can try to predict how an appeals judge will rule by finding out whether they were appointed by a Democratic or a Republican President, there's something that will predict their vote even more reliably: which party appointed the panel's other judges. Inevitably, the effect also manifests itself with juries. The amount in damages that juries award against plaintiffs is typically much higher than the average of what jurors individually say they would award before the discussion.

If group polarisation can affect even small groups of professionals trained to watch for biases – like judges – it's not hard to imagine the effect of certain internet subcultures, or even what our Facebook friends or Twitter followers may do to our own opinions. The filter bubble doesn't just shield us from dissenting opinions – it also carries us further away from the centre.

We conform with our groups, we signal our belonging in our groups and we are polarised by our groups. These factors begin to explain why bullshit information that supports our group identity may be more welcome than accurate and verifiable information which challenges it. More than this, though, we build an identity around the opposition of our groups to others – a habit referred to as 'in-group, out-group' behaviour, or 'realistic conflict theory'. Part of what makes us feel like a real member of one group can be rivalry, or even hatred, of another.

The most famous study of this kind of conflict – the details of which have been challenged by later studies – dates back to the 1950s, when researchers arranged an experimental summer camp for twenty-two boys in Robbers Cave State Park. The boys were split into two separate groups, not meeting each other for several days, instead having time to bond and establish themselves as groups, catching only the occasional glimpse of the other. After a few days, the groups named themselves the 'Rattlesnakes' and the 'Eagles'. Even before any attempt to introduce rivalry between the groups had begun, there was tension:

the Rattlesnakes came within earshot of the Eagles, who were playing ball. Their immediate reaction was to 'run them off' or 'challenge them', going on to make territorial claims to different parts of the park,[20] marking the baseball diamond with a team flag – and both teams said they wanted to challenge the other.

The pieces were in place for rivalry, and it took almost no effort from the researchers to bring it up to fever pitch: they simply offered a prize of some Swiss Army knives as a reward for the winners of a baseball match. The teams taunted one another before the game – fairly standard for sports – but after the end of the match, which the Rattlesnakes won, things escalated rapidly: a few hours after the game, the Eagles tore down and burned the Rattlesnakes' flag. In retaliation, the Rattlesnakes raided the Eagles' camp, shredding mosquito netting and stealing personal belongings. The Eagles planned (but didn't carry out) a retaliatory raid on their rivals, plotting to attack them with 'socks filled with rocks'. The Eagles referred to the Rattlers as 'bums', 'poor losers' and 'cussers', the Rattlers dubbing the Eagles 'sissies', 'cowards' and 'little babies'.[21]

This was a conflict between two very similar groups which had been arbitrarily created and which lasted only for a few days. Both groups were of boys of the same age from the same area – and yet it took several days of very deliberate effort on behalf of the researchers to reverse the divisions they'd created and at least partially reunite the groups. The adults changed the nature of the tasks given to the boys to require both teams to work together, rather than in competition, in order to get any kind of reward.

De-escalating conflict between short-lived, homogenous groups with no real differences required sustained effort from researchers. As such, it's not hard to see how difficult avoiding polarisation online could be. Trump supporters have Democrats and the media as out-groups. Corbyn supporters' out-groups often include centrists, Conservatives and (again) the media. Once an entity becomes an out-group, it's not only less likely to be taken seriously, but opposition to what it says also becomes part of group identity – and in the real world there are no researchers sitting waiting to try to reunify the people concerned.

Given all of these factors, it shouldn't come as a surprise that online radicalisation is a concern for governments across the world: even without anyone's deliberate effort, our membership of groups can move our views away from the political centre towards the extremes and increase our antipathy towards those with different views. If these natural trends are then being deliberately exploited by people to promote a cause, whether that's Islamic extremism or the far right, then social media has the potential to become a fertile source of recruits.

The UK think tank Demos connects the risk of online recruitment to ISIS, and even of lone-wolf terrorists becoming radicalised through a mishmash of online half-truths and conspiracies, with people's poor ability to distinguish between truth and lies on the internet. A prescient 2011 report concluded:

> Our research shows, however, that many young people are not careful, discerning users of the internet. They are unable to find the information they are looking for or trust the first thing they do. They do not apply fact checks to the information they find. They are unable to recognise bias and propaganda and will not go to a varied number of sources…
>
> The potential consequences of this on society as a whole are unknown. One danger is that young people are more likely to be

seduced by extremist and violent ideas ... many terrorist groups are fed by bogus online material circulating unchallenged on online echo chambers. Anders Breivik, the recent Oslo terrorist, is a devastating but only the most recent example of the power of internet material to radicalise.[22]

A UK parliamentary inquiry said social media – specifically Facebook, Twitter and YouTube – had become the 'vehicle of choice in spreading propaganda' and 'the recruiting platforms for terrorism'. The MPs called for the companies to hire more people to monitor and delete extremist content, and for greater efforts to proactively report people posting such material to law enforcement.[23] 'The modern frontline is the internet,' said Keith Vaz, then the chair of the parliamentary committee which ran the inquiry.[24] 'Its forums, message boards and social media platforms are the lifeblood of Daesh [ISIS] and other terrorist groups for their recruitment and financing and the spread of ideology.'

Blocking the most extreme content may be part of a solution, but given our ability to radicalise ourselves – and given that even content that may be within the realms of what's permitted to be published by the social networks could radicalise people – Demos, and other experts, warn this alone isn't nearly enough.

Demos researcher Louis Reynolds argues:

The government is putting more and more pressure on social media companies to censor content, on schools to restrict internet access, on the justice system to become more involved in policing social media, in order to counter jihadi content online. Yet ultimately trying to censor the internet can't be the principal solution to this problem.

There are next to no effective extremism-related efforts to improve young people's critical thinking ongoing in the UK … We have to teach young people, from an early age, how to spot manipulation, to counter grooming efforts, to challenge extremist views and spot falsehoods, online and offline. The recruitment of foreign fighters to the Islamic State movement represents a failure of reason and a victory for manipulation. If there is a counter-narrative, this should be the message.[25]

Online radicalisation is not something that only happens through sustained and deliberate effort. Instead, it's built into the architecture of how we interact online – meaning that ongoing efforts to take the most extreme content offline can only take us so far.

Much of how we deal with and process information online comes down to how we choose to think about it – and it's a decision that we often don't even realise we're making. The Nobel Prize-winning psychologist Daniel Kahneman set out a thorough explanation of how we can often deal with things reflexively rather than through deliberate consideration in his bestselling book *Thinking Fast and Slow*.

The idea is best illustrated with an example. Consider this maths problem: 2 x 2. For almost everyone reading this paragraph, the answer to the question will have immediately popped into your head – with no deliberate effort or action required. Now think about another maths problem: 19 x 23. Unless you're a polymath (or didn't even bother trying to solve the problem), tackling this one will have required some deliberate thought. You may have decided to try to work out 20 x 23 and then subtract 23 from the answer. You may have considered looking for a calculator. But unlike 2 x 2, the problem will have required some thought and some effort on your part.[26]

These are the two types of thinking Kahneman lays out. The first, effortless form of thinking is System One – our gut feelings, instincts and reflexive actions. System One thinking is easy and beyond our control: we don't decide to automatically solve 2 x 2, it just happens. System Two is our deliberate thought, requiring conscious mental effort. Thinking in this way feels much more intentional, like we're making a choice or working something out.

The two systems often fight with each other, as this famous puzzle illustrates: 'A bat and ball together cost £1.10. The bat costs £1.00 more than the ball. What does the ball cost?'

Many people reading this paragraph will have an instant answer of 10p jump into their head – it just looks right when you read the puzzle. But if you stop to consider the puzzle, that answer is wrong: if the ball costs 10p, the bat must cost £1 more, meaning the total cost of the two would be £1.20 rather than £1.10. The correct answer is that the ball costs 5p and the bat £1.05. Our System One thinking guides us towards a quick and obvious answer which is wrong. Our System Two thinking – if we give it time to kick in – lets us ignore that and work out the correct answer.

This gives us a good way to think about how we read and share online. When we see a quote that suits our political beliefs, it's easy for us to believe it and almost reflexively share it to our social circle – to stop and consider the source of the quote and maybe even check whether it's genuine requires a degree of effort. The former is, for social media addicts at least, a System One action. The latter requires us to make a considered decision to engage System Two to assess the information more carefully before sharing. This isn't something we can do without effort: we have to make a decision to think in this way, and that's not as relaxing or straightforward as the way we often browse. Engaging System Two is an act of self-control, and this is something we find tiring – a process called 'ego depletion'. Without deliberate forethought and self-control we will leave ourselves open to bullshit – and in a sense, we only have a certain stock of self-control in the tank each day,[27] and have to decide whether this is where we want to spend it.

There are many psychological reasons that bullshit works on us, even if we consider ourselves well-educated and able to discern good information from bad. Material may fall into our current worldview, suit our social norms, suit something we wish to signal, or reinforce a group identity. None of these mean we're doomed to believe bullshit, but they do mean we're predisposed to do so without deliberate effort. It shouldn't come as a surprise that bullshit works – if it didn't work, it wouldn't be so prolific – but knowing the mechanisms by which it catches us should help. That takes us some way towards understanding the demand side – why bullshit is an effective strategy. The next step is to tackle the supply: why it's financially worth spreading.

CHAPTER TEN

WHY IT'S PROFITABLE

Bullshit thrives when there are people and organisations around with an interest in spreading it, and an audience willing to accept it. The reasons for some politicians to spread bullshit are fairly self-explanatory, and have been tackled in previous chapters – they can help bring election victories, can mire opponents in nonsense scandals, and can crowd out unhelpful media narratives. As we've said elsewhere, bullshit can pave the path to power (which doesn't bode well for politicians' footwear).

The motivations for others tend to be less straightforward, but usually come down to money. For some outlets, letting through the occasional bullshit story is just a side-effect of shrinking newsrooms and cost-cutting. Other outlets, pushing for mass traffic whatever the consequences, are happy to run questionable but cheap stories alongside better-sourced information if that will boost their traffic. But behind the news outlets we visit as consumers lies a supply chain with an interest in passing on unverified stories, hoaxes and stunts and feeding them into the news ecosystem – and it's this array of business models, and the incentives of the players across the industry, that we're going to explore in more depth in this chapter.

Working out what gets spread by who and why is important: it's easy to just point at bad viral stories, or outlets credulously running sensational pieces, and purse our lips and say they're doing something wrong. That's also pointless – unless we work out why organisations have financial reasons for acting as they do, we'll miss many of the real solutions that could actually help us tackle the problem.

The place where most of us as consumers encounter questionable – or bullshit – stories is through media outlets. These are facing a huge number of challenges to their business model, virtually all of which encourage them to favour low-cost content that will appeal to huge audiences. The challenges of the shift to digital are most obvious for news outlets which are used to print revenues.

Print advertising is worth vastly more – in total and on a per reader basis – than digital advertising to most legacy newsrooms. Analysis of five of the largest US print groups by the Pew Research Center in 2016[1] found that digital made up around a quarter of total advertising revenues, much more than it had a decade before. But this apparent growth is exaggerated by decline elsewhere – digital's share of the total is growing because print is shrinking so fast. Not only are print revenues falling, at rates often at 10–20 per cent a year, but newspapers have suffered from losing job advertising and classified adverts to online rivals. We tend to focus on the challenge of newspapers getting less money for display adverts (banners, pop-ups etc.), and ignore all the other types of advertising they lost out on even more sharply.

Digital advertising makes only a tiny amount of money per click: a banner advert in a prime spot on a high-quality and big-name news website will make only a fraction of a cent, something around 0.5¢ to 0.7¢.[2] This is a premium price – other sites receive far less for each advertising spot. This gets even more difficult still when we start thinking about how we actually browse: a computer screen can show several large adverts around a news story, but a mobile screen cannot – but now around half of all news is viewed on mobile, and this share is growing.[3] This means digital revenues, which were already barely a fraction of print revenues, are themselves dwindling as desktop browsing is replaced by less lucrative mobile traffic. Advertisers are also sceptical of visits on many web pages, due in part to unscrupulous middlemen gaming the system by creating 'bots' to generate fake traffic (and therefore ad impressions) – and due in part to simpler concerns that many readers never actually saw an advert halfway down a page.[4]

The result is increasing desperation on behalf of sites to prove that visitors have definitely seen the adverts on the site. This includes buttons which require you to click to continue reading a story (which guarantees you've seen the advert that appears as you click), adverts that pop-up and appear before you can read a story, or annoying adverts which divert you to app stores on mobile. All of these are, if we're honest, pretty irritating to readers – and the result is that around one in five users now use software to block adverts, up from fewer than one in ten a few years ago.[5] People using ad blockers generate no revenue whatsoever for the sites they visit. The advertising problem just keeps getting worse.

Some sites – like the *New York Times*, *Financial Times*, and *Wall Street Journal* – have shown they can build subscriber bases to rebuild their revenues and become less reliant on advertising, but for the majority of sites that rely on adverts, the situation is difficult. There is a need for constant content to generate large traffic numbers, with not much money around for fact-checking or scrutiny – and the need to get large numbers of visitors may also incentivise running sensationalised versions of a story. It's a great habitat for bullshit to thrive.

Mark Thompson, the CEO of the *New York Times* and former director-general of the BBC, set this out in stark terms in a 2016 essay for the Reuters Institute at the University of Oxford.[6] 'Winter really is coming for many of the world's news publishers,' he wrote, with a nod towards *Game of Thrones*.

> Many publishers have responded to this challenge by putting their faith in a model based on audience scale and digital display advertising ... most of the new digital news providers were launched with business models which were parasitic versions of the same idea. They aimed to rewrite and repackage other people's journalism for much less money than it cost to originate it, and then to use superior technology to out-compete the legacy companies in distribution and advertising monetisation ... These models now look suspect.

The media outlets that we read and share are an obvious player in the bullshit game, and their difficult economics make it easy to see why they're amenable to running stories with minimal checking or with exaggeration. But there are layers of agencies and companies acting within this system that aren't visible to us as consumers who play a significant role in how unverified information spreads.

An apparently innocuous news story from February 2017 helps bring some of these players to light. The story centred on footage of a female cyclist in London, pulling up next to a white-van man at a traffic light. A man inside the van calls out to the cyclist asking for her number, gets rebuffed and then hurls abuse at her, asking if she's on her period. Furious, she pursues the van – which has now taken off as the light changes to green – pauses, and rips off one of its wing mirrors.

The story and footage were picked up by numerous major outlets: the *Daily Mail*, *Metro*, *The Independent*, *The Sun*, the *Sydney Morning Herald*, and more – attracting millions of video views on some. The issue is that none of them took any action to verify whether or not the video was real before running it, and when *The Sun* did later track down an eyewitness, he said that he thought the video was staged. Elena Cresci, a digital journalist at *The Guardian*, set out why there were obvious warning signs the outlets could have spotted without needing to speak to anyone. 'Even before this witness came forward a few things made the video seem suspect,' she wrote.

> It's extremely convenient that the motorcyclist managed to capture the whole thing – though, as many motorcyclists wear helmet cameras, it's not impossible. Some people also pointed out that it's a bit difficult to pull off a wing mirror so easily. The video itself seems to follow a model often seen on prankster sites that create outrageous situations and film them with the intention of going viral.[7]

Where had the video come from, to appear across numerous news sites within hours? Like a lot of content designed to spread virally on the internet, it had been promoted and sold by an agency specialising in finding and monetising video going viral on the internet. These agencies work by finding anything taking off on YouTube or similar sites, and acting as a middleman to help the creators monetise their (often accidental) hit – but such agencies can easily be passed content from hoaxers or others.

In the case of the cycling video we've been discussing, the agency concerned, Jungle Creations, was selling the video for £400 to be embedded on newspaper websites, or £150 for use on social media – netting thousands of pounds as dozens of outlets picked up the story. However, Jungle Creations said it had done no work to verify the footage. 'We do not have the resources available to do in-depth checks on every piece of content we get sent,' it said in a statement. The company later issued a second statement saying the video 'may be factually incorrect', and removed it from its own social feeds.[8]

This didn't provoke a wave of retractions or corrections in the outlets that garnered millions of views from the original dubious video. Some added '– but was it real?' to their original headlines, some did nothing and, audaciously, the *Daily Mail* left its original account untouched, but added a second story reporting on people's doubt about the video.

Women are routinely harassed during their commutes in London – whether the video is genuine or not, the issue it is highlighting is real. The fakery is not especially serious in this instance, but the compound effect of stories like it is damaging the news outlets which often demand their readers trust them more than politicians, and certainly more than 'niche' or 'fake' news outlets. If major sites routinely run unverified stories and videos fed by middlemen with no kinds of checks, why should readers trust them on other issues? How is the casual reader supposed to know which stories are carefully checked and which aren't?

The reason such videos are spread and run is that they're a great kind of content for news sites. Video advertising is one of the rosiest areas for digital advertising, creating far more revenue per user than standard banner adverts. Thanks to agencies searching and promoting videos which are already going viral, sites can buy near-guaranteed winners at a relatively low cost, boosting their traffic and hopefully their revenues. But no one in the food chain has any incentive to do too much checking – providing the claims in the video aren't likely to get anyone sued. The agencies are looking to turn a profit on the grabby videos they've sourced, and the news sites are looking for easy traffic. The financial incentives for both act against doing too much checking.

Other players in the industry have even stronger incentives to plant stories in the media – for the PR profession, that's long been part of the job, and it's one that has adapted to the new news environment. The joy of creating dubious – essentially fake – viral videos for such agencies is that the hoax itself often serves to promote the client, and then any admission that the video was staged promotes the client once again, and promotes the agency itself to new clients. They win both on the initial viral story and again on the debunk.

Such was the case with a story in 2016 where Twitter and Facebook users noticed a high-end white Range Rover parked outside Harrods and daubed with 'Cheater, it's over' and 'Hope she was worth it!'. The car, left in such a high-profile location, quickly and naturally began to be noticed and go viral on social media and was in turn quickly written up by multiple news outlets, with various degrees of scepticism as to whether or not there was more to the tale than met the eye.

A day later, as the initial PR hit faded, the car workshop behind the stunt admitted everything, securing a second set of write-ups which served their interests even better than the first. An *Evening Standard* article on the hoax referred to 'the brand new £90,000 white Range Rover', 'an advertising stunt for the new Revere Range Rover Vogue' and to the workshop behind the stunt as 'a luxury auto design and enhancement workshop'.[9] The article was also accompanied by a second video showing behind the scenes of the stunt and filming the reactions of passers-by as they examined the apparently trashed car. The news sites concerned got two stories for the price of one, the client of the PR company received generous mentions of their product (including yet another here), even in the story revealing they'd tricked the media, and the PR company got to plug itself as somewhere that can plant stories and net traffic – a great way to secure future work.

Specialist agencies and divisions now exist producing just this form of publicity. One Australian agency specialises in shock videos, with examples including 'Man Fights Off Great White Shark In Sydney Harbour', 'Crazy Guy Runs Into Outbreak Tornado To Take Selfie', 'Stormtrooper Falls Down Stairs On The Way To Star Wars Premiere' and 'Lightning almost strikes girl in Sydney!!!'

The agency began creating the videos to experiment in what kind of material would take off online, but quickly secured clients willing to promote their brand through the stunts, as the company's managing director Dave Christison told the Huffington Post: 'Our second video was client commissioned and it was on the same account. Roadshow Films was the client and we created it for an upcoming film called Into The Storm, on the release date, we revealed it was a hoax.'[10]

Despite posting the second film using exactly the same account as their first faked video, no one sussed out the PR agency was behind the films until they revealed themselves after six more viral videos and a total view count well in excess of 200 million – and the reveal itself was, of course, an effort to secure more clients.

These viral stunts are the latest manifestation of a years-long habit of PR agencies trying to find news hooks to secure coverage for their clients, which can result in good and high-quality stories but which can also lead to stories that are baseless or downright damaging. The science writer Ben Goldacre wrote for several years about 'Blue Monday' – the idea that there's a particular Monday in January which is 'the most depressing day of the year' – which has now been covered as an annual event in the UK for more than a decade, despite a lack of evidence for seasonal variation in mood, and an obvious total lack of evidence for an arbitrary date marking the low point.[11] The day began as a PR hook for Sky Travel, before being seized upon by other companies and then, eventually, mental health charities who presumably reasoned if you can't beat 'em, join 'em.

Goldacre, though, noted in 2011 that not all of this bullshit is harmless. A start-up offering counselling via webcam for £50 a pop claimed it had run a survey which found that 34 per cent teenagers faked serious mental health problems to gain attention – a serious allegation which could have negative consequences for vulnerable young people. Goldacre asked the PR agency behind the story for details on how they'd carried out this research, how many teens they'd contacted, how they'd checked demographics, and other details – and received no response.

'Bullshit is a slippery slope,' he concluded on the matter.

At the top is an okay charity endorsing fatuous PR nonsense as a one-off, and normalising it. At the bottom, the health correspondent of a major national newspaper is standing in a river of sewage, shouting at a million readers that teenagers are malingerers who invent serious mental health problems. All I suggest is that you should think a bit before you step onto the crest.[12]

There's every reason to expect more and more bullshit from this source: one way of measuring its impact through the years has been a metric referred to as 'advertising equivalent exposure', a way agencies try to show clients how much they would have to advertise to reach an audience the same size as that reached by the PR coverage – and these days directly through YouTube, Facebook and similar. As brands become sceptical of advertising, with audiences using ad blockers and seeing news directly on social sites, the PR route becomes more appealing – especially as it works. PRs are definitely a significant player in the economics of bullshit.

In the mainstream media, the business models of bullshit focus on advertising and PR, and the same is true for some on the fringes – particularly those who make conspiratorial or hyperpartisan videos, many of whom receive generous funding from YouTube (owned by Google) to do so. As Joseph Bernstein noted for BuzzFeed News,[13] while Facebook receives most of the public attention for the spread of bullshit, YouTube actually funds it. Videos produced by people pushing the pizzagate conspiracy theory (see Chapter Eight) attract millions of views, and draw advertising from brands including Uber and Quaker Oats – placed by YouTube's ad network. The internet's largest ad network – Google, a company with a stated mission to 'organise the world's information'[14] – and big brands are helping to make conspiracy theories and misinformation pay.

Elsewhere on the fringes, though, the financial models work quite differently – most notably with InfoWars, once at the very furthest of the political extremes, but now with a clear line into the White House. InfoWars is a site and show helmed by Alex Jones, a right-wing conspiracy theorist closely followed by people in the survivalist movement. Jones was a prominent backer of the theory that 9/11 was an inside job, that the Sandy Hook school massacre was a hoax, that the government was behind the Boston bombings, and more. All of these, Jones claims, were part of a sinister agenda of 'globalist' forces to take over the world.[15] He's claimed that Pepsi contains baby parts, that Obama is a member of al-Qaeda, that same-sex marriage is an attack on God and that the government plans to kill off half of the US population.

You may be imagining a man producing a show from a garden shed, but InfoWars has professional studios, syndication of its shows, and revenue in the millions, and has interviewed Donald Trump after his election win – Jones even claims Trump occasionally calls on him for advice.[16]

InfoWars pushes a hyper-masculine, paranoid agenda in which the audience are urged to 'be part of history', to man 'the new battleship of the fight' – its slogan is 'You are the re-sistance!'[17] Its income source is not standard banner adverts or subscriptions or any kind of outside advertiser: instead, the site and the shows relentlessly advertise an InfoWars range of sur-vivalist products – goods designed to help its audience survive an apocalyptic event, or to help them bulk up and prepare for such a conflict.

Products include 'Super Male Vitality', produced by 'InfoWars Life', which it is claimed 'has been used by Alex Jones in order to maximize vitality when working up to twelve hours a day or more in the fight for freedom', for a mere $44.95 for a month's supply.[18] Other products tap into the survivalist mindset – people who stock up and prepare to survive for months or years off-grid following a war or disaster. InfoWars sells iodine – a chemical which offers some protection against radioactive fallout – under the brand 'SURVIVAL SHIELD X-2', noting the supplement is 'tested for radiation'.[19] InfoWars even partners with the 'patriot pantry' to offer 'emergency storable foods' with a 25-year shelf life, in stockpiles designed to provide enough food for three, six or twelve months, for $499, $895 and $1,797 respectively.[20]

A cynic could summarise InfoWars' business model as constantly feeding its audience a diet of stories warning conflict and disaster is coming, while relentlessly advertising bespoke products useful only in the case of that kind of apocalyptic event – reminding them all the while that such purchases are necessary to further the struggle. The business model, as InfoWars points out to its audience, is a robust one, resistant to pressure from advertisers, search engines and others: brands can't pull their advertising from its site because they're not there in the first place.

If an outlet can gather an audience devoted enough, it can create its own economic system – which has even survived the transition to a friendly President. The struggle has shifted from the need to resist the government to the need to defend the President: audiences are told Obama has 'a new residence, some are calling it a compound', two miles from the White House, with 'a secret army in a secret bunker' – 30,000 people in service of a 'globalist deep state'.[21] 'They'll probably just kill him,' Jones says of their plans for Trump. Whoever is in the White House, the paranoia must be fuelled – without it, the InfoWars business model falls apart.

This kind of direct commerce is a big factor in the places which produce straightforwardly fake news. Leaving aside the hoaxers who set up sites for advertising clicks (covered in Chapter Six), there's a blurred mass of fake news versus other forms of fake sites designed simply to sell products or get-rich-quick schemes. These kinds of things – 'make $$$ in your spare time' – long pre-date the internet, when people would try to recruit unwitting targets into the schemes with leaflets and posters scattered around in streets. With the easy reach of the internet, these are everywhere: anyone who's spent more than ten minutes online will have seen pop-ups, adverts and more promising 'Millionaire Exposes Her Secret to Earning £127/Hr From Home' or 'How to Get Paid £387 Every Day Without A Job in the UK'.[22]

Following the link takes you to an apparent news article at a fictitious news outlet, 'Online Wealth News'. The site is sophisticated, using data from your web browser to modify the headline so it appears the subject of the story is from your local area – for me, it reads 'Millionaire Mum from Islington Tells All' – followed by an 'As seen on: Telegraph.co.uk, FT.com, BBC'. The story, a dummy interview, then explains how 'Leah Williams' got rich.[23] The trail eventually leads to a site facilitating the trade of ultra-high-risk 'binary options' – a way to gamble on market movements – which have led to 'thousands of British savers losing millions of pounds', according to reporting by the Bureau of Investigative Journalism.[24]

That the binary options trading site promotes itself with a fake news article isn't itself especially significant – a few years ago the same site may have promoted itself on a website not posing as news, or simply on an email thread. However, it does serve to warn that while some fake news is relatively harmless to its readers, misinforming them but not hitting their wallets, others could lead to serious financial loss.

But what's most significant of all when considering the business model of bullshit is where the first grabby headline that led to the fake news story appeared – and that was at the foot of an article on a mainstream news site.[25]

This is the bit of the fake news ecosystem that mainstream outlets tend not to mention when they rail against fake news, demanding that Google, Facebook or national governments take action to tackle it: the fact is that the overwhelming majority of major news sites make money from advertising networks which include either outright fake news or articles of very dubious quality.

These stories come from links you often see at the foot or at the side of an article, often headlined in small font 'sponsored links', 'promoted links from around the web', 'promoted stories' or 'more from the web'. The links differ from regular adverts as they match the design of the site they appear on – appearing to the casual viewer like a standard, unsponsored, related story link.

On the *Daily Mirror*, for example, sponsored links include 'Nick Berry Was Gorgeous In "Eastenders" … But What He Looks Like Today Is Incredible' and 'After Losing 170lbs Susan Boyle is Unbelievably Gorgeous'. Clicking through on the Susan Boyle link leads to a site crammed with adverts offering a generic list of 'Incredible Celeb Weight Transformations' – showing just one celebrity on the page, requiring a click to see who's next, handily reloading the adverts and increasing the site's revenues. Anyone wanting to actually see what Susan Boyle looks like would have to click seventy-one times, seeing only 'after dropping a few pounds … Boyle looks better than ever', accompanied by a dated photo of Susan Boyle looking much as she usually does – she has not, of course, lost 170lbs.[26]

The highbrow Foreign Policy site offers sponsored links including 'Here's How Spoiled Barron Trump Actually Is and He's Only Ten' and 'Republican Clint Eastwood Revealed Who He Voted For, And Fans Are In Complete Disbelief' (in reality, Eastwood said he supported Trump, to no one's surprise).[27] The Guardian's sponsored headlines include 'You Will Not Believe The Cars That are Coming Out This Year', 'The Furniture Site Other Retailers Don't Want You To Know About!' and 'What "Mary Smith" From Eastenders Looks Like Today Is Jaw Dropping'.

These sponsored content boxes are operated by a small group of specialist ad agencies, with Outbrain, Taboola and Revcontent dominating the market. Why are major news outlets who are supposedly committed to fighting fake news willing to let misleading and sometimes downright false headlines appear on their own pages? The short and predictable answer is revenue: even though these links often go to anonymously registered and little-known advertisers, they pay better than regular display adverts.

'The widgets, which hawk dubious dietary supplements and a wide variety of clickbait, have become an unfortunate staple of websites – both news-focused and otherwise – thanks largely to the ad rates they pay publishers, which tend to be higher than standard banner ads,' noted the Nieman Lab.[28] 'They are, to many, a necessary evil for publishers desperate for more revenue from wherever they can get it.'

The same piece quotes an anonymous executive at a major

online company saying: 'Publishers hate these companies but make too much money from them to stop working with them.' This is backed up with statistics: a 2016 report found forty-one of the top fifty news sites on the internet used at least one of the major 'promoted stories' advertising networks – exceptions include the *New York Times*, Slate, BuzzFeed and the *Boston Globe*. Others may find it difficult to wean themselves off this revenue, though, if Outbrain is to be believed. 'We have been told from major, major publishers that we have become their No. 1 revenue provider,' the company's VP of product marketing told Nieman Lab.[29]

Publishers sit on both sides of the 'promoted stories' ecosystem, though – UK news sites including the *Express* and the *Daily Star* appear in Taboola-sponsored content boxes on other sites, driving traffic towards stories about politicians trying to block Brexit in the *Express* and an article on woolly mammoth remains in the *Daily Star*. These kinds of content promotion networks are also used on occasion by some outlets to drive traffic towards sponsored content their sales teams have made for clients – to generate the minimum viewing figures promised to clients.

The dilemma for the publishers running the adverts is set out most clearly by Matthew Ingram in *Fortune*:

> If you just published a long investigative piece of journalism on an important topic like immigration or the U.S. political landscape, what message does it send when the reader gets to the bottom of that story and sees links to cheesy sites using photos of scantily-clad women and other gimmicks?[30]

At the minimum, any outlets campaigning or lobbying for action to be taken against fake news while running these adverts has a bullet to bite – like it or not, it's on both sides of the fight. Can they demand that others tackle fake news while not taking steps entirely within their own control do so?

The final source of financial tension comes from the way the priorities of technology companies clash with those of media companies. Facebook, like news sites, wants to keep its 1.8 billion users logging into the social network every day, and spending as long as possible on the network – the more engaged the audience, the better the revenue. Where once Facebook would link to videos, it now hosts them on its site and in its app. Facebook encourages publishers to offer their articles as 'instant articles' within its walled garden – and has the power to prioritise posts of these kinds in its algorithms, helping them reach a bigger audience. Facebook then gets a share of the revenues from such pieces – though it gives publishers at least 70 per cent of proceeds.[31] What publishers lose is control: they have to reshape their plans, their design and parts of their business model to suit big technology. Trickier still for traditional publishers is the uniformity of instant articles – if they homogenise the look of content, then the source (and its credibility) becomes even less obvious to a casual reader.[32]

Facebook's is not an ecosystem that tends to foster a culture of truth. Pages on the site benefit from trying to build huge communities of fans – and many of the largest work by lifting content from elsewhere, often without payment or attribution, and framing it to provoke nostalgia or humour. Some of the most egregious examples include pages stealing photographs of disabled children 'to gain followers and get shares', to the distress of their mothers.[33] Like it or not, publishers on Facebook are routinely competing for attention in an environment where small and unscrupulous players trade off sentiment and stolen content with little or no regard to truth – and where reputation matters less than you might hope.

Other decisions of the major technology companies can have negative consequences for the post-truth era. Google has constantly refined its search results page, putting more and more information directly on its own site where once it just offered a list of search results – resulting in the risk of falling traffic to outlets which once traded off searches asking, for example, who played a particular character in a TV show, or how old a politician is.

These algorithmic answers can fail badly: Google seems to take minimal steps to prioritise established outlets over niche ones. Peter Shulman, an associate professor at Case Western Reserve, set out an example that he'd encountered after a bad class.[34] He recounted how a student had announced in his history class that at least five Presidents had been members of the Ku Klux Klan. Searching 'Presidents in the Klan' showed in Google's info box – offering supposedly reliable information from sites Google in which has a high degree of trust – a list of Presidents including McKinley, Wilson, Harding and Truman, cited to a Nigerian news outlet and not backed up with any evidence. Just as Facebook's trending news feature backfired when it was automated (see Chapter Seven), Google's information box does the same. The technology companies end up, perhaps accidentally, competing with news outlets on their own turf and adding to the misinformation mess.

The biggest economic issue for news outlets with Facebook and Google is that the technology companies on which they rely to reach an audience are also their competitors. In many instances, it's easier and more effective for brands to spend their digital advertising budget directly with Facebook and Google than it is to spend it with news outlets: the sites have such scale that they have the ability to make adverts that work well and are easy to target. That's hard for news outlets to compete with.

The dominance of Facebook and Google in digital advertising provoked the UK's News Media Association – the trade body of UK newspapers – to call on the government to take action. In a briefing to ministers, it warned that 'the online news environment is characterised by aggregation of news stories by third party players who repackage, serve, link to and monetise that content', adding that 'Google dominates these activities in search and Facebook dominates in social'. It warned: 'Significant value is being captured by companies who do not invest in original journalism at the expense of those who do.'[35] Google and Facebook make up around 75 per cent of the US digital display advertising market and more than 50 per cent of the UK market – and the share is increasing.[36]

None of this is to try to paint either Google or Facebook as pantomime villains. Among other journalism projects, Google funds the Digital News Initiative, helping fund efforts to 'support high quality journalism' and 'encourage a more sustainable news ecosystem' in Europe, which has funded €24 million of projects from newsrooms big and small.[37] Facebook has launched a journalism project looking to work with newsrooms to develop new products, support local news and help build new business models.[38] Cynics may say the internet giants are trying to act on the problem so as to stave off attempts by governments to add regulations or introduce levies to fund news outlets – but senior figures in both companies are aware that their sites rely on high-quality content, and so it's in their interest that the media survives. But these relatively small efforts don't change the current underlying reality. On the internet, it's not creating original content that pays off – it's having the scale and the ability to exploit it.

These are the various business models of bullshit, and when they work together in tandem they're corrosive to mainstream outlets and to trust. News organisations face a funding crunch from all sides: ad revenue is low and squeezed by consumer backlash, the shift to mobile and the dominance of search and social media giants. The resulting newsroom economics encourage outlets to run dubious viral stories and staged videos alongside the articles we're meant to value as high-quality journalism – and surrounding both are sponsored links to questionable advertisers and, on occasion, outright fake news.

The mainstream media is facing simultaneous crises in trust and in business models – and the two pressures are pushing many outlets in opposing directions. Elsewhere in the bullshit ecosystem, outright fakery can pay off, either through advertising – it's so cheap to make that digital adverts pay enough to make it profitable – or by promoting dubious products and services. Fringe sites can pay off by feeding the very paranoia and division the mainstream would like to tackle. Looking at the financial models of the internet might not be a heartening experience, but understanding why places act as they do is the first step to working out how to tackle it.

You might notice that we haven't talked much about sites trading off subscriptions or other business models this chapter, and that's because for a few sites that can generate enough revenue in this way, this model can serve as a counterweight to producing mass-market, low-cost news. There are still well-re-sourced newsrooms which work in this way – but if this alone was enough to tackle bullshit, the crisis would not have arisen in the first place. That takes us to the question of our next chapter: why isn't it?

CHAPTER ELEVEN

A BULLSHIT CULTURE

The previous chapters of this section have looked at why cash-strapped outlets may spread bullshit, and why we might buy into it, but we haven't looked much into why the remaining well-funded and high-quality outlets are failing to stop the tide – until now. First, though, this chapter risks creating a misconception: that there are outlets which only produce bullshit and outlets which only produce quality news. In reality, almost everyone produces some proportion of both.

Even without any bad intent, we've seen how news outlets run headlines that can mislead, struggle to challenge dubious claims from Trump, Brexit, or other campaigns, and rush out viral stories. It would be a nonsense, though, to suggest that places like the *Daily Mail* do no original or investigative journalism – even if it doesn't suit our political agendas. The *Mail* was the driving force in revealing the people behind the killing of a black teenager, Stephen Lawrence, in 1993 and, in a campaign and coverage spanning more than a decade, it was the *Mail* who spurred inquiries into police failings, uncovered police spying operations on Lawrence's family as they campaigned for justice, and reported on the trials of those who were ultimately found guilty of the murder.[1] This chapter is not intended as an example of 'good' outlets versus 'bad' outlets.

However, some sections of the media have fewer financial incentives to publish bullshit than others. The BBC, for example, receives its funding from an annual license fee of just under £150 per UK household, showing no adverts within the UK. Another handful of newspapers and magazines – particularly but not exclusively in finance – have built up substantial revenue from digital subscriptions, filling the gap left by falling advertising sales. These produce no shortage of high-quality journalism – but that's not what we're here to discuss. Our key question is: given that these outlets don't have the same kind of pressures as many others in the industry, why can't they stem the tide? Partly, of course, it's that asking just a handful of outlets – even huge and powerful ones – to shape the rest of the industry is expecting a lot, but there are also aspects in how these places produce their content that may help bullshit spread unchecked.

The subscription business model is a pretty simple one, and returns to a business model that print newspapers are familiar with: readers pay for their news. The challenge with trying this online is that there are dozens of news outlets immediately available for free, which are able to re-write versions of any original story within minutes. For a successful subscription model, news sites need to be able to attract a dedicated and engaged audience with an attachment to the brand. This favours sites which produce distinctive, high-quality and original content – a good counterweight to other business models which favour quick turnaround and questionable stories.

The *New York Times* has exploited this model more successfully than most, and benefited from a huge bump in interest and sign-ups during the rise of Donald Trump. Digital subscriptions at the *NYT* rose by more than 500,000, to 1.6 million – for all Trump likes to call the paper 'failing', it's doing better than most online.[2] The *Washington Post*, *Wall Street Journal* and *Financial Times* are all pursuing similar strategies, all relatively successfully. This might now seem like the easy and obvious fix to the news ecosystem, but the reality is a bit more complex. The *New York Times* is the second largest newspaper website in the world, and had a huge boost in digital subscriptions thanks in large part to a huge and unique running news story – but even this failed to compensate for falling print revenues. Overall revenue at the *NYT* fell around 2 per cent in 2016. For the very biggest outlets, subscriptions are helping make falling print revenues survivable, but they're still facing decline. For outlets without those huge audiences and large newsrooms to produce enough original content to encourage large numbers of subscriptions, the revenue will provide only a small fraction of the total funding mix.

This is perhaps illustrated by *The Guardian*, another of the world's biggest online newspapers, which offers membership as an alternative to subscription. Readers are urged to support the paper: 'More people are reading the Guardian than ever. But far fewer are paying for it. And advertising revenues are falling fast. So you can see why we need to ask for your help,' says a call to action at the foot of many stories. Members are asked to contribute at least £5 a month to secure *The Guardian*'s future. The initiative has had some success: fuelled by Brexit and Trump, membership in 2016 rose from 15,000 to 200,000, implying up to around £15 million a year in total revenue from the initiative. That's no bad thing, but *The Guardian*'s print revenues are around £120 million, digital makes around £80 million, and the paper loses around £60 million a year.[3] The membership money helps, but is dwarfed by advertising – leaving *The Guardian* aiming to increase subscriptions fivefold by 2019, a vastly ambitious target.[4]

For places that opt for a strict paywall which bars non-subscribers from reading their journalism, the model can also serve against the interests of countering low-quality information across the internet with better material. If the best outlets all hide their content behind paywalls, the mass audience doesn't see it, as Mathew Ingram set out in 2012:[5]

'One thing is for sure: while metered paywalls may help to save specific newspapers, they aren't going to save journalism – if by "journalism" you mean the process of informing as many people as you can about news that is important to their lives,' he argued. 'By definition, paywalls restrict the reach of a newspaper and that has very real implications for the social aspects of journalism as opposed to the business of one specific newspaper. In the end, we have to answer the question: What is journalism for?'

Paywalls and subscriptions work well for some sites, but they aren't a saviour of journalism, and they risk hiding the best-quality material away from the mass public conversation they might hope to influence. But many of the barriers that prevent quality news outlets having the impact they would hope for stem from factors inside the culture of journalism, rather than its economics.

One aspect of this is the culture of objectivity held sacred by UK broadcasters (who are required to behave this way by law) and most US newspapers (who aren't). This rule holds that news outlets and their journalists should act as if they hold no opinions of their own, instead seeking to reflect and question all sides of a debate while never taking a side of their own. The rationale is that this creates outlets that are trusted by everyone, giving the public the facts they need to debate issues and make their own decisions.

In a world where not everyone follows these values, though, this can look sterile and anodyne: partisan outlets and politicians speak passionately, launching attacks in clear and human terms – and outlets respond in a stilted on-the-one-hand, on-the-other-hand kind of way, which may sound authoritative but is far less relatable. The habit of this form of journalism to question all sides carries other risks, too. Outlets often confuse objectivity with balance: if one political campaign makes an untrue or niche claim, there's a temptation not to judge it on its merits, but instead to leave it for opponents to challenge – not reporting the facts, but instead reporting the argument. The other risk reflects the old Margaret Thatcher quote: 'Standing in the middle of the road is very dangerous; you get knocked down by the traffic from both sides.' Outlets start to look like an enemy to partisans on both sides, rather than a trusted voice for either.

A final and substantial risk of this 'objective' style of journalism is that it becomes, largely accidentally, a reflection of the view of establishment sources – perhaps most egregiously in the run-up to the 2003 war on Iraq. In an admirable confession of its mistakes, the *New York Times* acknowledged that it had been over-reliant on administration sources and Iraqi defectors, both of whom were determined to sell a particular narrative on Iraq having and being ready to use weapons of mass destruction.[6] And while the BBC faces relentless (and often unfair) accusations of bias from all sides, there's reasonable evidence to suggest that if it does have a bias, it leans towards the status quo and the current government of the day[7] – simply by virtue of the fact that they create policy and statements, and so by their actions shape much of the resulting coverage.

The culture of objectivity has been challenged by New York journalism professor Jay Rosen for more than a decade. Rosen, who refers to it as the 'view from nowhere', says it came to dominate quality journalism culture in the twentieth century as the craft professionalised and displaced the campaigners and pamphleteers who became the first newspapermen. Thus partisan or campaigning journalism is referred to by Rosen as 'Old Testament' journalism, and 'objective' reporting is 'New Testament'. But, as Rosen set out in a 2013 speech, New Testament journalism may not be the right tool for a post-truth era marked by collapsing trust in public institutions and experts, and a collapse of the old media business models.

'In new testament journalism, the media's financial security is the norm, made possible by high barriers to entry and large capital costs required to deliver news,' he said.[8]

The new testament style is risk-averse because the news delivery franchise is so valuable. The mission is not to move public opinion but to maintain trust or, to put it another way, to protect the brand. Audiences tend to be stable. The authorities learn to regularize their relationship with the journalists. Professionalism in journalism and broadcasting interlocks well with professionalism in politics and other knowledge fields. Thus, the rolodex of reliable experts.

This argument is not a no-brainer: plenty of courageous journalism comes from outlets with the culture of objectivity, and its proponents say it helps make sure reporting is trusted as fair and accurate. But there's a counterpoint: this model takes passionate and engaged reporters who become experts on their fields of coverage year after year but who spend those decades muzzled from giving their own assessments or opinions, risking appearing to be automatons. A final question: as the internet brings us closer together, do we still think the audience believe that reporters at the BBC or the *New York Times* have absolutely no opinions of their own? Social media and comment feeds across the internet suggest otherwise.

There's another risk factor among the outlets that consider themselves to be 'quality' journalism – that writers become more concerned with the opinion of other journalists than with that of the audience. This is a concern that dates back at least to the 1970s. 'Journalists write for other journalists, the people they have lunch with rather than the reader,' an unnamed journalist said at the time, leading one academic to conclude: 'Their image of the audience is hazy and unimportant … they care primarily about the reaction of the editor and their fellow-reporters.'[9]

This tendency is exacerbated in US awards culture, where the most prestigious prizes favour journalism written at great length – often 10,000 words or more and presented in a dense, discursive fashion. These pieces are often, for a journalist like me, a joy to read and are produced over the course of months. They are often the very best articles their outlets produce – but it's not hard to argue that they're not as accessible or impactful as they could be. UK journalism culture favours relatively short, punchy write-ups of investigations with a sharp top news line. The US format of long stories, often with their top line buried a dozen or more paragraphs in, seem designed for the devoted reader but leave the mass audience behind. An open question: if the Pulitzers, Polks, Scripps Howard and other awards were scrapped tomorrow, would newsrooms present their best stories differently?

Sometimes some of the ways mainstream outlets present stories are restricted by laws or regulations, in a way that journalists understand but which audiences may not. The UK's environment gives a good outline of how this can happen. Reforms to the UK's libel laws made it easier for outlets to run public service investigative journalism. Previously, outlets would have to be able to prove every claim in a story as true – a hugely difficult bar when journalists were trying to find out complex stories with limited information and contradictory sources.

The shift in the law lets news outlets defend a story on the basis that it was fair, based on information which they had good reason to believe was accurate, and where everyone concerned had a chance to respond to the information and allegations therein. This change lets far more stories make their way to the public, but comes with a sting: the journalists concerned can't adopt the allegation – the piece has to be approached in a neutral, 'view from nowhere', kind of way – and any correspondence and memos sent during the reporting of it must be similarly free of bias: if the journalists concerned looked enthusiastic at the prospect discrediting the politician or company they were writing about, they can't appeal to this libel defence. These restrictions account for the reporting style of quite a lot of modern UK investigative journalism: phrasing is often careful; the newspaper or TV show carefully avoids (in its news section at least) expressing an opinion on its revelations; and any comment on them is left to politicians or other outlets. The article also typically contains quite extensive denials or explanations from the targets of a story – which may be good for fairness, but risks leaving the article looking confusing to a casual reader.

For broadcasters, these obligations are even more onerous, as TV news and channels are bound to comply with rules set by the regulator Ofcom, which requires coverage to show 'due impartiality' and – especially in the run-up to elections – give fair, measured amounts of airtime to all major political parties.[10] The rules aren't intended to be too rigid – they don't require equal time to be given to all opinions, for example – but they do risk leaving broadcasters leaning towards caution. This presents TV news with a dilemma in the run-up to elections or referenda, when there is an obligation to give airtime to, and reflect the views of, all major parties and campaigns. Navigating the lines of those legal obligations, especially if a candidate or campaign says things that are untrue, is a substantial challenge – and often a source of frustration to those watching from the other side of the political divide. To take Vote Leave's £350 million-a-week NHS claim (covered at length in Chapter Two) as an example: broadcasters are unable not to talk about this, as it was a central and daily plank of an official campaign's platform during the campaign. But calling it out as inaccurate on every mention would not feel impartial to many listeners. The result tends to be that longer broadcasts, like half-hour current affairs shows, note that the claim is disputed, but shorter broadcasts and clips, which hit a mass audience, often let dubious claims run unchallenged. Keeping broadcast impartial can help keep people of all political views agreed on some central shared view of reality – but does it also risk letting bullshit pass unchecked?

This reminder of restrictions on the media from law and

from regulation should also serve as an antidote to politicians making accusations about how outlets use anonymous sources. US newspapers haven't opted to sign up to (or even create) industry-wide regulators, but they have internal ombudsmen and other safeguards, and they remain subject to libel laws and other restrictions. This should cast attacks from Donald Trump against the media using 'anonymous sources' in a new light; the President has suggested that news outlets should only use on-the-record sources in their stories.[11] Many government staff have no permission to talk to the media without explicit permission, so the only way people can hear a view other than the administration's official line is if off-the-record sources are allowed. Donald Trump himself has used anonymous sources to claim that Obama faked his birth certificate and applied to university as a foreign student, that 'Clinton's hacked emails' led to Iran's execution of a nuclear scientist, and more.[12] Anonymous sources do risk making it possible for politicians and outlets to invent 'news' from nowhere – but this is less true for mainstream outlets than for others. If a UK publication runs a big story based on an anonymous source, it is saying it's confident its anonymous source would – if necessary – back up their claims in court or in front of the regulator. There are reasons to be sceptical of anonymous sources, but for most mainstream outlets, they're not wholly invented when they're making major claims – though former tabloid reporters have admitted fabricating quotes on stories where it was unlikely to lead to lawsuits.[13]

And then there's climate change, and how the media covers it – an issue with the ability to reshape the world, leading to tens of millions of extra deaths by the end of the century,[14] and which would require major action by government, business and citizens to tackle. In terms of expert opinion, more than 97 per cent of published climate scientists agree climate change is real and is caused by the activities of humans.[15] The picture is very different in politics, where the issue has become a cause of controversy between the religious right, pro-business right and liberals, especially in the USA.

The media is more used to covering issues through debate and argument, and many flagship news programmes rely on this format to produce segments on issues. This means even well-intentioned programmes looking to produce good-quality news can be left covering climate change badly, as a 2014 parliamentary report into coverage of the issue found.[16] 'The producers of the recent Today Programme piece on the new IPCC report tried, we are told, more than a dozen qualified climate scientists willing to give an opposing view but could not find a single one (a hint, perhaps, that there is indeed a scientific consensus on global warming),' said the report, quoting Professor Steve Jones, author of a report for the BBC Trust on climate change coverage. 'Instead, they gave equal time to a well-known expert and to [an] Australian retired geologist with no background in the field: in my view a classic [case] of "false balance".'

Another issue across newspapers and broadcasters is that news desks aren't really set up to cover something like climate change, a serious issue which develops slowly and unsurprisingly, as James Randerson – then an environmental journalist at *The Guardian* – told the committee, speaking of the 'tendency for news desks to like things that are new and surprising and favour the underdog. A general issue with science reporting is that mavericks tend to get more coverage than perhaps they deserve.'[17]

Science journalists have been covering topics where false or fringe views challenge established and well-evidenced mainstream consensuses for far longer than most political journalists. The media were among the most enthusiastic boosters of the anti-vaccination movement, but were also instrumental in exposing the scientific fraud at its core. Some media outlets enthusiastically boost climate conspiracy theories while others battle to cover the issue fairly and accurately while also reflecting the political rows and debates around it. If political discourse is indeed facing a new high tide of bullshit, talking to science reporters and editors might serve as a good way to find what will and won't work – they've been in the trenches of this battle for years.

The instinctive response of many US outlets to the rise of Trump, the fall of trust in their output, and the polarisation of US discourse seems to be promising to double-down, committing to doing even more of the type of reporting they've always been doing. News outlets have reported how Trump and his White House spokesman told an average of around four untruths a day in the early days of the administration.[18] And yet most of the battles on the ground between White House reporters and the administration are to keep open access to the briefings in which they're told these untruths and half-truths. The fight is to maintain the illusion of business-as-usual, a status quo which arguably no longer exists.[19]

It's clearly a temptation for some in the mainstream to use the rise of Trump as an I-told-you-so, and some have taken the bait. 'This is what happens when we stop paying for quality journalism,' says Asha Dornfest in a Medium post warning that 'authoritarian governments choke off access to information. By abandoning quality news sources, we've already done much of that work ourselves.'[20] Dornfest tells her readers to stop getting news from Facebook, start paying for local and national newspaper subscriptions, and pay for public radio. Her calls to action may be helpful, but they're also exactly what mainstream journalists would like to hear: if the public are divided and believing in bullshit, it's their own fault for not reading us any more. Sure, why not. But how many Trump supporters are going to read that post and return to elite media on bended knee?

Others have been more questioning: veteran *Washington Post* report Dan Balz, who's had more than 1,000 front-page stories, warned against the rise of polling-driven and model-driven news – where every headline was based on a shift in a forecast in elaborate models aimed to predict the election. 'We have all come to rely on data which turned out not to be specifically accurate, whether it was polling, predictive modelling, almost anything you looked at in one way or another broke down in the end,' he told CNN.[21] 'I think we have to re-examine a lot of the ways we go about doing journalism.'

Others are blunter still. Margaret Sullivan, the *Washington Post* columnist and respected former public editor of the *New York Times*, warned that Trump's presidency would be 'hellish' for journalists, that he would be a 'gaslighter in chief' who would 'relentlessly manipulate' the media and 'punish journalists for doing their jobs'. Her conclusion was less business-as-usual than some of her colleagues. 'Journalists are in for the fight of their lives. And they are going to have to be better than ever before, just to do their jobs,' she said.[22] 'They will need to work together, be prepared for legal persecution, toughen up for punishing attacks and figure out new ways to uncover and present the truth.'

This hope that journalists may unite to respond to a new kind of President may prove as futile as hoping the public will spontaneously regain their trust in traditional journalism. In a somewhat despairing post, Russian journalist Alexey Kovalev warned his 'doomed colleagues in the American media' that they 'can't hurt this man with facts and reason', urged them not to expect any camaraderie as some outlets would always go along with Trump's conferences, and advised them to 'expect a lot of sycophancy and softballs' from colleagues towards the President.[23]

We have to hope Kovalev's counsel is one of despair, and too far on the negative side – but other responses are evidently leading too far towards business-as-usual. While giving up won't help tackle the rise of bullshit, we do have to acknowledge that while messages like 'let's keep on doing our jobs, with more energy and determination than ever' might be in journalists' comfort zones, there's no reason to believe they will work either. So far, the principal weapon against bullshit in the mainstream press has been the rise of the fact-checker. In our next and final section, we're going to look at how they've fared – and then look into what else might help get us through the post-truth era.

PART IV

HOW TO STOP BULLSHIT

CHAPTER TWELVE

DEBUNKING THE DEBUNKERS

If we're worried that politicians, campaigns, the press and the public are playing fast and loose with the facts, then boosting fact-checking is something of a no-brainer. What better antidote to misinformation could there be than sources of balanced, impartial information looking for evidence behind political and media claims and judging them on truth? The same could hold for viral hoaxes and misinformation – we tend to refer to 'debunks' for these, rather than 'fact-checks', though the two are much the same thing – why shouldn't these be fixable by getting accurate information out there quickly?

The reality is much more complex, but is hinted at in the very old saying that 'a lie can travel halfway around the world before the truth has got its boots on'. Everything we've seen so far in this book should warn us why fact-checks – even if they're put together meticulously, written well and released promptly (as they often are) – will struggle to hold back bullshit. Bullshit grabs us, it pulls us by our existing beliefs and triggers our impulses to share. We tend to believe information that confirms our beliefs, and we tend to find a sensational piece grabbier than a careful and fact-based one. When we do look for fact-checks, we tend to do it for things we were already inclined to doubt: how many of us regularly look for fact-checks on things we believe in? And even in the wake of terrorist attacks or natural disasters, we want to know what's going on quickly – which news outlet is likely to do better: the one which says honestly that it knows very little and is looking for confirmation from official channels, or the ones speculating on unverified information from the internet? None of this is intended as an attack on fact-checkers – even a casual glance at the references section of this book will show what a great resource they can be – but instead will hopefully serve as a warning: these can, at most, only be a small part of a solution to our current misinformation ecosystem.

One cautionary note to those who hope that fact-checks will be their salvation is just to look at which area of the world already has the most active fact-checking corps – and that's the USA, especially its political coverage. The US public is served by the *Washington Post*'s Fact Checker, by NPR's Fact Check, by FactCheck.org (run by the Annenberg Public Policy Center) and by PolitiFact, a Pulitzer Prize-winning site established by the *Tampa Bay Times*. All present themselves as non-partisan and examine claims made by both major political parties.

The sites have hardly stood idle through the rise of Donald Trump, either. PolitiFact had, at the time of writing, fact-checked more than 370 claims made by Trump on a scale running from 'True' to 'False', with a special category of 'Pants on Fire' – a rating it saves for what it says are 'ridiculous claims'.[1] PolitiFact found just fifteen of the 373 (just 4 per cent) Trump claims it checked could be classed as 'True', while 123 merited 'False' and sixty-three rated 'Pants on Fire'. These pants-on-fire claims included allegations of voter fraud, of Clinton aides rigging the polls, that Clinton had lost or stolen $6 billion when she was Secretary of State, and denials that Trump had suggested people look at a 'sex tape' of a woman mentioned by Clinton during a presidential debate – in reality, he had literally tweeted 'check out sex tape', and the woman concerned had never made such a tape.[2] By contrast, PolitiFact checked 293 claims from Hillary Clinton, classing seventy-two as 'True', versus twenty-nine as 'False' and just seven as 'Pants on Fire'.

The *Washington Post*'s Fact Checker blog scores on a scale of Pinocchios, with the (rarely awarded) score of zero signalling a claim was essentially entirely accurate, while four Pinocchios signal a politician's claim was entirely baseless. The blog posted its own round-up of the presidential candidates a few days before the election in November. Trump was fact-checked ninety-two times by the blog, scoring zero Pinocchios on three occasions, and four Pinocchios fifty-nine times. Clinton, meanwhile, was fact-checked forty-nine times, scoring zero Pinocchios on seven of those occasions, and four Pinocchios again on seven occasions.[3] Trump bust the bullshit meters of the USA's established fact-checkers, scoring dramatically worse than any previous major party candidate, and being shown up as playing fast and loose with the facts – if not telling outright falsehoods – week after week. And then he won an election and became the President of the USA.

There is at least anecdotal evidence that many of Trump's supporters knew that much of what he said as a candidate wasn't true, and simply didn't care[4] – and some simply wanted a change from the status quo, while some were social conservatives who would never vote for Clinton, and some hoped for tax breaks and less regulation (Trump voters were, on average, richer than Clinton voters).[5] Sometimes, entertaining bullshit which signals a politician's priorities is more important than the details of the facts: a candidate who will claim he'll build a wall and Mexico will pay is clearly making the right noises on immigration, even if the details don't pan out.

But there is also a numbers game at play, as the chart of top fifty fake news stories we looked at in Chapter Six makes clear. Almost half of 2016's most viral stories related to US politics, and the one at the top of the charts had more than 2 million Facebook engagements (likes, shares or comments). The fiftieth-placed fake news story on the 2016 ranking managed more than 198,000 Facebook engagements – and remember, these don't include hyper-partisan or biased posts: this is just outright fakery.[6] Even these outright made-up stories, posted by fake news sites and without the machinery of major outlets behind them, comprehensively defeated the fact-checking sites when it came to blowing up in front of an online audience. The most-shared *Washington Post* Fact Checker piece (on Paul Ryan and Obamacare) got 162,400 Facebook engagements,[7] while PolitiFact's most shared individual article (on whether the public care about Trump's tax returns) got just 75,800.[8] The best-performing pieces of content on both sites were comprehensively beaten by the fiftieth-placed fake news story. Even if people who read and believe claims from or about Trump were the same ones reading the fact-checking blogs – and there's every reason to believe they're not, though this is hard to prove – not many of them are doing so. The facts are out there, but they're not what's getting shared.

This is often just as true when outlets are trying to tackle misinformation, jokes and hoaxes emerging on social media in the wake of terror attacks, riots and natural disasters. One of the earliest UK incidents to be reported first through social media was the London riots of 2011: several nights of protests, looting and chaos provoked by the killing by police of Mark Duggan in Tottenham. Such was the furore – and the mistaken belief that Twitter and Facebook were being used to coordinate the riots – that police even asked for the power to 'turn off' the social networks in times of crisis.[9] While it wasn't used to coordinate the riots, Twitter in particular was used to spread often bizarre misinformation, as the *Guardian* reporting team on the 'Reading the Riots' project uncovered.

Shortly after midnight on Tuesday 9 August, one Twitter user posted a picture of the London Eye set alight – 'Oh my god! This can't happening!' The blatant hoax (the Eye is made from steel, which is difficult for any mob to set alight) nonetheless spread despite being immediately debunked. Others claimed tanks had been deployed at Bank station, using a photo from Egypt as 'evidence', or that tigers had escaped London Zoo.[10] Another apparent hoax – that rioters had broken into McDonald's and were now cooking their own food – was picked up by the *Mail on Sunday*, despite never being corroborated. More than five years later, the story remains uncorrected.[11]

The London riots happened before newsrooms were used to dealing with social media as a source for reporting – and as a rival source of information during these kinds of breaking stories. But there's good evidence that even years later misinformation often spreads despite being corrected or coming from dubious sources, as outlined in a 2015 report for the Tow Center for Digital Journalism, produced by Craig Silverman.

The report notes how mainstream outlets can accidentally launder fabricated claims through a series of retweets, eventually making them appear as if they'd been checked by credible sources. This included an anonymous claim that the New York Stock Exchange was under 3ft of water, tweeted by an anonymous account during Hurricane Sandy in 2012. This was retweeted inside quote marks by the Weather Channel (which made no other comment), which seemed a credible source for other outlets – including NBC and CNN. There was no truth to the claim.[12]

Silverman's reports also looked at efforts to correct misinformation being spread in the wake of the Boston bombings in 2013, when wholly innocent people had been wrongly named as suspects, and when false claims suggested an eight-year-old girl had been killed and that the US government had been involved in the attacks. The research showed that tweets containing misinformation outnumbered those containing corrections by ratios up of 44 to 1, and even after accurate information was available, it was still outweighed by misinformation. 'Misinformation is often more viral and spreads with greater frequency than corrective information,' the report concluded.[13] 'One reason for this is that false information is designed to meet emotional needs, reinforce beliefs, and provide fodder for our inherent desire to make sense of the world.'

Part of the challenge facing fact-checkers and debunkers alike is that they're not engaged in a fair fight. It takes mere seconds to think up a very specific and completely bullshit claim – say, 'I have received credible information that there are 1,650 active ISIS agents in the USA right now.' If I run a fake or fringe news site and make this claim, I can be spreading it in less than a minute and it may catch on – it will suit the agenda of those looking to support tighter border controls, or those who feel Obama was soft on radical Islamic terror groups. Proving the claim is fabricated, though, is a tougher job.

If a fact-checker was looking into my just-now-invented claim, their first step would likely be to ask me for any evidence supporting it. I could, in turn, claim it was from a confidential source I cannot reveal. This would leave them able to say my claim was 'baseless' or 'unevidenced' (especially if I had a track record of making such claims), but not 'false'. To show it up as false would require extensive work, speaking to the FBI or other agencies and asking them to comment on the figure – and no one could say for certain there definitely aren't that many ISIS operatives, even if it is vanishingly unlikely and there's not a shred of evidence for it. Inventing bullshit is easy. Fighting it is hard.

'There's a reason this battle is often likened to asymmetric warfare,' says *Guardian* assistant media editor Jasper Jackson.[14]

Media organisations are used to having absolute dominance via their power of distribution, and they are also constrained by the equivalent of the Geneva Convention (those journalistic principles). But those spreading fake news have none of those constraints, and can pick the weakest points to exploit without any of the difficulties of trying to follow journalistic procedure.

Tackling bullshit on a story-by-story, claim-by-claim basis is the equivalent of trench warfare in the information conflict: it quickly leads to a quagmire, and a war that's unwinnable. Fact-checking a bullshit claim takes a lot more time and effort than making one does, and even then the fact-check spreads to a much smaller audience, and doesn't stop the spread of the original claim. That's not the turf the mainstream should be aiming for.

There's another risk of shifting fact-checking to specialist teams of reporters, and specific sections of a website – and that's separating it from the bulk of coverage. Many news desks will by instinct seek to minimise overlap between different stories they commission, especially if they're still working in print: if the paper is going to run a 600-word fact-check, it will be keen that it's not repeated in the main political coverage of the day. The political write-up of a campaign speech is the story likely to be put on the front page of the newspaper, and the top of the website. The fact-check will sit on an inside page, or a smaller link online. As a result, many people will only see the main story, which may have only minimal challenges against the dubious claims therein. The dilemma was perhaps put most clearly by comedian Jon Stewart: 'When did fact-checking and journalism separate?'[15]

This is neither inevitable or unfixable: as discussed earlier in the book, US newspapers have become more aggressive in terms of flagging 'bogus' or 'baseless' claims in major headlines and in their main news items. There are also ways to move debunking and reporting efforts more closely together. One innovation from BuzzFeed News during some of the major terror attacks in 2015 and 2016 (in Paris, Brussels and Nice) was to combine debunking rumours with reporting efforts. In addition to sending reporters to the affected cities, staff sought out and shared apparent eyewitness accounts, information and claims from social media. If these were corroborated, they were incorporated into reporting – but if they were found to be hoaxes, rather than being ignored or saved for later, they were marked as 'FALSE' and shared through social media and gathered in a post. The reporting and debunking processes were combined, and the expertise of a broad field of staff specialisations (people with local knowledge, security knowledge, specialists in spotting hoaxes etc.) brought to bear quickly – hopefully to the benefit of both the reporting and tackling misinformation.

Despite these reasons for concerns over the power of fact-checking, their role is set to become all the more integral in the years to come. In January 2017, the BBC announced it would be creating a permanent fact-checking team with a series of hugely ambitious aims. 'The BBC can't edit the internet, but we won't stand aside either,' said James Harding, the director of news for the BBC, at its launch.[16]

> We will fact check the most popular outliers on Facebook, Instagram and other social media. We are working with Facebook, in particular, to see how we can be most effective. Where we see deliberately misleading stories masquerading as news, we'll publish a Reality Check that says so. And we want Reality Check to be more than a public service, we want it to be hugely popular. We will aim to use styles and formats – online, on TV and on radio – that ensure the facts are more fascinating and grabby than the falsehoods.

The goals are laudable, but given the evidence on the popularity of fakery versus debunks – and that the BBC itself is often mistrusted among the people most likely to believe fake news – its success is far from a given, and it remains to be seen if the fact-checking model will prove the most effective in this new information ecosystem. However, the BBC is not alone in prioritising this approach: Facebook, having faced criticism and calls for action on fake news from all sides, is planning to incorporate fact-checking into how it presents news.

Facebook will partner with AP, ABC News, FactCheck.org, PolitiFact and Snopes to flag and check stories that appear to be going viral on its network. Facebook is adding a tool to allow users to flag a story as potentially dubious, and if enough users flag a story it will alert the various fact-checkers, Facebook's vice-president for the News Feed announced in a post. 'We'll use the reports from our community, along with other signals, to send stories to these organizations. If the fact-checking organizations identify a story as fake, it will get flagged as disputed and there will be a link to the corresponding article explaining why.'[17]

Facebook's action does go beyond simply providing fact-check – stories flagged as disputed may be less likely to show in users' feeds, and cannot be promoted by advertisers. People will still be able to see and spread the story, but will receive a warning saying the story is 'disputed by third-party fact-checkers' before doing so. The move may very well slow the spread of such stories among casual and mainstream audiences, but could prove counterproductive among audiences already mistrustful of the mainstream media and big technology – and may even compound allegations of bias, or of deliberate cover-ups of 'what's really going on'.

'Flagging of fake news on social media may work well for people who trust the "authority" flagging them, and should be useful for helping people unable to distinguish an established outlet from one set up specifically to deceive,' *Guardian* assistant media editor Jasper Jackson explains.[18]

But it won't have much impact on those who distrust authority and want to believe false stories … The solutions to fake news currently being discussed, it's pretty clear they don't deal with that fundamental problem, and bad actors spreading fake news will be able to overcome them, or simply ignore them. Debunking or fact-checking can be challenged with a counter-narrative, normally one which deflects by questioning the broader context rather than addressing the facts.

As they grow in prominence, and especially as they gain the power to regulate how prominently information appears in the Facebook news feed, the fact-checkers themselves can expect to become the target of ever-more scrutiny. The reputation of fact-checkers – and their access to the News Feed – relies on their adherence to a code of conduct and their being seen as politically neutral. This has, generally speaking, been accepted by most – but there are already signs that they may need to get used to a higher degree of pressure.

One of the best-known debunkers and myth-busters on the internet – and one of the fact-checkers working with Facebook – is Snopes, which has been around for more than twenty years. Unlike many of the sites previously mentioned, Snopes is run by a small, independent team and is not backed by a major news organisation or university. The site, which had been debunking chain emails, hoax Facebook posts and fake news for two decades, suddenly became the target of much more ferocious scrutiny following its sign-up to Facebook's plan to tackle fake news.

It was MailOnline which led the way, with a characteristically lurid headline:[19] 'Facebook "fact checker" who will arbitrate on "fake news" is accused of defrauding website to pay for prostitutes – and its staff includes an escort-porn star and "Vice Vixen domme".

The article was largely filled with details of Snopes' staff personal lives and finances, based on court filings in the divorce of the site's two founders, but also hinted at the integrity of the site's fact-checks, noting its administrator had run for Congress as a libertarian 'despite claims [the] website is non-political' and alleged Snopes' 'main "fact checker"' had 'posted on Snopes. com while smoking pot'. Politics – both online and offline – has become an increasingly vicious game in recent years. Fact-checkers have generally managed to stay somewhat out of the fray – but as their role grows and they're pushed to centre-stage, that seems unlikely to last. Can their 'neutral' reputation withstand the potential onslaught?

The other challenge to fact-checking's reputation will come from the proven ability of the internet's bullshit merchants to move with the times: whatever their motivation for doing so, people spreading dodgy information will do what successfully connects with an audience. This is already starting to be seen with the rise of what are, in essence, fake fact-checkers.

This can be seen with sites offering the internet's current favourite get-rich-quick scheme, 'binary options'. These sites – as discussed in Chapter Eight – have used fake news and other tactics to boost traffic to their sites. A further technique used by some relates to dubious 'reviews' and 'scambuster' sites, which give assurances that the site under review is safe, reliable and one of the best in the business – with links which give the reviews site a fixed fee, or a cut of any takings, for anyone who then signs up. Searching some binary options providers gives a Google autocomplete with the word 'scam' as the first result – but searching for this then results in as many as three different reviews sites, all at the top of search rankings thanks to paid advertising slots, all of which reassure customers the site is safe. By feeding into the reviews ecosystem, these efforts not only provide would-be customers to the ultra-high-risk sites (many experts call binary options an outright scam)[20] with 'evidence' that they're safe, but also crowd out genuinely independent warnings against using the brokers.

These simulacra of respected fact-checkers or reviewers are starting to creep into the political domain. Late in 2016, Mediekollen, an apparently new fact-checking organisation aimed at a Swedish audience, launched on Facebook. However, rather than impartially fact-checking claims, the page instead appeared determined to push a particular political agenda, spreading discredited online theories about the origins of a dossier of information on Donald Trump published by BuzzFeed News, and defending claims on 'no-go areas' made by a Swedish author on Czech TV – despite the fact that she herself had retracted many of her comments when faced with evidence that her claims were untrue.[21] The page did not disclose who had created it, or who (if anyone) was funding it. 'Much of the information Mediekollen uses in its version of a fact check is indeed based on fact,' *The Guardian* noted. 'But unlike most established fact checkers, which pick out figures or statements to verify or debunk, it creates a different narrative using other pieces of evidence or opinion to support or knock down a statement or story. It is argument, often deliberately misleading, dressed up as verification.'

Mediekollen also attacked articles produced by other fact-checkers focusing on Sweden, as the editor of Viralgranskaren ('viral examiner') told thelocal.se: 'We noticed that after we wrote the article, they wrote an article saying our article was fake,' he said.[22] 'I then posted some comments under that article, and five minutes later it was taken down.'

Mediekollen was subsequently removed from Facebook following the row, but does serve to highlight the potential turf war coming: the page borrowed the visual and narrative style of an established Swedish fact-checking site and secured an audience on Facebook. Other players able to push their agendas more subtly, or those who don't rely on Facebook for hosting, may not prove nearly so easy to get rid of. Given the pace of change on the internet, everyone who is trying to fight misinformation is gunning at a number of targets, all of which are fast-moving.

Finally, when it comes to politics and public policy, most statements are neither 'true' nor 'false', but somewhere in between – statements can easily be largely true with a degree of exaggeration, or largely false but with a grain of truth. Differentiating one from the other isn't really a question of fact, but one of judgement or opinion – if we delegate tackling bullshit to merely tackling what's outright false, we may leave the bulk of bullshit entirely unchallenged.

This is an issue some of those at the forefront of the fact-checking movement are well aware of and have spoken on. David Mikkelson, one of the two founders of Snopes, laid this out in a blogpost around a week after the US results, titled 'We Have a Bad News Problem, Not a Fake News Problem'.[23]

'There is much bad news in the online world, but not all of it is "fake" …' he writes, ahead of a cogent list of the baffling array of misinformation with which his site contends.

There are also partisan political sites that take nuggets of real news and spin them into highly distorted, clickbait articles.

There are sites that misleadingly repackage old news as if it were current information. There are sites that aggregate articles from a variety of dubious and questionable sources. There are sites (especially in the fields of health and science) that believe they're presenting pertinent information but are woefully inaccurate in their information-gathering and reporting. These forms of news are all bad in one way or another, but broadly classifying all such information as 'fake news' clouds an already confusing issue.

Mikkelson's post continued by warning of the dangers of tagging Fox News or MSNBC reporting as 'fake news' – because of its partisan spin which political opponents may find outright misleading – as 'entering perilous territory', but did say that partisan reporting risked falling into his category of 'bad' news, which he said should be a non-partisan issue to tackle.

This is a commendable viewpoint, and one which may well be right – but it's worth taking a step back and looking at the situation realistically: if the current information system is serving one side of the political divide better than the other, what's their incentive to try to tackle it? If our premise is that Donald Trump is a source of misinformation and bullshit, can tackling that really be regarded as non-partisan? If we believe the UK's Brexit debate featured the Leave campaign far more skilfully exploiting partial truths and spin than the Remain campaign did, can tackling those problems be a non-partisan issue here? There is fake news, spin and misinformation on all sides of the political divide – this is an easy and uncontroversial thing to say, just as it's easy and uncontroversial to say that people from all sides of the divide should work to fix it. The question is whether that's actually true, or whether it's asking certain politicians and campaigns to unilaterally disarm, and ditch one of the most politically effective weapons in their arsenal. If there is currently an imbalance in who can best use bullshit, is tackling it (in the short term at least) really a non-partisan issue – and if it isn't, what does that mean for fixing the problem?

People within respected fact-checkers and verification outlets are well aware that the misinformation ecosystem is more complex than just true and false, and that fact-checking outlets can only be part of a solution. Claire Wardle, the research and strategy director of First Draft News, set out in a blogpost how 'fake news' is just the most visible part of a much broader problem, with related problems including false context, misleading rather than outright false facts, or drawing false connections between items – issues much harder to deal with in a fact-check format. She noted:

> We all play a crucial part in this ecosystem. Every time we passively accept information without double-checking, or share a post, image or video before we've verified it, we're adding to the noise and confusion. The ecosystem is now so polluted, we have to take responsibility for independently checking what we see online...
>
> This is about teaching people to second guess their instinctual reactions. If you find yourself incredibly angry at a piece of content or feeling smug (because your viewpoint has been reaffirmed), take another look.[24]

Will Moy, the director of the independent UK fact-checker FullFact, also speaks about the need to go beyond the traditional fact-check. Speaking at a panel debate hosted by the Royal

Statistical Society, he spoke of the need to make reliable information easier to use, and unreliable information more difficult, as well as launching training for journalists and other professionals. FullFact is also working to build automated fact-checking tools,[25] to tackle the asymmetry of effort involved in tracking down and addressing bullshit – ideally with the aim of having such posts flagged in Google results and on Facebook. Moy did add, though, that post-truth can only get a politician so far – eventually, he argued, reality catches up with you.

'What we talk about when we talk about post-truth as a problem is that suddenly there are more people and more powerful people that have decided that telling the truth simply doesn't matter,' he said.[26]

And that's a problem, and that's a problem for all of us – when the Committee for Standards in Public Life asked people what do you think are the most important qualities in your public servants, telling the truth came out as the single most important thing we expect from MPs. And it's a problem because having some grasp on reality is quite important if you're going to run the country – there is only so long you can govern in a post-truth way, even if you might be able to campaign in a post-truth way.

There comes a point, too, where you have to step back and realise that bullshit and distortions are part of a much bigger series of phenomena: against globalisation, against elites and against the liberal social order which has seemed to be winning the culture wars for the past few decades. For one, we should remember what's been argued elsewhere in this book – that there are financial and economic drivers behind the way Trump and other post-truth causes are covered. Even early in the election contest, as the primaries were ongoing, outlets devoting lots of coverage to Trump were doing better financially than ones who didn't. 'It's one thing to be high-minded about your journalistic principles, but it's another to do so while outlets like CNN are raking in billions of dollars for their wall-to-wall Trump coverage, and you are trying to keep the lights on as your ad revenue vanishes with breathtaking speed,' noted Mathew Ingram in *Fortune*.[27] The result was that even as early as March 2016, Trump had picked up media coverage which would have cost $2 billion in ad buys – almost three times as much as Clinton, and six times as much as Republican primary rival Ted Cruz.[28] This storm of wall-to-wall media coverage is far too powerful to be fixed around the margins. There is another reason why fact-checking won't prevent future campaigns operating like the Trump campaign, or Brexit campaigns did – there are much broader cultural factors at play behind the shock elections of 2016, and bullshit and spin have been just one part of the problem.

With regard to Trump, this was spelled out early in the presidential election campaign by the media theorist Clay Shirky in a lengthy series of tweets the day after Trump's speech at the Republican convention. 'I want to say something to my liberal white friends: Trump talked a lot of shit last night, but not one word of "I am your voice!" was a lie,' he posted.[29]

Trump IS the voice of angry whites. He wasn't on stage because he has unusual views. He was on stage because he has the usual ones, loudly. He is the voice of whites who want their neighbors deported if they speak Spanish. He is the voice of whites terrorized by seeing a hijab. He is the voice of people who think legal

& cultural privileges for white conservative Protestants are God's plan, not a bias to be overcome. He is the voice of people who hear 'hard-working' as a synonym for 'white'. He is the voice of people who think black lives matter less. He speaks for millions. During the speech, a lot of white liberals in my timeline – people like me – were reacting in disbelief. We can't afford disbelief, not now … We've brought fact-checkers to a culture war. Time to get serious.

So far as the media and so far as post-truth is concerned, there is a battle of competing narratives. We've seen that emotive narratives that play to people's pre-existing beliefs work best on social media, reaching the biggest audience and working best to be believed. This is almost the antithesis of fact-checking culture, which aims to be even-handed and measured and to avoid becoming a partisan in a debate – and we've also seen that even the most viral fact-checks have nothing like the reach of the fake news or bullshit they exist to battle.

This was spelled out by *The Guardian*'s social and new formats editor Martin Belam, who noted that 'fact checkers are terrible at telling stories' while 'the neo-Nazi "alt-right" movement is great at building and maintaining a narrative'.[30] Belam's conclusion is (my paraphrase) to suggest that fact-checking in the current political climate may be futile, as it doesn't challenge the broader narratives the misleading information is being used to advance. Instead, the media should focus on building its own truth-based narratives. 'As we get to grips with living in an era in which the White House is going to call the press "very, very dishonest" people who are suppressing information, we, as journalists, are going to have to wrestle with how to deal with this,' Belam says.

Infowars, Breitbart, Britain First – the sort of websites and organisations that are spreading the far right's anti-Muslim, conspiracy-theory-ridden ideology – are not going to be afraid to double-down on spreading their message. Fact-checking their spurious claims is one thing – but what does it achieve? To really challenge the spread of this nonsense we need to work out what we are going to do about more effectively spreading the truth.

Fact-checkers are definitely on the side of the angels in the post-truth battle, and have a substantial role to play: those of us who are looking for which claims are true, which claims are questionable, and which are downright false need reliable first ports of call, and there are far worse places to go than most of these blogs. But in a world of shifting targets, and given the scale of the issue, we should avoid placing too much pressure on fact-checkers – they might be part of a solution, but placing all of our hopes on them is just another version of the head-in-the-sand approach that's too tempting to follow: if we keep on doing a bit more of what we've been doing already, the problem will go away. The answer is likely to be rather more difficult than that, and won't involve just one (or even just half a dozen) fixes – but let's now take a look at a few ideas that might work.

CHAPTER THIRTEEN

STOPPING THE SPREAD

We've spent the last twelve chapters looking at what makes bullshit so effective, why the internet is a great breeding ground for it, how it taps into modern politics, and why there's a big business model behind it. We've also discovered that there's unlikely to be one easy fix: fact-checking alone won't be a salvation, and nor is there some straightforward crackdown on 'fake news' that will fix the bullshit ecosystem. But simply setting out problems without any discussion of what might work to tackle them would be nothing more than a counsel of despair, a book-length howl into the void. I'm going to try to be just a touch less bleak than this.

This chapter, then, is a list of suggestions for politicians and policy makers; for media outlets and journalists; and for us as citizen and news consumers. These shouldn't all be taken as original ideas or even as coherent: instead, this is a collection of ideas and conclusions which follow on from everything discussed in the previous chapters, which respond to different pressures in different ways. People have different incentives to take different actions: the right response for a political rival to a candidate deploying bullshit will be different to that of a media outlet covering the race. What they do assume is that the reader is on the side of fighting bullshit, rather than spreading it – which is not necessarily a given: bullshit clearly has power as a political and commercial strategy, and some will be tempted to use it.

Our first batch of fixes are those aimed at political candidates and campaigns, some of them looking at how to take on a rival using these tactics, and others looking at what policy makers currently able to change laws, practices or even education syllabuses might be able to do.

POLITICIANS

Don't explain: It's a very old saying in politics that if you're explaining, you're losing. This did not stop the Remain campaign in the UK repeatedly trying to take down Vote Leave's £350 million-a-week claim on the details, explaining the UK's rebate, money spent by the EU inside the UK, trying to explain the effect of economic growth on public finances, and more. The result for many voters was simply that Vote Leave's core message was repeated more often and more widely than before. The same is true for many of Donald Trump's claims: taking on the details of, for example, his claim that the media were ignoring numerous terrorist attacks just served to remind the public of numerous terror attacks around the world – serving his broader narrative. Learning when to engage and when not to take the bait, or to offer a rival narrative instead of an attack on details, is going to become a key political skill. Being shown up as wrong on the details weakens some politicians, but not others. It's certainly not going to prove to be Donald Trump's Achilles heel.

Don't complain: Complaining about the media isn't restricted to one side of the political divide, or to one country. Labour leader Jeremy Corbyn's team have made attacking the bias of the mainstream media part of their communications strategy – motivated in part by a genuine right-wing lean in the UK's newspaper market, though extending to the BBC and centre-left publications. And no more needs to be said here about Donald Trump's persistent attacks on the media. It's becoming part of the anti-establishment political playbook – but there are good reasons it shouldn't. For most politicians, attacking the media just looks weak: as shown elsewhere in the book, polling evidence shows a majority of the population across multiple democracies are looking for a strong national leader. Someone complaining about the difficulties of the media may not fit that description, but such complaints do serve to drive their own core supporters away from the centre and diminish their trust in public institutions. Attacking the media alone isn't going to win elections, and would not be a good way – in terms of the long-term health of a democracy – to do so. For a political leader who *does* come across to many as strong, like Trump, the negative effects still hold, but the positives are more apparent. Attacking the media might help rouse the troops, boost donations and drive supporters towards friendlier outlets – but we're best served by politicians who don't need to resort to these tactics. The most confident ones, from across the political divide, simply don't need to.

Don't just focus on fake news: Lots of the media debate on post-truth has focused on tackling fake news, and many politicians have followed suit. This was most obvious in the UK, where a parliamentary committee launched an official inquiry looking only at the narrowest definition of fake news – fabricated stories on fake news sites – despite there being little evidence of a fake news problem affecting the UK. To do this is to imagine that if we tackle only the bit of the iceberg we can see floating above water (even if that's tiny), then the course ahead will be smooth sailing. If any part of the bullshit ecosystem is subject to technological fixes, then it's fake news: advertising networks and social media may be able to take steps to address fake sites that they couldn't adopt for the broader problems – though even this is questionable, as fake sites make their money in a variety of ways and adapt rapidly in a changing online environment. But to focus on just this aspect of bullshit is to avoid the bigger and harder problems which won't be subject to technological solutions: distorted news, viral hoaxes and hyper-partisan memes, bullshit from political campaigns and more don't fall under the fake news umbrella and will need tackling. Fake news is only a small part of the barrage of BS we're facing – it should only be a small part of the debate on how to fix these things.

Teach media literacy in schools: Most school systems include at least some tuition on things expected to be good for public health or citizenship, whether that's sex education or basic teaching about the structure of government, national values, or health and nutrition advice. There's a good case for adding some basic tools of media literacy to that list – how to evaluate sources, how to judge claims by basic rules of thumb, and even some practical statistics to help us judge what's really going on rather than what suits what we want to believe in the heat of a moment. These lessons don't need to be partisan, don't need to connect to what any current politician or media group says, and don't need to take up all that much class time. Anywhere which already teaches PSHE (personal, social and health education) or similar topics could put this into its syllabus – and given these are already being expanded to include awareness of other online issues (online dangers, sexting etc.), this is a relatively easy first step towards long-term fixes for the world's bullshit problem.

Don't bring down the edifice on top of yourself: It's generally a vote-winning tactic to present yourself as a 'change' candidate who can reform the system, and this in itself is not a damaging tactic. But when this turns into claims that everyone already in the political establishment is corrupt or self-interested, the risk is that the campaign attacks faith in mainstream institutions, setting up expectations that can't be met. Blanket attacks on the political system – or the media establishment – as being corrupt and venal may well be believed, but they diminish faith in those institutions. When they're heard every four years from every candidate, only for things to then continue pretty much as they did before, that faith just keeps dropping – and who might the public look to the next time around, after being let down again? This isn't to say that no one should ever call out corruption or bad practice when it happens: we might be outraged by money in politics, by access to lobbyists, by particular politicians seeming to fill their pockets, and more. We can and should call these out. Most people who work in politics (or cover it) don't think this is the norm – but if that's all most of the public hear, that's what they'll believe. This is a case of what economists call the 'tragedy of the commons': any individual politician benefits from attacking the system, but they're all hurt by the collective effect of the attacks.

Bring targeted ads into the public eye: It's possible their effect has been exaggerated, but targeted Facebook adverts pose a significant risk to how elections are conducted. The ability of campaigns to send messages to some voters which are almost impossible for the media or the electorate at large to see and scrutinise could have numerous damaging effects. It opens the door to targeted messages aimed at discouraging supporters of a political rival to turn out, whether through crude outright deception (false polling days etc.), or more subtle messages designed to put them off the candidate. It opens the door to a new era of dog-whistle politics where overtly racist, sexist or homophobic messages could be sent without the risk that they'll fall on the wrong ears and cause a political backlash. It opens the door to bullshit campaigns. The tempting thing to call for is simply a ban on such tactics, but this seems unlikely to work, especially in the USA, where calls to take money out of politics or bar certain types of adverts have generally failed in the courts – often falling foul of the First Amendment. What might be a much more doable start would be to require any communication coming from a registered campaign, PAC or similar institution to be registered with an official body, who immediately makes it public and openly accessible. This would be a minor extension of current rules, such as those which state materials must show who's promoting it, but could make a big difference to keeping campaigns accountable to the public.

Don't look like part of the establishment unless you have to: Donald Trump is the billionaire son of a millionaire, who used to present and produce a huge show on US network television. Nigel Farage is a privately educated former City trader who has been a member of the European Parliament for eighteen years. Michael Gove is an Oxford-educated *Times* columnist and former Cabinet minister and before the final days of the Brexit campaign was regarded as a close friend of the Prime Minister. Yet all three managed to present themselves as outside the political establishment, as figures of change, and as people somehow outside of the elite. When it comes to who is and isn't a political elite, it seems to have very little to do with the facts on the ground, instead being a state of mind. The current political mood is against the establishment: if once being part of this was an asset, gathering the respect of the electorate, that doesn't seem true now. If candidates want to break through – wherever they are on the political spectrum – appearing to stand outside the establishment seems both possible and beneficial, as French presidential hopeful Emmanuel Macron demonstrated in the early months of 2017.[1]

MEDIA

Watch your headlines: We've always suspected that people often only read the headlines, and in the era of much more robust online metrics, we now know this to be true. People share stories they haven't read, comment on stories they haven't read, and believe stories they haven't read – or at least believe what the headline suggests. When we have such solid proof that some people will only read the headline (sometimes accompanied by a sentence or so of text knows as a 'deck' or 'standfirst') that appears on Facebook, Google or Twitter, we have to make sure these work in isolation. That's restrictive – it means we can't play on expectations or set up a joke in the first line of the article – but is an easy and concrete course of action. If we're reporting on dubious or flat-out untrue claims, we need to note that in the headline. If a political quote is baseless, we need to say so at the top. It may lose the ability to keep people in suspense waiting for the reveal, but it tackles one vector of misinformation.

Complexity is not a virtue: Some of us in the media seem to think more words, or longer words, means a better article. It shows off our own depth of knowledge as writers, or it lets us show off our talents. But if what we're trying to do is challenge a short and simple – but false – claim, this may not be a virtue. We can be clearer. If we're fact-checking a claim (if we're still going to do fact-checking), why not put the short answer at the top of the piece, and then walk through the reasoning and the caveats lower down, for those who are interested? If we've got an exposé, the UK habit of putting the most significant facts at the top of the story might lack the elegance of the US investigative writing style – but might get the facts across to a bigger audience. We shouldn't over-simplify – almost every real-world problem is complex and has multiple causes – but we should try to work out what's pertinent for any given story or narrative, and try to focus just on the information that's necessary. Lots of the people who build bullshit narratives are great at being clear. The rest of us should aspire to be clear, too.

Reconsider the 'view from nowhere': The rationale for a church/state divide in US journalism – impartial news versus comment sections – has been that this is the basis of getting the audience's trust. By reporting in an 'objective' and balanced way, outlets will be seen as authoritative and will be trusted. We've tackled in detail why some now object to this view, but it's worth thinking about whether some places might want to consider revising that view. Do we really think the average Trump voter currently thinks the *New York Times* or CNN present news impartially? Do Clinton supporters think the same of the *Wall Street Journal* or Fox News (which arguably pays only lip service to neutrality)? Meanwhile in the UK, the BBC faces angry accusations of bias from left and right alike. 'Objective' news is a hold-over from the era when people trusted authorities and had respect for brands – an era which may still exist to an extent. But there may be a new model, familiar to UK broadsheet readers, based on being clear about source material, still striving for accuracy and fairness, but being honest about the biases of staff and maybe even the institution itself. Might this not be more plausible to a modern audience than the idea of newsrooms full of people with no personal politics?

Explain how we work: In the autumn of 2016, the *Washington Post* faced accusations that it had thrown NSA whistle-blower Edward Snowden 'under the bus', becoming 'the first paper to call for the prosecution of its own source'.[2] The paper had in 2014, shared the Pulitzer Prize for Public Service – the highest honour in US journalism – with *The Guardian* for reporting based on documents leaked by Snowden. But two years later, it ran an editorial calling for Snowden to be prosecuted and claiming his leaks weren't in the public interest. On the surface, this was a clear betrayal – but the reality was different. The reporting team who worked on the Snowden material distanced themselves from the editorial, which in US papers come from an entirely different team from the newsroom. Reporters had to watch as their own organisation attacked their source. That's difficult for many journalists to wrap their head around – so it must be incomprehensible to most typical readers. This is an extreme example of how lots of newsroom norms may not make sense to readers. Journalists know why all stories include statements from the target of the piece. They know what certain phrasings, in-jokes etc. mean. They know the limits imposed by laws and by regulators. These limits affect how stories are presented and how news organisations act – and we should try to do more to explain these in simple terms where they're relevant.

Cross the bubble, and help the audience do the same: Journalists are people too, and we have our own filter bubbles. These make us susceptible to miss trends and misreport issues on the opposite side of cultural divides to our own. A decent thought experiment to illustrate this would be to imagine how many newsrooms in the UK have a 50/50 mix of journalists who supported Remain *v.* Leave during the EU referendum; or how many US newsrooms have anything close to a 50/50 divide in terms of supporting or opposing Trump. Without that kind of diversity of opinion within an organisation, we'll struggle to report on such movements – and struggle to see which controversies connect with supporters, rather than just opponents, of campaigns and candidates. In the UK, for example, this would also mean breaking the dominance of London over the national media, and thus the national conversation. More broadly, news organisations can also work to break readers out of their own bubbles – one experiment on this front is being tried by

BuzzFeed News, which is trying out presenting a curated sample of Facebook posts from diverse viewpoints at the bottom of some political reports, to bust readers 'outside your bubble'.[3] This is just one approach – there will surely be many others – but the effort seems worthwhile.

Rethink fact-checking: Sometimes fact-checking backfires: when dozens of news outlets meticulously checked whether or not they'd reported each of the seventy-eight terror incidents White House press secretary Sean Spicer claimed had received less coverage than they merited,[4] they created a highlights reel of attacks connected to extreme Islamic terror, while being unable to definitively debunk his claim: outlets could show they'd covered most, if not all, of the attacks, but how could they prove whether they'd covered them 'enough'? By trying to challenge Spicer on the details, media outlets (unwittingly) instead just spread his narrative on the threat from Islamist terror. This is one of the reasons fact-checking can be counterproductive – others are covered at length in the previous chapter – and why it's worth at least some assessment. When are they effective, and how might they hit the same audience who believe a claim? How can outlets make sure that producing fact-checks as a separate entity doesn't mean that claims aren't assessed for truth in mainstream political reporting? At the most radical end, could some fact-checking be centralised to non-partisan outlets subject to independent audit? A solution like this ends the problem of dozens of reporters spending hundreds of man-hours scrabbling to fact-check a claim made in ten seconds – and may also prove easier for Facebook and Google to incorporate into technological fixes – but this may be something of a moon shot.

If you want to be trusted, be trustworthy: Mainstream outlets are lamenting falling public trust in their output, and questioning why fringe and fake news is so often believed. But while they do this, they're running unchecked viral material, laundering hoaxes and then, upon discovering these stories are false or questionable, either doing nothing or just invisibly changing a headline – with no acknowledgement of any error – to suggest they'd always had some doubt. This kind of practice is not conducive to building public trust. Inside the newsroom, these pieces may seem a long way away from the original or 'high-quality' reporting produced by those same outlets, but to the readers the difference is not nearly so obvious: they appear under the same brand, in the same layout, with the same presentation as hard news. One way to stop this kind of question mark over trustworthiness might be simply to stop running these kinds of stories – but if they're what generates the traffic to fund elsewhere in the newsroom, this won't be likely. If outlets are going to carry on running viral pieces without checking, and without correction, then one fix might be to find a new way of presenting or flagging such stories – different colour coding, branding or other visual signs to try to make a clear distinction between what's being presented as matching top editorial standards and what is not.

Find ways to push corrections as far and wide as errors: If a news outlet runs a story that turns out to be an error or hoax, or to contain some other serious error, simply deleting the social post is unlikely to have much of an effect: why would people who read or re-posted it even notice that a day later? For posts which got widely shared, this is even more difficult – even if the outlet publishes a correction on its Facebook page, this is unlikely to get anything like the shares of the original piece, and gets seen by far fewer people. This is something Facebook and media outlets could work together to fix. Facebook could either give a few trusted outlets (at first) the ability to push corrections or retractions to anyone who saw an original post, or even look for volunteers to sign up to a third-party independent arbiter who could send them. In turn, Facebook could reward such outlets with slightly better visibility on the platform. It might be a small fix, but it would be a step along the way to making sure accurate information travels to everyone who gets misinformed.

Think about where you get your content: In Chapter Ten we looked at the agencies that exist just out of the view of the audience, who find and repackage viral videos and sell them on to newsrooms. If these are going to be treated as sources of content which are then published without independent verification and checking, they should be held to the same standards as traditional wire services and picture agencies. At the moment, viral agencies who don't check content themselves are a point of weakness for anyone trying to get bullshit or fake news into the mainstream media: if a hoaxer or a guerrilla marketing campaign targets the agency, they can get into every newsroom. Outlets should be on guard against this risk.

Stop funding fake news outlets: 'Content promotion agencies' (like Outbrain and Taboola, see Chapter Ten) might provide a good source of income, but their recommendations – which often look a lot like regular links on most news pages – diminish the reputation of major outlets and directly drive content towards fake news websites. The mainstream media can't win a war on fake news when it's fighting on both sides of it.

Talk to science reporters: If you're looking for grizzled veterans of many post-truth issues, look no further than any long-serving science or health reporter. Science desks have tackled issues where a vocal but evidence-light minority have challenged fact-based consensuses frequently over the past few decades, and if we're looking for lessons on what to do – and what not to do – we could do much worse than looking at the rise (and partial fall) of the anti-vaccination movement, and of how the mainstream media has tackled climate change. Lots of what these reporters and editors have learned will surely be transferable.

Build a new public media: This idea comes from Tow Center for Digital Journalism director Emily Bell, in the *Columbia Journalism Review*.[5] Social networks need quality content, as do search engines. All of them are dealing with reputational (and regulatory) problems over fake news, extreme content and mis-information. So, Bell suggests, 'instead of scrapping over news initiatives, the four or five leading technology companies could donate $1 billion in endowment each for a new type of engine for independent journalism'. Bell argues this endowment could produce a new form of public service journalism outlet, a 21st-century answer to the BBC or NPR, unburdened by the legacy of their old business models and structures. She concludes:

> There is a singular opportunity to write a better path for the broken model of American journalism, and it has landed at the feet of a small number of technology companies, who like

a moon shot, and who are rapidly learning that the real value of journalism is seldom monetary. Journalism likes long reads, but right now it needs the money more.

Look at why parts of the audience are leaving: There is an anti-establishment mood among much of the public across the world right now, and the mainstream media is struggling to capture most of it. Ellie Mae O'Hagan, a journalist and campaigner on the left of UK politics, explains how fringe outlets have proven more able at catching this mood than their traditional rivals. 'Over the last eight or nine years, in the UK at least, there has been an endemic scandal in pretty much every major institution: the banks, the media, the police, Westminster and so on,' she says.[6]

These combined issues have led to a massive fall in trust in the traditional establishment. A lot of people now simply see a broad elite class that is self-interested, incompetent, scheming and not fit for purpose. The Canary and co. consciously takes advantage of this, marketing themselves as outlets that can peek behind the curtain, if you like, and tell their readers what is really going on. Most of The Canary's headlines are variants on the theme that some part of the establishment is acting in a machiavellian or corrupt way at the expense of ordinary people – and it is The Canary that is brave enough to expose it … They can articulate the anger of their readers because they empathise with it. Meanwhile, those who inhabit the traditional media tend to come from the traditional establishment, they are used to seeing their views in public discourse all the time (not least because they shape discourse), and they have little contact with people who feel abandoned or rejected by politics. Thus, they have been completely wrong-footed by the politics of the last few years. They don't understand why people are beginning to reject the institutions they feel at home in. And they've reacted to this by either becoming defensive and contemptuous or by treating the whole thing as a fascinating anthropological experiment.

On one level, this attitude from readers may seem unfair to the traditional media – it was mainstream reporting that exposed phone hacking, the MPs' expenses scandal, police's undercover spying on left-wing and green groups, and more. But somehow, despite doing the reporting and providing the information, they've failed to capture the public anger these collective crises have created. Working out why even outlets uncovering these kinds of stories can't tap into the mood they create is integral to explaining the rise of fringe outlets – why doesn't the media sound authentic to so many people they're writing about? Blaming the audience for not reading us any more isn't going to help.

READERS/VOTERS

Burst your bubble: This, like the other suggestions in this section, works on the assumption that anyone who's got this far into a book on the dangers of bullshit has an earnest interest in tackling it – this is meant to be things you and I can do for ourselves, not suggestions to make people with no interest in BS as a problem suddenly start to care. If most of us exist in online filter bubbles, and those filter bubbles can shift our views away from the political mainstream (Chapter Nine), making an effort to break out of our own bubble can only be helpful. This needn't be too drastic: following a handful of thoughtful people – not the people shouting most loudly – from the other side of an issue you care about on Facebook or Twitter is a good start. Trying to watch programmes or read articles from outlets on the other side of your own politics helps too. Knowing what people we disagree with actually say and think – rather than the straw men and caricatures we create in our heads – helps us bridge gaps, and makes it harder to demonise people whose politics are different from our own.

Engage System Two: We talked about System One – our instinctive reaction – and System Two – our considered response – in Chapter Nine. System One is effortless, and often quite satisfying to leave in the driving seat. When we're browsing in this mode, it's really easy just to click and share anything outrageous or heart-warming which reaffirms our worldview. That's why this sort of material – which is often bullshit – performs so well on the internet. If we want to stop ourselves sharing this kind of material, just making ourselves stop and think, even for five or ten seconds – in other words, engaging System Two – makes us much less likely to share nonsense. Even just a few seconds' thought lets us make several quick assessments. What's the source of the information – is it from a major news outlet? A named politician? An anonymous account? Can we verify the claim that's made? If we're about to share a screenshot, does it seem credible – would the person concerned really say that? If we have doubts, we can easily and quickly Google for facts and find out what's happening. Slowing down for even just a few seconds makes us much less likely to share bullshit.

Learn some stats: This one does not sound much fun, I'll admit. But even a very basic grasp of statistics makes you much harder to fool. It's not so much about memorising dozens of figures about the economy, but rather about being able to build up a series of mental shortcuts about whether or not numbers are plausible, or big. If we hear that the cost of benefit fraud is £1.3 billion a year,[7] this number on its own doesn't tell us much – it's quite a lot of money, and more than any of us can really visualise. If we happen to know the rough amount the government spends on working-age benefits, or even just the total amount of government spending (around £780 billion), we can put the figure in context. Knowing the basics of how averages work, how percentages work and how to put figures in context gives us a lot of power to independently assess what we read – and doesn't even require us to do too much maths. If this has grabbed your interest, the 1954 book *How to Lie with Statistics* by Darrell Huff is a great (and accessible) place to start.

Treat narratives you believe as sceptically as ones you don't: By instinct, we tend to look for fact-checks and sceptical takes on narratives that conflict with our existing politics: if we're liberal, we're unlikely to have thought Clinton's email scandal was a big deal, and would likely be sceptical of the Benghazi probes from Congress. If we're a Trump supporter, we're not all that likely to think the allegations around Trump's ties to Russia are particularly credible. We need to try to jump back from this and look for sceptical takes on the attack lines we believe – and also try to give credence to attack lines on causes and candidates we like. It may even help to try to mentally swap in a different politician or cause when reading a story and see if it would change our view. This is a big ask: it's really tough to try to leave our politics behind when looking into a scandal, but if we can manage it, it's great for our ability to actually assess facts and evidence – and to see why people we disagree with might be fired up by a scandal we've dismissed, and vice versa.

Try not to succumb to conspiratorial thinking: In the run-up to the Brexit vote, Leave supporters online urged one another to use pens in the voting booth, lest the authorities rub out their vote and change it to keep the UK in the EU. Left-wingers share stories of Theresa May directing contracts towards G4S because her husband owns shares in it (he doesn't). Before the US election, Trump supporters warned of efforts to rig the vote, whether with millions of fake votes, with outright fraud or by denying Trump supporters their votes. After the election, elaborate and detailed (but evidence-free) anti-Trump theories – 'time for some game theory' – went viral time and again. Conspiracy theories are the enemy of reality-based coverage. These theories take isolated facts and use conjecture to join the dots, building elaborate narratives showing up their targets as malign and dangerous. Almost no real political scandal could ever live up to the imaginary ones conspiratorial thinking creates. The results are all damaging: they normalise bad behaviour – real malpractice is rarely as exciting as imagined scandal – while diminishing trust in political institutions and driving those who believe them to the political fringes. The post-truth era is accompanied by a rise in conspiratorial thinking on all sides. The more we can resist it, the better for all of us: we should fight to hold our politicians and our media accountable, but this should be based on hard evidence and thorough investigation. This might be less exciting than the conspiratorial version of history, but it's surely more productive.

There will be no single solution to the rise of bullshit, and different players in the information ecosystem will all have to respond in different ways. We cannot build a solution which relies on good faith of everyone involved: we need to start from the politics and the media that we have, so proposals that rely on asking media outlets to reinvent their business model, or require millions of people who don't pay for news to spontaneously start, are doomed. This chapter has, hopefully, offered some starting points for realistic strategies to deal with the new world we're in – there will doubtless be dozens of other ways the problem can be tackled. But, one way or another, tackle it we must – a shared sense of reality, a counter to conspiracies, and some basic consensus are vital to a healthy democracy. A truly post-truth world is in none of our interests.

CONCLUSION

Clarity is the cornerstone of democracy. Confusion is the tool of the autocrat. A fug of bad information, paranoia and misinformation undermines the institutions of democracy and creates an atmosphere of uncertainty – an infosmog – which makes any attempts to get a consensus on what's true and what isn't an exhausting and futile task.

This serves the agenda of the strongman and of the autocrat: Kremlin-watchers are agreed that much of the purpose of Russia's information strategy is not to have its propaganda believed, but to cast division and uncertainty to avoid anyone producing an effective counter-narrative to Putin or his agenda.

Russia's military campaign in eastern Ukraine – and its annexation of the Crimea – brought its concurrent information warfare tactics into stark relief for a Western audience. 'The information war tactics deployed by Russia in the Ukraine conflict and adopted by governments in many of the former Soviet republics has been called the "weaponisation of information",' explains Andrew Puddephatt, chair of International Media Support, in a blogpost.[1]

The core of the strategy is not to persuade people that the Kremlin's view of events is correct. Indeed, some of the propaganda issued by the Kremlin is so laughable this would be difficult (viz. the contrary claims regarding the shooting down of Malaysia Airlines flight MH17). Instead the goal is to persuade people that there is no objective truth, that no media can be relied upon, that all news, including western news media, is simply propaganda.

This is echoed in a 2016 report from the NATO Defense College, titled 'Handbook of Russian Information Warfare'.[2] 'A key element of subversion campaigns is "spreading disinformation among the population about the work of state bodies, undermining their authority, and discrediting administrative structures", the report states. 'This contributes to the "dismay" effect in former NATO press officer Ben Nimmo's short characterisation of Russian disinformation aims as to "dismiss, distort, distract, dismay," and can be achieved by exploiting vulnerabilities in the target society, particularly freedom of expression and democratic principles.'

The post-truth approach is the approach of the autocrat: by a campaign of attrition, trust in institutions such as the state, the judiciary and the media are undermined, until public discourse is simply a clash of competing narratives: a contest which can then be won by the side willing to make the boldest plays towards emotion and mass-appeal – often, history has taught us, through the demonisation of minority groups.

This approach is hardly restricted to Russia. Even Nazi Germany, long held as the ultimate example of an organised and evil regime, had chaos and confusion at its core. Rising through a populist movement (though only ever becoming part of a

coalition government through democratic means), the administration had long delegitimised the media and cracked down on
press freedom very early in their term, in 1933. But the chaos and
the confusion of the regime was not just a cynical tactic – it was
a function of how Hitler's regime operated, a combination of the
Fuhrer's laziness and his chaotic governing style.

'Hitler normally appeared shortly before lunch, read through
the newspaper cuttings with Reich press chief [Otto] Dietrich
and then went into lunch,' testimony of Fritz Wiedemann,
Hitler's personal adjutant, states.[3] 'When Hitler stayed [at his
summer residence] it was even worse. There, he never left his
room until two in the afternoon – then he went into lunch. He
spent most afternoons taking a walk. In the evenings, straight
after dinner, there were films.'

The results were a messy form of government. 'In the twelve
years of his rule of Germany, Hitler produced the biggest confusion in government that has ever existed in a civilised state,'
said testimony of Otto Dietrich, Hitler's aforementioned chief
press secretary. 'I've sometimes secured decisions from him,
even ones about important matters, without his ever asking to
see the relevant files.'

These decisions had calamitous and catastrophic consequences for the people they affected. The Nazi policy of killing disabled
infants and children reportedly grew out of a single comment
from Hitler granting permission to a man who had written to
him asking permission to kill his disabled son. Seemingly without any further instruction or planning from Hitler, this was
extended into a national programme – itself masked through
faked diagnoses of natural deaths in children's homes, among
other means. Discovering what was really being done, and who

had endorsed what decisions, was all but impossible. Hitler rose on a post-truth narrative, a brutal vilification of vulnerable scapegoats who were blamed for very real problems facing Germany. The chaotic information climate was part deliberate tactic, part just a necessary and inescapable component of that style of totalitarian rule.

Nazi Germany is an extreme even among autocratic regimes, let alone among practitioners of post-truth, but it serves as a sign of how far post-truth regimes can go. Narratives matter, but institutions matter too – and whether deliberate or otherwise, modern politicians and campaigns are acting in such a way as to fuel dangerous post-truth narratives.

Joel Simon, the executive director of the Committee to Protect Journalists, finds parallels between Donald Trump and a more contemporary populist (whom many would also call an autocrat): Hugo Chávez, the populist President of Venezuela for fourteen years, until his death in 2013 – and other Latin American leaders who modelled themselves on his leadership style.

Writing in the *Columbia Journalism Review*, Simon pointed out:

'The No. 1 enemies of Evo Morales are the majority of the media,' the Bolivian president said in September 2006, a day after his government published a list of the country's most hostile media outlets. Ecuadorian President Rafael Correa has described critics in the press as 'ignorant,' 'trash-talking,' 'liars,' 'unethical,' 'mediocre,' 'ink-stained hit men,' and 'political actors who are trying to oppose the revolutionary government.' Daniel Ortega calls journalists 'children of Goebbels' and enemies of the Nicaraguan people. Hugo Chávez frequently called the media opposition coup plotters and fascists … sound familiar? [4]

Simon's conclusion is a warning:

> Trump's intent is clear. Through his relentless attacks, he seeks to create an environment in which critical media is marginalized and the truth is unknowable. The experience in Latin America – which, unlike Russia, has a democratic tradition, a robust civil society, and a history of independent media – shows that the strategy can work.

Trump has shown himself willing to tap into the worst kinds of conspiratorial thinking to fire up his base. In 2012, long before he was taken seriously as a presidential candidate, this took root in Trump's fervent boosting of the 'Birther' movement, a fringe and baseless campaign based on the untrue belief that President Obama was born in Kenya. But Trump didn't abandon this kind of misinformation campaign upon entering the Oval Office. Speaking in February 2017, Trump appeared to endorse the view that Obama was engineering protests against his presidency, feeding into conspiracy theories advanced on InfoWars (see Chapter Ten) that Obama was building some form of illegitimate resistance to Trump's presidency – though not going as far as InfoWars did. 'I think President Obama's behind it, because his people are certainly behind it,' Trump told *Fox & Friends*.[5]

> And some of the leaks possibly come from that group. You know, some of the leaks, which are really very serious leaks, because they're very bad in terms of national security, but I also understand that's politics. And in terms of him being behind things, that's politics, and it will probably continue.

Trump's media strategy serves to fire up a core of supporters and polarise politics, rather than reach across divides – and the evidence suggests his efforts to paint the media as just another partisan are working, at least on his base: research by Public Policy Polling showed 69 per cent of Trump voters agreed the news media is an enemy of the American people.[6] Scrutiny is being painted as opposition, and illegitimate opposition at that.

This is mirrored in the aftermath of the Brexit debate in the UK. People who question the implementation of how the UK leaves the EU – or who say they would still prefer the UK doesn't leave – are accused of acting as enemies of democracy, attempting to block the will of the people, or simply of 'remoaning'. This should be a ridiculous position, suggesting that after a general election anyone who didn't vote for the governing party should cheer on its manifesto until the next election – which of course isn't what happens. Politicians, including the Prime Minister, have begun accusing one another (and the media) of spreading 'fake news' and 'alternative facts'.[7] The centre may not have fallen, but the cracks are showing.

The dangers of the sky-high expectations created by the Leave campaign – and some Brexit boosters in the months following the vote – and the consequences if those expectations aren't met were set out in a speech by former Prime Minister John Major in February 2017, warning of the dangers of delegitimising debate.

'I have watched with growing concern as the British people have been led to expect a future that seems to be unreal and over-optimistic. Obstacles are brushed aside as of no consequence, whilst opportunities are inflated beyond any reasonable expectation of delivery,' said Major.[8]

After decades of campaigning, the anti-Europeans won their battle to take Britain out of Europe. But, in the afterglow of victory, their cheerleaders have shown a disregard that amounts to contempt for the 48 per cent who believed our future was more secure within the European Union … They do not deserve to be told that, since the decision has been taken, they must keep quiet and toe the line. A popular triumph at the polls – even in a referendum – does not take away the right to disagree – nor the right to express that dissent. Freedom of speech is absolute in our country. It's not 'arrogant' or 'brazen' or 'elitist', or remotely 'delusional' to express concern about our future after Brexit. Nor, by doing so, is this group undermining the will of the people: they are the people. Shouting down their legitimate comment is against all our traditions of tolerance.

The phenomenon is not confined to one country or to one political persuasion, and it's one being egged on by our political leaders. Instead of talking to each other, we talk (or shout) about each other to people we agree with, believing the absolute worst of anyone we disagree with, and leaping to accept and share anything that seems to show them in a bad light.

The result is a fever that will be difficult to break. A few years ago, to suggest that an intelligence agency was pulling the strings behind the world's media, online giants and information would put you right at the edges of the political fringes alongside niche conspiracy theorists. Even now, suggesting that of CIA and US agencies – the best trained and funded in the world – would be far from an establishment viewpoint. But suggesting the same of Russia – a country with a GDP roughly that of Spain's – has become the conspiracy theory of the mainstream establishment.

Russia is behind every piece of fake news, spreading propaganda everywhere, tampering with elections, and is even directly tied to the US President's campaign.

This is what many people now believe – but, at the time of writing, it's not what the evidence suggests. Reality, as ever, is more complex. There are numerous motivations for making fake news, and profit is the leading one. Yes, Russia has bot armies which it sometimes deploys to advance its agenda on certain issues – but plenty of other people operate botnets too, for fun and for profit, and these have been seen to be pushing pro-Trump content as this is what works to reach an audience.[9] People involved in Trump campaigns may indeed have been in touch with people connected to Russia's FSB agency[10] – but any foreign policy expert speaking to Russian contacts is likely to have done the same: absent proof of deliberate cooperation, this isn't (yet) a smoking gun. Russia did attempt to influence and interfere in the USA's election, and may well try to interfere in others[11] – but the USA (and others) has regularly done the same in Eastern Europe and South America.[12]

As ever, reality is messier and more complex than a conspiracy narrative, and requires much more waiting around for hard evidence. Having comic-book villains for the post-truth era, a cabal of enemies we can dispatch, is much more satisfying then believing that this is a complex problem with numerous causes, and that we're all part of this problem. And yet accepting that is the only way we'll start to fix it. We need to resist the urge to always be cynical, to always think the worst of those we disagree with, to believe information we want to be true, rather than acknowledging inconvenient truths – and we need to work on how to make real information pay off better for politicians and for media than bullshit.

All of that is hard, but here's the good news: if we're all part of the problem, we can all be part of the solution – and we can start whenever we like. How about now?

REFERENCES

Where at all possible, I've given direct links to online sources for any factual claims made in this book – it's inevitable in a book on bias and bullshit that people will want to look into these, so I've tried to make it simple. Please don't hesitate to contact me (details are in the introduction) if there's anything that seems to be missing, or that you'd like extra details on.

INTRODUCTION
1   https://www.bostonglobe.com/news/politics/2016/11/05/west-virginia-citizens-paint-dystopian-picture-under-clinton-presidency/jDCbxZ0Dkz8Xd5B-2MUdp3O/story.html
2   https://twitter.com/duncanrobinson/status/796630733024595968
3   https://twitter.com/oneunderscore__/status/798269541344276481
4   https://twitter.com/evanchill/status/798212965573029888
5   http://www.boeing.com/company/about-bca/everett-production-facility.page
6   https://www.buzzfeed.com/jamesball/are-eu-telling-porkies?utm_term=.uydrmq3p#.yh4yoQYe
7   https://www.nytimes.com/2015/11/27/us/politics/donald-trump-says-his-mocking-of-new-york-times-reporter-was-misread.html?_r=0
8   http://www.bbc.co.uk/news/world-us-canada-38137630
9   https://www.buzzfeed.com/jamesball/heres-who-voted-for-brexit-and-who-didnt?utm_term=.mvj4y2zM#.uw4ynG1E
10 http://www.bbc.co.uk/news/uk-38655760

11 http://www.huffingtonpost.co.uk/entry/daily-mail-correction-were-from-europe-eu-referendum_uk_5763cfe6e4b01fb6586374d8

12 http://www.express.co.uk/news/weird/731823/Chemtrails-will-wipe-out-humans-causing-biblical-style-floods

13 http://www.politico.com/magazine/story/2017/01/tabloid-newspapers-trump-media-propaganda-214627

14 https://twitter.com/tomwills/status/801807511548522497

15 http://edition.cnn.com/2016/11/10/politics/trump-quote-facebook-trnd/

CHAPTER ONE: TRUMPED: HOW THE DONALD WON AMERICA

1 http://www.forbes.com/sites/rickungar/2012/08/20/the-dirtiest-presidential-campaign-ever-not-even-close/#769d30b3fea2

2 http://edition.cnn.com/2016/09/23/politics/election-2016-personal-attacks/

3 http://www.salon.com/2015/10/23/obamacare_is_the_worst_thing_since_slavery_and_hitlers_gun_control_caused_the_holocaust_the_bizarro_world_of_iowa_republicans_propelling_ben_carsons_surge/

4 https://www.theguardian.com/world/2015/jul/26/huckabee-iran-nuclear-deal-obama-marching-israelis-to-door-of-the-oven

5 http://www.factcheck.org/2015/05/huckabee-repeats-discredited-claims/

6 https://www.washingtonpost.com/news/fact-checker/wp/2015/08/21/trumps-absurd-claim-the-real-unemployment-rate-is-42-percent/?utm_term=.c773343b5063

7 https://www.washingtonpost.com/news/fact-checker/wp/2016/02/18/trumps-truly-absurd-claim-he-would-save-300-billion-a-year-on-prescription-drugs/?utm_term=.b3443d76c56f

8 https://www.washingtonpost.com/news/fact-checker/wp/2015/11/18/repeat-after-me-obama-is-not-admitting-100000-200000-or-250000-syrian-refugees

9 http://www.taxpolicycenter.org/publications/analysis-donald-trumps-tax-plan/full

10 http://www.pewhispanic.org/2015/11/19/more-mexicans-leaving-than-coming-to-the-u-s/

11 http://www.newstalk.com/Trump-claims-border-wall-cost-will-come-way-down

12 http://www.politifact.com/truth-o-meter/statements/2015/nov/22/donald-}trump/fact-checking-trumps-claim-thousands-new-jersey-ch/

13 http://www.factcheck.org/2016/08/trumps-revised-911-claim/

14 https://www.theguardian.com/us-news/video/2015/nov/26/donald-trump-appears-to-mock-disabled-reporter-video

15 https://www.washingtonpost.com/news/fact-checker/wp/2016/08/02/donald-trumps-revisionist-history-of-mocking-a-disabled-reporter/?utm_term=.670c4a2468d4

16 http://www.huffingtonpost.com/entry/donald-trump-reporter-disability_us_58738c2fe4b043ad97e473f2

17 http://www.ibtimes.co.uk/white-house-adviser-kellyanne-conway-says-president-trump-wont-release-his-tax-returns-1602470

18 https://www.thisamericanlife.org/radio-archives/episode/601/master-of-her-domain-name

19 http://www.politico.com/story/2016/10/2016-presidential-debate-transcript-229519

20 https://www.fbi.gov/news/pressrel/press-releases/statement-by-fbi-director-james-b-comey-on-the-investigation-of-secretary-hillary-clinton2019s-use-of-a-personal-e-mail-system

21 https://motherboard.vice.com/en_us/article/how-hackers-broke-into-john-podesta-and-colin-powells-gmail-accounts

22 http://www.vox.com/2016/7/27/12297304/donald-trump-russia-hack-hillary-clinton-email-dnc

23 https://www.donaldjtrump.com/press-releases/crooked-hillary-question-of-the-day17

24 https://www.nytimes.com/interactive/2016/10/28/us/politics/fbi-letter.html?_r=0

25 http://www.huffingtonpost.com/entry/edward-snowden-hillary-clinton-emails_us_581fe27de4b0aac62485334d

26 http://apps.washingtonpost.com/g/page/politics/washington-post-abc-news-tracking-poll-october-25-28/2115/

27 https://www.nytimes.com/2016/10/02/us/politics/donald-trump-taxes.html

28 http://www.slate.com/blogs/the_slatest/2016/10/07/donald_trump_2005_tape_i_grab_women_by_the_pussy.html

29 https://qz.com/804528/the-republican-leaders-who-no-longer-endorse-trump/

30 http://www.pewresearch.org/fact-tank/2016/11/09/why-2016-election-polls-missed-their-mark/

31 http://www.politico.com/story/2016/10/full-transcript-third-2016-presidential-debate-230063

32 https://www.theguardian.com/us-news/2016/oct/20/donald-trump-us-election-result

33 http://www.cbsnews.com/news/googles-top-search-result-for-final-election-numbers-leads-to-fake-news-site/

34 http://www.npr.org/2016/12/11/505182622/fact-check-trump-claims-a-massive-landslide-victory-but-history-differs

35 https://www.theatlantic.com/politics/archive/2017/01/gregg-phillips-trump-voter-fraud/515046/

36 http://www.nydailynews.com/news/politics/alex-jones-doubles-completely-fake-sandy-hook-claims-article-1.2878305

37 https://www.youtube.com/watch?v=pDZR-t0Vr7E

38 http://www.cnbc.com/2017/01/30/trumps-voter-fraud-expert-registered-in-3-states.html

39 https://www.nytimes.com/2017/01/27/us/politics/trump-cabinet-family-voter-registration.html

40 https://www.dhs.gov/news/2016/10/07/joint-statement-department-homeland-security-and-office-director-national

41 https://www.theguardian.com/us-news/2016/dec/10/cia-concludes-russia-interfered-to-help-trump-win-election-report

42 http://www.nbcnews.com/politics/first-read/trump-has-been-strikingly-consistent-denying-russian-hacking-role-n703866

43 https://today.yougov.com/news/2016/12/27/belief-conspiracies-largely-depends-political-iden/

44 http://ew.com/article/2016/12/16/barack-obama-russia-campaign-hack/

45 https://www.buzzfeed.com/craigsilverman/viral-fake-election-news-outperformed-real-news-on-facebook?utm_term=.ouo59aZV#.rtDYAKw8

46 http://www.snopes.com/mike-pence-allowing-rape-victims-to-have-abortions-will-lead-to-women-trying-to-get-raped/

47 https://www.buzzfeed.com/ishmaeldaro/trump-fake-quote-people-magazine

48 https://twitter.com/duncanrobinson/status/796630733024595968

49 https://www.buzzfeed.com/claudiakoerner/people-noticed-that-crowds-were-a-lot-smaller-for-trumps-ina?utm_term=.xs70OgwJ#.gq5lnVDW

50 https://www.theatlantic.com/politics/archive/2017/01/the-pointless-needless-lies-of-the-trump-administration/514061/

51 http://www.independent.co.uk/news/world/americas/donald-trump-us-president-false-claims-inauguration-white-house-sean-spicer-kellyanen-conway-press-a7541171.html

52 https://www.theatlantic.com/politics/archive/2017/01/inauguration-crowd-size/514058/

53 https://www.whitehouse.gov/the-press-office/2017/01/21/statement-press-secretary-sean-spicer

54 https://twitter.com/revjjackson/status/822566447692005377

55 http://www.npr.org/sections/thetwo-way/2017/01/27/511983884/trump-reportedly-called-national-park-service-over-inauguration-crowd-photos

56 https://www.theatlantic.com/science/archive/2017/01/how-curiosity-bursts-our-political-bubbles/514451/

57 http://www.politico.com/story/2017/01/full-text-trump-pence-remarks-cia-headquarters-233978

58 https://twitter.com/realdonaldtrump/status/819164172781060096

59 https://twitter.com/realDonaldTrump/status/832708293516632065

CHAPTER TWO: BREXIT: TAKING BACK CONTROL

1   https://yougov.co.uk/news/2016/06/23/yougov-day-poll/

2   http://uk.businessinsider.com/nigel-farage-remain-will-edge-it-2016-6?r=US&IR=T

3   https://ig.ft.com/sites/brexit-polling/

4   https://www.ipsos-mori.com/researchpublications/researcharchive/3566/EconomistIpsos-MORI-April-2015-Issues-Index.aspx

5   Craig Oliver, *Unleashing Demons*, p. 42

6   Tim Shipman, *All Out War*, pp. 55–6

7   http://blogs.ec.europa.eu/ECintheUK/euromyths-a-z-index/

8   http://www.staffordshirenewsletter.co.uk/boris-johnson-visits-hixon-burns-350m-cheque/story-29284015-detail/story.html

9   http://www.itv.com/news/update/2016-04-15/gove-350m-sent-to-brussels-is-better-spent-on-nhs/

10 http://www.telegraph.co.uk/news/2016/04/02/furious-row-over-future-of-the-nhs-as-health-becomes-latest-eu-b/

11 https://fullfact.org/europe/our-eu-membership-fee-55-million/

12 https://www.statisticsauthority.gov.uk/wp-content/uploads/2016/04/Letter-from-Sir-Andrew-Dilnot-to-Norman-Lamb-MP-210416.pdf

13 https://www.youtube.com/watch?v=5EdKJfNRqsI

14 https://dominiccummings.wordpress.com/2017/01/09/on-the-referendum-21-branching-histories-of-the-2016-referendum-and-the-frogs-before-the-storm-2/

15 https://www.buzzfeed.com/jamesball/are-eu-telling-porkies?utm_term=.ejy5v-JVD#.knnGAadl

16 https://www.ons.gov.uk/peoplepopulationandcommunity/populationandmigration/internationalmigration/bulletins/migrationstatisticsquarterlyreport/dec2016

17 https://twitter.com/BBCDanielS/status/743207295883055104?ref_src=tws-rc%5Etfw

18 http://blogs.spectator.co.uk/2011/02/why-av-will-cost-250-million/

19 https://www.buzzfeed.com/jimwaterson/fake-news-sites-cant-compete-with-britains-partisan-newspape?utm_term=.lfQMQzKw#.hxl01DQ6

20 http://www.bbc.co.uk/news/uk-politics-eu-referendum-36534192

21 Chapter 21

22 https://www.ipsos-mori.com/Assets/Docs/Polls/pm-16-june-2016-tables.pdf

23 https://www.buzzfeed.com/jamesball/heres-who-voted-for-brexit-and-who-didnt?utm_term=.kjynxPlN#.pooxGQeY

24 pp. 285–6

25 Philip Cowley and Robert Ford (eds), *More Sex, Lies and the Ballot Box*, Chapter 28

26 http://www.wired.co.uk/article/developer-rebuilds-wiped-vote-leave-website

27 http://www.independent.co.uk/news/uk/politics/eu-referendum-result-nigel-farage-nhs-pledge-disowns-350-million-pounds-a7099906.html

28 http://edition.cnn.com/2016/12/19/europe/cnn-brexit-poll/

29 https://www.buzzfeed.com/jamesball/3-million-brexit-tweets-reveal-leave-voters-talked-about-imm?utm_term=.itedPGBQ#.fr5OlMzb

CHAPTER THREE: POLITICIANS

1 https://www.ipsos-mori.com/researchpublications/researcharchive/15/Trust-in-Professions.aspx

2 http://www.people-press.org/2015/11/23/1-trust-in-government-1958-2015/

3 https://www.buzzfeed.com/andrewkaczynski/how-trump-tricked-the-press-into-reporting-the-royals-were-j?utm_term=.qo0mXabZ#.ifrY6nz2

4 http://tyndallreport.com/comment/20/5778/

5 https://www.nytimes.com/2016/11/11/opinion/what-i-got-wrong-about-the-election.html?_r=0

6 *Would They Lie to You? How to Spin Friends and Manipulate People*, Robert Hutton, p. x

7 https://twitter.com/realDonaldTrump/status/232572505238433794

8 https://twitter.com/realDonaldTrump/status/232923697009278976

9 https://twitter.com/realDonaldTrump/status/232573681736503298

10 Credit is due to Conor Friedersdorf at *Slate* for noticing this comparison: https://www.theatlantic.com/politics/archive/2016/12/all-the-president-elects-pseudo-events/509630/

11 http://www.columbia.edu/itc/journalism/j6075/edit/boor.html

12 http://www.politico.com/magazine/story/2016/04/donald-trump-roy-cohn-mentor-joseph-mccarthy-213799

13 http://www.weeklystandard.com/article/15381

14 http://miami.cbslocal.com/2016/10/12/trump-ally-roger-stone-admits-back-channel-tie-to-wikileaks/

15 http://www.mediaite.com/online/roger-stone-confirms-rafael-cruz-was-tied-to-jfk-in-the-most-roger-stone-way-imaginable/

16 http://www.independent.co.uk/news/media/my-greatest-mistake-boris-johnson-mp-for-henley-and-editor-of-the-spectator-189322.html

17 https://blogs.ec.europa.eu/ECintheUK/category/euromyths/page/45/

18 http://www.telegraph.co.uk/news/uknews/1441470/Europe-my-part-in-its-downfall.html

19 http://metro.co.uk/2016/07/14/11-things-boris-has-said-that-make-him-the-perfect-foreign-secretary-6005960/

20 Tim Shipman, *All Out War*, p. 164

21 http://www.standard.co.uk/news/politics/boris-johnsons-article-backing-britains-future-in-the-eu-a3370296.html

22 http://blogs.spectator.co.uk/2016/04/has-boris-finally-realised-why-turkey-shouldnt-join-the-eu/

23 https://yougov.co.uk/news/2016/05/09/eu-referendum-trust-boris-slides/

24 http://www.politico.eu/article/boris-johnson-free-movement-as-a-fundamental-freedom-bollocks-brexit-trump/

25 https://www.politicshome.com/news/europe/eu-policy-agenda/brexit/news/80530/german-foreign-minister-%E2%80%98not-amused%E2%80%99-boris-johnson

26 http://www.bbc.co.uk/news/uk-36798992

27 http://nltimes.nl/2016/11/16/dutch-finance-min-boris-johnson-misleads-british-brexit

28 https://www.thesun.co.uk/news/2113892/theresa-may-threatens-to-exterminate-boris-johnson-in-brutal-public-slap-down/

CHAPTER FOUR: OLD MEDIA

1 http://www.express.co.uk/news/weird/731823/Chemtrails-will-wipe-out-humans-causing-biblical-style-floods

2 http://www.express.co.uk/news/weird/766792/Illuminati-card-game-Donald-Trump-assassination

3 http://www.express.co.uk/news/weird/762353/NASA-UFO-JPL-California

4 https://www.thesun.co.uk/news/2690331/google-earth-satellite-pictures-show-moment-brit-was-punched-in-the-face-by-a-grey-alien-before-he-was-abducted/

5 https://www.thesun.co.uk/news/2878041/millions-of-humans-doomed-to-become-cannibals-as-drought-and-famine-sweep-the-world-expert-warns/

6 https://twitter.com/DailyMail/status/824278005379952642
7 Author interview
8 http://www.dailymail.co.uk/news/article-4155480/Was-Trump-s-bodyguard-wearing-prosthetic-hands.html?ito=social-twitter_dailymailus
9 https://twitter.com/JamesLiamCook/status/801449014411620352
10 https://twitter.com/josephdrennan/status/801813867953352704
11 http://www.independent.co.uk/news/world/middle-east/20-million-muslims-march-against-isis-arbaeen-pilgrimage-iraq-karbala-a7436561.html
12 https://twitter.com/JamesLiamCook/status/813383666881667072
13 http://www.mirror.co.uk/3am/celebrity-news/britney-spears-dead-according-sony-9515808
14 https://www.buzzfeed.com/aishagani/muslim-leaders-do-not-want-to-ban-peppa-pig?utm_term=.krb37V8R#.hm0lg03d
15 https://www.theguardian.com/world/2017/jan/19/press-publishing-consistent-stream-of-inaccurate-stories-about-muslims
16 https://twitter.com/miqdaad/status/826483372750946304
17 https://twitter.com/miqdaad/status/814366513000017920
18 http://www.dailymail.co.uk/news/article-3903436/Enemies-people-Fury-touch-judges-defied-17-4m-Brexit-voters-trigger-constitutional-crisis.html
19 https://fullfact.org/law/daily-mail-headine-comparison-to-nazis/
20 http://www.adweek.com/tvnewser/fox-news-conservative-audience-is-more-loyal-than-msnbcs-liberal-audience/229494
21 http://www.endersanalysis.com/content/publication/news-brands-rise-membership-advertising-stalls
22 https://www.theguardian.com/media/2016/apr/26/uk-ad-market-booms-but-newspapers-lose-155m-in-print-advertising
23 2006 circulation: https://www.theguardian.com/media/presspublishing/table/0,,1991715,00.html; 2016 circulation: http://www.pressgazette.co.uk/print-abcs-seven-uk-national-newspapers-losing-print-sales-at-more-than-10-per-cent-year-on-year/
24 https://www.theguardian.com/tv-and-radio/2016/apr/17/tv-news-audience-decline-fast-as-newspaper-circulation-fall
25 http://asne.org/content.asp?pl=140&sl=129&contentid=129
26 http://www.gallup.com/poll/195542/americans-trust-mass-media-sinks-new-low.aspx
27 https://www.ipsos-mori.com/Assets/Docs/Polls/ipsos-mori-veracity-index-2016-charts.pdf
28 https://twitter.com/brianstelter/status/823864939517513728
29 https://twitter.com/ktumulty/status/823608598496481281
30 http://www.newyorker.com/news/news-desk/sean-spicers-abnormal-press-conference
31 https://www.nytimes.com/2017/01/25/business/media/donald-trump-lie-media.html
32 http://www.independent.co.uk/voices/don-t-call-donald-trump-a-liar-new-york-times-hillary-clinton-tony-blair-a7563001.html
33 https://www.nytimes.com/interactive/2016/01/28/upshot/donald-trump-twitter-insults.html

34 https://www.nytimes.com/2016/10/15/us/politics/trump-media-attacks.html?_r=0

35 http://abcnews.go.com/Politics/history-donald-trump-megyn-kelly-feud/story?id=36526503

36 http://www.politico.com/story/2017/01/trump-presser-slams-buzzfeed-233483

37 https://www.buzzfeed.com/tomnamako/donald-trump-presser-media?utm_term=.cy3NrKM1#.kt6MQv3Y

38 https://www.washingtonpost.com/lifestyle/style/the-traditional-way-of-reporting-on-a-president-is-dead-and-trumps-press-secretary-killed-it/2017/01/22/75403a00-e0bf-11e6-a453-19ec4b3d09ba_story.html

39 https://www.washingtonpost.com/blogs/plum-line/wp/2017/01/23/dear-media-the-trump-white-house-has-total-contempt-for-you-time-to-react-accordingly/?utm_term=.76089f3454fd

40 http://pressthink.org/2017/01/send-the-interns/

41 http://www.politico.com/story/2017/02/trump-tv-ad-rates-morning-joe-oreilly-234647

42 https://www.nytimes.com/2017/02/02/business/media/new-york-times-q4-earnings.html

43 http://www.cnbc.com/2016/11/29/new-york-times-subscriptions-soar-tenfold-after-donald-trump-wins-presidency.html

44 Credit to Kadhim Shubber for this insight: https://twitter.com/kadhimshubber/status/798575111947374593

CHAPTER FIVE: NEW MEDIA

1 https://www.newswhip.com/2013/12/article-length/#KjAXS7qUUCVLYcaG.99

2 https://www.thecanary.co/values/

3 https://www.buzzfeed.com/marieleconte/the-rise-of-the-canary?utm_term=.kqPR3VZl#.rdyvXD5M

4 https://app.buzzsumo.com/research/most-shared?type=articles&result_type=total&num_days=365&general_article&infographic&video&guest_post&giveaway&interview&q=thecanary.co&page=1

5 http://www.thecanary.co/2016/11/04/major-media-outlet-just-revealed-won-us-election-week-advance/

6 http://www.huffingtonpost.co.uk/entry/portman-communications-jeremy-corbyn-death-threat-the-canary-plot_uk_577c0fc3e4b0f7b5579618cd

7 http://www.breitbart.com/london/2016/10/05/breitbarts-raheem-kassam-run-ukip-leader/

8 https://www.bloomberg.com/politics/graphics/2015-steve-bannon/

9 http://www.thedailybeast.com/articles/2016/08/22/steve-bannon-trump-s-top-guy-told-me-he-was-a-leninist.html

10 http://time.com/4657665/steve-bannon-donald-trump/

11 https://yiannopoulos.net/

12 https://www.theguardian.com/books/2017/jan/03/milo-yiannopoulos-250000-book-deal-fury-leslie-jones-simon-schuster-breitbart-alt-right

13 https://www.theguardian.com/books/2017/jan/25/roxane-gay-simon-schuster-milo-yiannopoulos

14 https://idledillettante.com/2015/10/12/milo-yiannopoulos-in-his-own-words/
15 https://web-beta.archive.org/web/20060814212842/http://www.milowagner.com:80/
16 https://www.waterstones.com/author/milo-andreas-wagner/312874
17 http://www.houstonpress.com/music/gamergate-journalist-milo-yiannopou-loss-self-published-poetry-book-contains-unattributed-tori-amos-lyrics-6497169
18 https://web-beta.archive.org/web/20080306202815/http://counterknowledge.com:80/?cat=13
19 https://en.wikipedia.org/wiki/User:Milo_Andreas_Wagner
20 https://www.worldfuturecouncil.org/bianca-jagger-chair-world-future-coun-cil-urges-world-leaders-wealthiest-industrialised-nations-stop-playing-rus-sian-roulette-future/
21 https://www.theguardian.com/media/2011/may/17/telegraph-wonga-startup-award
22 Author interviews; https://maxdunbar.wordpress.com/2013/01/09/milo-yiannopoulous-and-the-kernel/
23 http://www.dailymail.co.uk/news/article-3696975/Ghostbusters-star-Leslie-Jones-forced-quit-Twitter-sad-heart-receiving-vile-racist-insults.html
24 https://www.theguardian.com/media/2013/mar/05/kernel-close-debts-unpaid-sentinel-media
25 http://kernelmag.dailydot.com/comment/column/5344/am-i-too-old-for-video-games/
26 https://www.reddit.com/r/ShitRedditSays/comments/3qip6z/brdcast_milo_yiannopoulos_cant_name_3_video_games/?st=iz9eg3mk&sh=f18954e0
27 http://www.breitbart.com/london/2014/12/15/i-m-writing-a-book-about-gamergate/
28 https://www.theguardian.com/books/2017/feb/14/milo-yiannopoulos-delays-memoir-to-add-details-of-protests-against-it
29 http://www.politico.com/story/2017/02/trump-cpac-milo-yiannopoulos-tape-235204
30 http://www.usatoday.com/story/life/books/2017/02/20/could-milo-yiannopoulos-now-lose-his-lucrative-book-deal/98156040/

CHAPTER SIX: FAKE MEDIA

1 http://nymag.com/selectall/2016/11/fake-facebook-news-sites-to-avoid.html
2 https://docs.google.com/spreadsheets/d/1sTkRkHLvZp9XlJOynYMXGslKY9fuB_e-2mrxqgLwvZY/edit#gid=652144590
3 http://baltimoregazette.com/
4 https://www.buzzfeed.com/craigsilverman/how-macedonia-became-a-global-hub-for-pro-trump-misinfo?utm_term=.uv7ealor#.bgvYNl92
5 http://www.dailymail.co.uk/news/article-3972662/The-16-year-old-Macedonia-just-one-faces-spread-fake-news-social-media.html
6 http://www.bbc.co.uk/news/magazine-38168281
7 https://www.theguardian.com/uk/2012/nov/25/sham-directors-woman-companies-caribbean
8 https://www.buzzfeed.com/jamesball/fake-news-site-uses-professor-stephen-hawking-to-sell-get-ri?utm_term=.eg98grWP#.rw6OQB6N

9 Credit for this spot goes to Dan Newling

10 http://web.archive.org/web/20141030135629/http://www.nytimes.com/2000/12/14/technology/14DOGG.html

11 https://www.washingtonpost.com/news/the-intersect/wp/2016/11/17/facebook-fake-news-writer-i-think-donald-trump-is-in-the-white-house-because-of-me/?utm_term=.253ff68d7bc6

12 https://www.buzzfeed.com/albertonardelli/italys-most-popular-political-party-is-leading-europe-in-fak?utm_term=.trAq15OW#.jx5zVAm0

13 Author's analysis

14 https://www.theguardian.com/world/2015/apr/02/putin-kremlin-inside-russian-troll-house

15 http://europe.newsweek.com/german-suspect-russia-behind-fake-news-propaganda-540501?rm=eu

16 https://www.buzzfeed.com/craigsilverman/viral-fake-election-news-outperformed-real-news-on-facebook?utm_term=.xeJ89x2w#.iw1rPv5Y

17 http://www.cjr.org/analysis/fake-news-facebook-audience-drudge-breitbart-study.php

18 http://www.poynter.org/2017/did-fake-news-help-elect-trump-not-likely-according-to-new-research/445724/

19 Author interview

20 https://twitter.com/jeffjarvis/status/797062174959161345

21 Author interview

22 https://www.buzzfeed.com/jimwaterson/fake-news-sites-cant-compete-with-britains-partisan-newspape?utm_term=.qo0mXabZ#.lvXrnlYj

23 https://www.buzzfeed.com/jamesball/how-550-facebook-users-spread-britain-first-content-to-hundr

24 https://www.buzzfeed.com/jimwaterson/campaigners-keep-flooding-the-fake-news-inquiry-with-complai?utm_term=.ovymY7WO#.dg7G2NP1

CHAPTER SEVEN: SOCIAL MEDIA

1 http://www.telegraph.co.uk/news/bbc/12126571/BBCs-News-at-Ten-extends-ratings-lead-over-ITV-after-launching-assault-on-its-rival.html

2 http://www.adweek.com/tvnewser/evening-news-ratings-week-of-february-6-2/320609

3 http://www.pressgazette.co.uk/category/media_metrics/

4 http://newsroom.fb.com/company-info/

5 https://www.wsj.com/articles/SB10001424127887324653004578650390383666794

6 https://order-order.com/2016/09/05/telegraph-digital-chief-admits-trashing-brand/

7 http://fortune.com/2015/08/18/facebook-google/

8 http://www.cjr.org/analysis/fake-news-facebook-audience-drudge-breitbart-study.php

9 https://www.ft.com/content/28cfe2a6-28eb-11e6-8b18-91555f2f4fde

10 http://fortune.com/2016/08/16/facebook-traffic-media/

11 http://newsroom.fb.com/news/2016/06/building-a-better-news-feed-for-you/

12 https://www.buzzfeed.com/charliewarzel/facebooks-unsettling-referendum-on-news?utm_term=.pneYy1wX#.sgmOoMJp

13 http://fortune.com/2016/04/07/facebook-sharing-decline/

14 http://www.recode.net/2016/11/2/13497376/google-facebook-advertising-shrinking-iab-dcn

15 http://gizmodo.com/want-to-know-what-facebook-really-thinks-of-journalists-1773916117

16 http://gizmodo.com/former-facebook-workers-we-routinely-suppressed-conser-1775461006

17 http://newsroom.fb.com/news/2016/08/search-fyi-an-update-to-trending/

18 https://www.theguardian.com/technology/2016/aug/29/facebook-fires-trending-topics-team-algorithm

19 https://inews.co.uk/essentials/news/technology/facebook-trying-combat-fake-news-winding-back-time-biggest-decisions-year/

20 http://www.theverge.com/2016/11/16/13653026/filter-bubble-facebook-election-eli-pariser-interview

21 https://www.facebook.com/JeremyCorbyn4PM/posts/1663622113931861

22 https://www.facebook.com/OfficialBritainFirst/photos/a.346633882148546.1073741826.300455573433044/1263684787110113/?type=3

23 https://www.ons.gov.uk/economy/inflationandpriceindices/bulletins/consumerpriceinflation/jan2017

24 https://www.facebook.com/leaveeuofficial/posts/1185653294866243

25 https://www.bloomberg.com/news/articles/2016-10-27/inside-the-trump-bunker-with-12-days-to-go; https://medium.com/startup-grind/how-the-trump-campaign-built-an-identity-database-and-used-facebook-ads-to-win-the-election-4ff7d24269ac#.vqrxp6udl

26 http://www.thetimes.co.uk/edition/thetimesmagazine/the-truth-sort-of-about-fake-news-j6n2lnvgx?CMP=Sprkr-_-3-_-TimesMagazine-_-Magazine-_-Unspecified-_-Unspecified-_-Unspecified-_-TWITTER&linkId=34853813

27 https://www.buzzfeed.com/susancheng/love-for-leslie-jones?utm_term=.hgvqGRYN#.aoNdMWmK

28 http://www.newyorker.com/magazine/2017/03/06/trump-putin-and-the-new-cold-war

29 https://www.theguardian.com/media/2017/feb/06/liberal-fake-news-shift-trump-standing-rock

30 http://www.journalism.org/2016/05/26/news-use-across-social-media-platforms-2016/

31 https://www.demos.co.uk/blog/infosmog-and-the-us-election/

32 http://fortune.com/2016/11/11/facebook-election-fake-news-mark-zuckerberg/

33 https://www.theguardian.com/technology/ng-interactive/2017/feb/17/mark-zuckerberg-facebook-letter-annotated-what-he-said-what-he-didnt?CMP=twt_a-technology_b-gdntech

34 http://blogs.lse.ac.uk/polis/2017/02/17/that-facebook-vision-thing-a-platform-still-grappling-with-political-realities/

35 https://www.theatlantic.com/technology/archive/2017/02/the-mark-zuckerberg-manifesto-is-a-blueprint-for-destroying-journalism/517113/

CHAPTER EIGHT: ... AND YOU

1   http://www.people-press.org/2007/08/02/public-blames-media-for-too-much-celebrity-coverage/

2   https://www.theguardian.com/media/2016/mar/06/new-day-editor-alison-phillps-normal-women

3   https://www.theguardian.com/media/2016/may/04/new-day-newspaper-shut-two-months-launch-trinity-mirror

4   https://www.theguardian.com/media/2010/nov/15/mailonline-daily-mail-website

5   https://d25d2506sfb94s.cloudfront.net/cumulus_uploads/document/3jomlll-c6m/YG%20Trackers%20-%20Top%20Issues.pdf

6   All examples in this paragraph are from Ipsos Mori's Perils of Perception survey: https://www.ipsos-mori.com/researchpublications/researcharchive/3188/Perceptions-are-not-reality-the-top-10-we-get-wrong.aspx

7   Jefferson Cowie, *The Great Exception: The New Deal and the Limits of American Politics*: http://press.princeton.edu/titles/10583.html

8   https://www.vice.com/en_uk/article/bad-politics-maps-memes-local-elections-2016

9   http://voxpoliticalonline.com/wp-content/uploads/2016/07/160721-This-is-Owen-Smith.jpg

10 https://keithpp.files.wordpress.com/2016/07/owen-smith.jpg?w=450

11 https://pbs.twimg.com/media/CUVdb0tWsAAckCz.jpg

12 http://voxpoliticalonline.com/2015/11/26/g4s-categorically-states-theresa-mays-husband-is-not-an-officer-director-or-shareholder/; https://www.vice.com/en_uk/article/g4s-theresa-mays-husband-shares

13 https://fabiusmaximus.com/2015/05/03/fake-quootes-by-conservatives-83837/

14 http://www.politifact.com/truth-o-meter/article/2016/mar/23/hillary-clinton-quotes-Internet-complete/

15 http://us4palin.com/fake-sarah-palin-quotes-hannity-interviews/

16 http://www.snopes.com/trump-back-to-africa/

17 https://www.buzzfeed.com/craigsilverman/fever-swamp-election?utm_term=.isRgEY1N#.ruNJR4b5

18 https://www.buzzfeed.com/johnstanton/pizza-gate-arrest?utm_term=.va4391zN#.leJjebzG

19 http://www.cjr.org/tow_center/memes-trump-articles-on-breitbarts-facebook-page.php

20 http://datascience.columbia.edu/new-study-highlights-power-crowd-transmit-news-twitter

21 https://www.washingtonian.com/2017/01/18/journalists-dont-know-how-to-cover-a-president-who-denies-basic-reality-donald-trump-lies/

22 https://www.washingtonpost.com/blogs/plum-line/wp/2016/12/29/memo-to-the-media-stop-giving-trump-the-headlines-he-wants/?utm_term=.6afbc68427be

23 https://blogs.chapman.edu/wilkinson/2016/10/11/what-arent-they-telling-us/

24 http://www.publicpolicypolling.com/main/2013/04/conspiracy-theory-poll-results-.html

25 https://yougov.co.uk/news/2016/05/27/conspiracies/

26 http://www.slate.com/articles/news_and_politics/politics/2016/12/what_the_hell_is_wrong_with_america_s_establishment_liberals.html

27 http://www.politico.com/magazine/story/2016/11/the-cure-for-fake-news-is-worse-than-the-disease-214477

28 https://twitter.com/brianstelter/status/798182485351952384

CHAPTER NINE: WHY WE FALL FOR IT

1   Stuart Sutherland, *Irrationality*, pp. 121–3

2   https://web.archive.org/web/20120324141249/http://psychsystems.net/lab/06_Westen_fmri.pdf

3   Stuart Sutherland, *Irrationality*, p. 127

4   http://www.dartmouth.edu/~nyhan/nyhan-reifler.pdf

5   https://www.poynter.org/2016/fact-checking-doesnt-backfire-new-study-suggests/436983/

6   https://youarenotsosmart.com/2011/06/10/the-backfire-effect/#more-1218

7   http://www.nhs.uk/Conditions/vaccinations/Pages/mmr-vaccine-when-needed.aspx

8   https://www.statnews.com/2017/01/21/andrew-wakefield-trump-inaugural-ball/

9   http://www.chicagotribune.com/news/opinion/commentary/ct-donald-trump-anti-vaxxer-20170116-story.html

10 http://www.independent.co.uk/life-style/health-and-families/health-news/processed-meat-and-cancer-link-just-two-rashers-of-bacon-per-day-increases-risk-of-bowel-cancer-says-a6709811.html

11 Michael Blastland and David Spiegelhalter, *The Norm Chronicles*, p. 37

12 http://dragonsofthinair.com/2014/04/how-many-people-are-afraid-to-fly/

13 https://www.theguardian.com/commentisfree/2014/jul/24/avoid-air-travel-mh17-math-risk-guide

14 https://www.theguardian.com/world/2011/sep/05/september-11-road-deaths

15 Margaret Heffernan, *Wilful Blindness*, p. 163

16 Ibid., pp. 262–3

17 http://www.spectator.co.uk/2015/10/i-invented-virtue-signalling-now-its-taking-over-the-world/

18 http://www.newstatesman.com/helen-lewis/2015/07/echo-chamber-social-media-luring-left-cosy-delusion-and-dangerous-insularity

19 All of the information on group polarisation comes from this excellent paper from Hastie and Sunstein: http://review.chicagobooth.edu/magazine/spring-2015/one-reason-groups-fail-polarization

20 http://psychclassics.yorku.ca/Sherif/chap4.htm

21 http://psychclassics.yorku.ca/Sherif/chap5.htm

22 https://www.demos.co.uk/files/Truth_-_web.pdf

23 https://www.publications.parliament.uk/pa/cm201617/cmselect/cmhaff/135/135.pdf

24 https://www.bloomberg.com/news/articles/2016-08-24/google-twitter-facebook-failing-on-extremism-u-k-panel-says

25 https://www.demos.co.uk/blog/theres-no-silver-bullet-to-prevent-radicalisation/

26 Based on p. 19 of *Thinking Fast and Slow* by Daniel Kahneman

27 See pp. 41–3 of *Thinking Fast and Slow* for a broader discussion of ego depletion

CHAPTER TEN: WHY IT'S PROFITABLE

1   http://www.journalism.org/2016/06/15/newspapers-fact-sheet/

2   http://www.comscore.com/Insights/Press-Releases/2010/6/The-New-York-Times-Ranks-as-Top-Online-Newspaper-According-to-May-2010-U.S.-comScore-Media-Metrix-Data?cs_edgescape_cc=GB

3   https://www.theguardian.com/technology/2016/nov/02/mobile-web-browsing-desktop-smartphones-tablets

4   http://www.economist.com/news/international/21565931-doom-beckons-online-ads-clicked

5   http://www.cnbc.com/2016/05/31/ad-blockers-posing-serious-threat-as-1-in-5-smartphone-users-using-tech-study.html

6   https://reutersinstitute.politics.ox.ac.uk/sites/default/files/Digital-News-Report-2016.pdf

7   https://www.theguardian.com/lifeandstyle/2017/feb/22/why-a-viral-video-of-a-cyclists-revenge-on-catcallers-may-not-be-all-it-seems

8   http://www.bbc.co.uk/news/uk-39051213

9   http://www.standard.co.uk/news/london/revealed-the-truth-behind-cheaters-spray-painted-range-rover-left-outside-harrods-a3248406.html

10 http://www.huffingtonpost.com.au/2016/07/11/your-favourite-viral-video-was-probably-faked-by-the-woolshed-co/

11 http://www.badscience.net/2009/01/part-432-in-which-i-get-a-bit-overinterested-and-look-up-waaay-too-many-references/

12 http://www.badscience.net/2011/01/tell-me-now-how-do-i-feel/

13 https://www.buzzfeed.com/josephbernstein/youtube-has-become-the-content-engine-of-the-internets-dark

14 https://www.cnet.com/uk/news/larry-page-google-probably-needs-a-new-mission-statement/

15 https://www.splcenter.org/fighting-hate/extremist-files/individual/alex-jones

16 http://www.independent.co.uk/news/world/americas/donald-trump-alex-jones-calls-phone-advice-infowars-conspiracy-theorist-far-right-sandy-hook-a7595136.html

17 http://www.infowars.com/watch-alex-jones-show/

18 https://www.infowarsstore.com/super-male-vitality.html

19 https://www.infowarsstore.com/survival-shield-x-2-nascent-iodine.html?ims=ybieu&utm_campaign=Survival+Shield+X-2+&utm_source=Infowars+Widget&utm_medium=Infowars.com

20 https://www.infowarsstore.com/infowars-life-select-3-month.html

21 http://www.infowars.com/watch-alex-jones-show/ – 23 February 2017

22 Both real examples captured on 18 February 2017

23 http://onlinewealthnews.com/uk2/quantum.php?city=Sheepland&did=202335&cid=29783&adid=1778947&sxid=r1607m9142dy

24 https://www.thebureauinvestigates.com/projects/binary-options

25 According to AdSpider,io, the headline in the example given was seen on at least 277 news sites: https://adspider.io/details/ads/7620013/how-to-get-paid-387-every-day-without-a-job-in-the-uk

26 http://www.iflmylife.com/health/weight-transformations/72/

27 https://www.washingtonpost.com/politics/2016/live-updates/general-election/

real-time-updates-on-the-2016-election-voting-and-race-results/clint-eastwood-trump-trump-trump/?utm_term=.7f38f3860976

28 http://www.niemanlab.org/2016/09/recommended-content-widgets-still-have-major-disclosure-and-clickbait-problems-says-a-new-report/?relatedstory

29 http://www.niemanlab.org/2016/10/slate-and-the-new-yorker-dump-outbrain-and-taboola-links-but-way-more-publishers-still-use-them/

30 http://fortune.com/2016/11/01/outbrain-taboola/

31 https://adexchanger.com/ad-exchange-news/facebook-instant-articles-a-trojan-horse-for-audience-network/

32 http://www.theverge.com/2016/12/6/13850230/fake-news-sites-google-search-facebook-instant-articles

33 https://www.buzzfeed.com/krishrach/stolen-disability-photos-catfish-facebook

34 https://twitter.com/pashulman/status/834577016464760832

35 https://www.theguardian.com/media/greenslade/2016/sep/22/publishers-government-google-facebook-newspaper

36 https://www.theguardian.com/media/2016/dec/15/google-facebook-uk-online-ad-revenue

37 https://www.digitalnewsinitiative.com/

38 https://media.fb.com/2017/01/11/facebook-journalism-project/

CHAPTER ELEVEN: A BULLSHIT CULTURE

1 http://www.bbc.co.uk/news/uk-26465916

2 https://www.nytimes.com/2017/02/02/business/media/new-york-times-q4-earnings.html

3 https://uploads.guim.co.uk/2016/07/27/GMG_Group_&_Company_Accounts_2016.pdf

4 http://digiday.com/uk/guardian-draws-200000-paying-members/

5 https://gigaom.com/2012/08/22/no-metered-content-walls-wont-save-journalism/

6 https://www.theguardian.com/world/2004/may/27/media.iraq

7 http://www.newstatesman.com/broadcast/2013/08/hard-evidence-how-biased-bbc

8 http://pressthink.org/2013/11/old-testament-and-new-testament-journalism/

9 Carol Weiss and Eleanor Singer, *Reporting of Social Science in the National Media*, pp. 61–2

10 https://www.ofcom.org.uk/__data/assets/pdf_file/0024/49308/Ofcom-broadcast-code-May-2016.pdf

11 http://fortune.com/2017/02/25/trump-anonymous-media-sources/

12 https://twitter.com/jamesrbuk/status/835150515843526656

13 https://www.ft.com/content/a462ee8c-2a7f-11e1-8f04-00144feabdc0

14 http://www.who.int/mediacentre/factsheets/fs266/en/

15 https://climate.nasa.gov/scientific-consensus/

16 https://www.publications.parliament.uk/pa/cm201314/cmselect/cmsctech/254/254.pdf

17 Ibid.

18 Accurate as at 25 February 2017, from https://www.washingtonpost.com/graphics/politics/trump-claims/

19 WHCA statement, 24 February 2017: http://www.whca.net/

20 https://medium.com/@ashadornfest/this-is-what-happens-when-we-stop-pay-ing-for-quality-journalism-9be9c8d49dea#.d39m7i5ot

21 https://twitter.com/brianstelter/status/797800015569698816

22 https://www.washingtonpost.com/lifestyle/style/a-hellscape-of-lies-and-distort-ed-reality-awaits-journalists-covering-president-trump/2017/01/15/3656a17e-d90f-11e6-b8b2-cb5164beba6b_story.html

23 http://www.huffingtonpost.com/alexey-kovalev/a-message-to-my-doomed-col-leagues-in_b_14138842.html?1484264929

CHAPTER TWELVE: DEBUNKING THE DEBUNKERS

1   Figures correct as at 26 February 2017: http://www.politifact.com/personalities/donald-trump/

2   http://www.politifact.com/personalities/donald-trump/statements/byruling/pants-fire/

3   https://www.washingtonpost.com/graphics/politics/2016-election/fact-checker/

4   http://money.cnn.com/2016/10/17/technology/donald-trump-deception/

5   https://www.theguardian.com/us-news/2016/nov/09/white-voters-victory-donald-trump-exit-polls

6   https://docs.google.com/spreadsheets/d/1sTkRkHLvZp9XlJOynYMXGslKY9fuB_e-2mrxqgLwvZY/edit#gid=652144590

7   https://app.buzzsumo.com/research/most-shared?type=articles&result_type=total&num_days=365&general_article&infographic&video&guest_post&givea-way&interview&q=www.washingtonpost.com%2Fnews%2Ffact-checker%2F&page=1

8   https://app.buzzsumo.com/research/most-shared?type=articles&result_type=total&num_days=365&general_article&infographic&video&guest_post&givea-way&interview&q=politifact.com&page=1

9   https://www.theguardian.com/uk/2011/dec/07/twitter-riots-how-news-spread

10 https://www.theguardian.com/uk/2011/dec/07/how-twitter-spread-rumours-riots

11 http://www.dailymail.co.uk/news/article-2023254/Tottenham-riot-Mark-Dug-gan-shooting-sparked-police-beating-girl.html

12 http://towcenter.org/wp-content/uploads/2015/02/LiesDamnLies_Silverman_TowCenter.pdf, pp. 40–41

13 http://towcenter.org/wp-content/uploads/2015/02/LiesDamnLies_Silverman_TowCenter.pdf, pp. 43–5

14 Author interview

15 https://www.americanpressinstitute.org/publications/reports/survey-research/fact-checking-journalism-changing-politics/

16 https://www.theguardian.com/media/2017/jan/12/bbc-sets-up-team-to-debunk-fake-news

17 https://newsroom.fb.com/news/2016/12/news-feed-fyi-addressing-hoaxes-and-fake-news/

18 Author interview

19 http://www.dailymail.co.uk/news/article-4042194/Facebook-fact-checker-arbitrate-

fake-news-accused-defrauding-website-pay-prostitutes-staff-includes-escort-porn-star-Vice-Vixen-domme.html#ixzz4Zoq2jJnA

20 http://labs.thebureauinvestigates.com/binary-options-real-risks-investigation/
21 https://www.theguardian.com/media/2017/jan/19/in-the-post-truth-era-swedens-far-right-fake-fact-checker-was-inevitable
22 http://www.thelocal.se/20170122/facebook-deleted-swedish-fake-fact-checker-page
23 http://www.snopes.com/2016/11/17/we-have-a-bad-news-problem-not-a-fake-news-problem/
24 https://firstdraftnews.com/fake-news-complicated/
25 https://fullfact.org/automated
26 https://www.statslife.org.uk/features/3202-event-report-post-truth-what-is-it-and-what-can-we-do-about-it
27 http://fortune.com/2016/11/07/trump-media-broken/
28 https://www.nytimes.com/2016/03/16/upshot/measuring-donald-trumps-mammoth-advantage-in-free-media.html?_r=0
29 https://twitter.com/cshirky/status/756569741020377088
30 Belam is (approvingly) quoting Hussein Kesvani in the first half of that quote: https://www.theguardian.com/commentisfree/2017/feb/07/fact-checking-far-right-media-truth-donald-trump-terrorist

CHAPTER THIRTEEN: STOPPING THE SPREAD

Much of what is discussed in this chapter has been raised elsewhere in the book, so I've avoided repeating references – those below are for the handful of points made for the first time here.

1 http://www.spectator.co.uk/2017/02/lanti-trump-can-emmanuel-macron-live-up-to-his-hype/
2 http://gizmodo.com/washington-post-throws-snowden-under-the-bus-1786775622
3 http://www.adweek.com/digital/buzzfeed-is-exposing-readers-to-opposing-viewpoints-with-outside-your-bubble-initiative/
4 http://www.bbc.co.uk/news/world-us-canada-38890090
5 http://www.cjr.org/tow_center/mark-zuckerberg-facebook-fix-journalism.php
6 Author interview
7 This is the cost of benefit fraud – around 0.8 per cent of the benefit bill, markedly less than the public estimate of around 15 per cent of benefits being fraudulently claimed: https://www.gov.uk/government/uploads/system/uploads/attachment_data/file/473968/fraud-and-error-stats-release-fy-2014-15.pdf

CONCLUSION

1 https://www.mediasupport.org/blogpost/weaponisation-information/
2 http://www.ndc.nato.int/download/downloads.php?icode=506
3 This and the following quote from Otto Dietrich are from *The Nazis: A Warning from History*, episode 2.

4   http://www.cjr.org/opinion/trump-chavez-media.php

5   https://www.buzzfeed.com/mbvd/trump-claims-obama-is-behind-protests-against-him-and-white?utm_term=.jjpmNb7v#.vgLdkmQJ

6   http://www.publicpolicypolling.com/pdf/2017/PPP_Release_National_22417.pdf

7   May on Corbyn: http://www.independent.co.uk/news/uk/politics/theresa-may-jeremy-corbyn-alternative-facts-pmqs-leaked-texts-tory-council-leader-a7568811.html – and Corbyn on May: http://www.independent.co.uk/news/uk/politics/jeremy-corbyn-theresa-may-alternative-facts-iraq-war-us-speech-visit-donald-trump-voting-for-a7549051.html

8   http://blogs.spectator.co.uk/2017/02/john-majors-brexit-speech-full-transcript/

9   https://medium.com/@DFRLab/portrait-of-a-botnet-12fa9d5d6b3#.uuztlrs1p

10   https://www.nytimes.com/2017/02/14/us/politics/russia-intelligence-communications-trump.html

11   https://www.buzzfeed.com/albertonardelli/german-spies-are-alarmed-over-threat-to-election-from-fake-n

12   http://www.globalresearch.ca/money-and-intervention-in-venezuela-wikileaks-us-embassy-requests-funding-for-anti-chavez-groups/25444

BIBLIOGRAPHY AND FURTHER READING

Below is a selected bibliography of the books relied on in the research of this book, as well as a few not cited herein but which offer good background or further reading on some of the topics covered. This isn't comprehensive – it doesn't include books or papers cited in passing – but these are included in the full list of references above.

Blastland, Michael, and D. J. Spiegelhalter. *The Norm Chronicles: Stories and Numbers about Risk*. London: Profile Books, 2014.

Boorstin, Daniel J. *The Image: A Guide to Pseudo-Events in America*. New York: Vintage Books, 1992.

Cowley, Philip, and Robert Ford. *More Sex, Lies & the Ballot Box: Another 50 things you need to know about elections*. London: Biteback Publishing, 2016.

Davies, Nick. *Flat Earth News: An award-winning reporter exposes falsehood, distortion and propaganda in the global media*. London: Vintage, 2009.

Frankfurt, Harry G. *On Bullshit*. Princeton, NJ: Princeton University Press, 2005.

Heffernan, Margaret. *Wilful Blindness: Why we ignore the obvious at our peril*. London: Simon & Schuster, 2012.

Huff, Darrell. *How to Lie with Statistics*. London: Penguin Books, 1991.

Hutton, Robert. *Would They Lie to You?: How to Spin Friends and Manipulate People*. London: Elliott and Thompson, 2014.

Kahneman, Daniel. *Thinking, Fast and Slow*. London: Penguin Books, 2012.

Oborne, Peter. *The Rise of Political Lying*. London: Free Press, 2005.

Oliver, Craig. *Unleashing Demons: The Inside Story of Brexit*. London: Hodder & Stoughton, 2016.

Shipman, Tim. *All Out War: The Full Story of How Brexit Sank Britain's Political Class*. London: William Collins, 2016.

Sutherland, N. S. *Irrationality: The enemy within*. London: Pinter & Martin, 2013.

Thompson, Damian. *Counterknowledge: How We Surrendered to Conspiracy Theories, Quack Medicine, Bogus Science and Fake History*. London: Atlantic, 2008.

Walker, Jesse. *The United States of Paranoia: A Conspiracy Theory*. New York: Harper Perennial, 2014.

Wheen, Francis. *How Mumbo-Jumbo Conquered the World: A Short History of Modern Delusions*. London: Harper Perennial, 2004.

ACKNOWLEDGEMENTS

Writing a book is never straightforward, and writing one at speed on a topic as fast-moving as post-truth, Trump and Brexit has been anything but – and it would have been an impossible task without the goodwill and help of far more people than I have space to name here. Special thanks, though, must go to everyone at Biteback Publishing for agreeing to publish this book so quickly, and for doing so on such an expedited timescale. Thanks are also due to my editors at BuzzFeed News for allowing me the time and space to produce this book, and for much else besides.

My gratitude also goes out to the people who proofread, edited and offered fact-checks of chapters of the book as they came together – particularly Luke McGee, Tom Chivers, Tom Phillips and my mum (thanks Mum!). Any mistakes, big or small, which remain are entirely mine. Special credit also goes to Francis Wheen, author of *How Mumbo-Jumbo Conquered the World*, for his graciousness over my shameless riffing on his book title. Finally, thanks go to all of those who spared their time to chat with me – whether on or off the record – about the topics in this book. Everything in here worth reading is built from your insights.